The
CONSTITUTION
of the State of
CALIFORNIA

PREAMBLE:..5

ARTICLE I DECLARATION OF RIGHTS 5

ARTICLE II VOTING, INITIATIVE AND REFERENDUM, AND RECALL..............28

ARTICLE III STATE OF CALIFORNIA..38

ARTICLE IV LEGISLATIVE 46

ARTICLE V EXECUTIVE 68

ARTICLE VI JUDICIAL...75

ARTICLE VII PUBLIC OFFICERS AND EMPLOYEES 89

ARTICLE IX EDUCATION...96

ARTICLE X WATER 106

ARTICLE X A WATER RESOURCES DEVELOPMENT.......................109

ARTICLE X B MARINE RESOURCES PROTECTION ACT OF 1990...................114

ARTICLE XI LOCAL GOVERNMENT 123

ARTICLE XII PUBLIC UTILITIES 132

ARTICLE XIII TAXATION..135

ARTICLE XIII A [TAX LIMITATION] 174

ARTICLE XIII B GOVERNMENT SPENDING LIMITATION 197

ARTICLE XIII C VOTER APPROVAL FOR LOCAL TAX LEVIES..........209

ARTICLE XIII D [ASSESSMENT AND PROPERTY-RELATED FEE REFORM] 212

ARTICLE XIV LABOR RELATIONS 219

ARTICLE XV USURY 223

ARTICLE XVI PUBLIC FINANCE 226

ARTICLE XVIII AMENDING AND REVISING THE CONSTITUTION 264

ARTICLE XIX MOTOR VEHICLE REVENUES 266

ARTICLE XIX A LOANS FROM THE PUBLIC TRANSPORTATION ACCOUNT OR LOCAL TRANSPORTATION FUNDS.......................................272

4

ARTICLE XIX B MOTOR VEHICLE FUEL SALES TAX REVENUES AND TRANSPORTATION IMPROVEMENT FUNDING 276

ARTICLE XIX C [ENFORCEMENT OF CERTAIN PROVISIONS].........................281

ARTICLE XIX D VEHICLE LICENSE FEE REVENUES FOR TRANSPORTATION PURPOSES 283

ARTICLE XX MISCELLANEOUS SUBJECTS 284

ARTICLE XXI REDISTRICTING OF SENATE, ASSEMBLY, CONGRESSIONAL AND BOARD OF EQUALIZATION DISTRICTS..293

ARTICLE XXII [ARCHITECTURAL AND ENGINEERING SERVICES]..................298

ARTICLE XXXIV PUBLIC HOUSING PROJECT LAW.......................................300

ARTICLE XXXV MEDICAL RESEARCH 302

PREAMBLE:

We, the People of the State of California, grateful to Almighty God for our freedom, in order to secure and perpetuate its blessings, do establish this Constitution.

ARTICLE I DECLARATION OF RIGHTS
[SECTION 1 - SEC. 32]
(Article 1 adopted 1879.)

SECTION 1.

All people are by nature free and independent and have inalienable rights. Among these are enjoying and defending life and liberty, acquiring, possessing, and protecting property, and pursuing and obtaining safety, happiness, and privacy.
(Sec. 1 added Nov. 5, 1974, by Proposition 7. Resolution Chapter 90, 1974.)

SEC. 2.

(a) Every person may freely speak, write and publish his or her sentiments on all subjects, being responsible for the abuse of this right. A law may not restrain or abridge liberty of speech or press.
(b) A publisher, editor, reporter, or other person connected with or employed upon a newspaper, magazine, or other periodical publication, or by a press association or wire service, or any person who has been so connected or employed, shall not be adjudged in contempt by a judicial, legislative, or administrative body, or any other body having the power to issue subpoenas, for refusing to disclose the source of any information procured while so

connected or employed for publication in a newspaper, magazine or other periodical publication, or for refusing to disclose any unpublished information obtained or prepared in gathering, receiving or processing of information for communication to the public.

Nor shall a radio or television news reporter or other person connected with or employed by a radio or television station, or any person who has been so connected or employed, be so adjudged in contempt for refusing to disclose the source of any information procured while so connected or employed for news or news commentary purposes on radio or television, or for refusing to disclose any unpublished information obtained or prepared in gathering, receiving or processing of information for communication to the public.

As used in this subdivision, "unpublished information" includes information not disseminated to the public by the person from whom disclosure is sought, whether or not related information has been disseminated and includes, but is not limited to, all notes, outtakes, photographs, tapes or other data of whatever sort not itself disseminated to the public through a medium of communication, whether or not published information based upon or related to such material has been disseminated.

(Sec. 2 amended June 3, 1980, by Prop. 5. Res.Ch. 77, 1978.)

SEC. 3.

(a) The people have the right to instruct their representatives, petition government for redress of grievances, and assemble freely to consult for the common good.

(b) (1) The people have the right of access to information concerning the conduct of the people's business, and, therefore, the meetings of public bodies and the writings of public officials and agencies shall be open to public scrutiny.

(2) A statute, court rule, or other authority, including those in effect on the effective date of this subdivision, shall be

broadly construed if it furthers the people's right of access, and narrowly construed if it limits the right of access. A statute, court rule, or other authority adopted after the effective date of this subdivision that limits the right of access shall be adopted with findings demonstrating the interest protected by the limitation and the need for protecting that interest.

(3) Nothing in this subdivision supersedes or modifies the right of privacy guaranteed by Section 1 or affects the construction of any statute, court rule, or other authority to the extent that it protects that right to privacy, including any statutory procedures governing discovery or disclosure of information concerning the official performance or professional qualifications of a peace officer.

(4) Nothing in this subdivision supersedes or modifies any provision of this Constitution, including the guarantees that a person may not be deprived of life, liberty, or property without due process of law, or denied equal protection of the laws, as provided in Section 7.

(5) This subdivision does not repeal or nullify, expressly or by implication, any constitutional or statutory exception to the right of access to public records or meetings of public bodies that is in effect on the effective date of this subdivision, including, but not limited to, any statute protecting the confidentiality of law enforcement and prosecution records.

(6) Nothing in this subdivision repeals, nullifies, supersedes, or modifies protections for the confidentiality of proceedings and records of the Legislature, the Members of the Legislature, and its employees, committees, and caucuses provided by Section 7 of Article IV, state law, or legislative rules adopted in furtherance of those provisions; nor does it affect the scope of permitted discovery in judicial or administrative proceedings regarding deliberations of the Legislature, the Members of the Legislature, and its employees, committees, and caucuses.

(7) In order to ensure public access to the meetings of public bodies and the writings of public officials and agencies, as specified in paragraph (1), each local agency is hereby required to comply with the California Public Records Act (Chapter 3.5 (commencing with Section 6250)

of Division 7 of Title 1 of the Government Code) and the Ralph M. Brown Act (Chapter 9 (commencing with Section 54950) of Part 1 of Division 2 of Title 5 of the Government Code), and with any subsequent statutory enactment amending either act, enacting a successor act, or amending any successor act that contains findings demonstrating that the statutory enactment furthers the purposes of this section.

(Sec. 3 amended June 3, 2014, by Prop. 42. Res.Ch. 123, 2013.)

SEC. 4.

Free exercise and enjoyment of religion without discrimination or preference are guaranteed. This liberty of conscience does not excuse acts that are licentious or inconsistent with the peace or safety of the State. The Legislature shall make no law respecting an establishment of religion.

A person is not incompetent to be a witness or juror because of his or her opinions on religious beliefs.

(Sec. 4 added Nov. 5, 1974, by Prop. 7. Res.Ch. 90, 1974.)

SEC. 5.

The military is subordinate to civil power. A standing army may not be maintained in peacetime. Soldiers may not be quartered in any house in wartime except as prescribed by law, or in peacetime without the owner's consent.

(Sec. 5 added Nov. 5, 1974, by Prop. 7. Res.Ch. 90, 1974.)

SEC. 6.

Slavery is prohibited. Involuntary servitude is prohibited except to punish crime.

(Sec. 6 added Nov. 5, 1974, by Prop. 7. Res.Ch. 90, 1974.)

SEC. 7.

(a) A person may not be deprived of life, liberty, or property without due process of law or denied equal protection of the laws; provided, that nothing contained herein or elsewhere in this Constitution imposes upon the State of California or any public entity, board, or official any obligations or responsibilities which exceed those imposed by the Equal Protection Clause of the 14th Amendment to the United States Constitution with respect to the use of pupil school assignment or pupil transportation. In enforcing this subdivision or any other provision of this Constitution, no court of this State may impose upon the State of California or any public entity, board, or official any obligation or responsibility with respect to the use of pupil school assignment or pupil transportation, (1) except to remedy a specific violation by such party that would also constitute a violation of the Equal Protection Clause of the 14th Amendment to the United States Constitution, and (2) unless a federal court would be permitted under federal decisional law to impose that obligation or responsibility upon such party to remedy the specific violation of the Equal Protection Clause of the 14th Amendment of the United States Constitution.

Except as may be precluded by the Constitution of the United States, every existing judgment, decree, writ, or other order of a court of this State, whenever rendered, which includes provisions regarding pupil school assignment or pupil transportation, or which requires a plan including any such provisions shall, upon application to a court having jurisdiction by any interested person, be modified to conform to the provisions of this subdivision as amended, as applied to the facts which exist at the time of such modification.

In all actions or proceedings arising under or seeking application of the amendments to this subdivision proposed by the Legislature at its 1979–80 Regular Session, all courts, wherein such actions or proceedings are or may hereafter be pending, shall give such actions or proceedings first precedence over all other civil actions therein.

Nothing herein shall prohibit the governing board of a school district from voluntarily continuing or commencing a school integration plan after the effective date of this subdivision as amended.

In amending this subdivision, the Legislature and people of the State of California find and declare that this amendment is necessary to serve compelling public interests, including those of making the most effective use of the limited financial resources now and prospectively available to support public education, maximizing the educational opportunities and protecting the health and safety of all public school pupils, enhancing the ability of parents to participate in the educational process, preserving harmony and tranquility in this State and its public schools, preventing the waste of scarce fuel resources, and protecting the environment.

(b) A citizen or class of citizens may not be granted privileges or immunities not granted on the same terms to all citizens. Privileges or immunities granted by the Legislature may be altered or revoked.

(Subdivision (a) amended Nov. 6, 1979, by Prop. 1. Res.Ch. 18, 1979. Other Source: Entire Sec. 7 was added Nov. 5, 1974, by Prop. 7; Res.Ch. 90, 1974.)

SEC. 7.5.

Only marriage between a man and a woman is valid or recognized in California.

(Sec. 7.5 added Nov. 4, 2008, by Prop. 8. Initiative measure. Note: Ruled unconstitutional per Perry v. Schwarzenegger (N.D.Cal. 2010) 704 F.Supp.2d 921.)

SEC. 8.

A person may not be disqualified from entering or pursuing a business, profession, vocation, or employment because of sex, race, creed, color, or national or ethnic origin.

(Sec. 8 renumbered from Sec. 18 (of Art. 20) on Nov. 5, 1974, by Prop. 7. Res.Ch. 90, 1974.)

SEC. 9.

A bill of attainder, ex post facto law, or law impairing the obligation of contracts may not be passed.
(Sec. 9 added Nov. 5, 1974, by Prop. 7. Res.Ch. 90, 1974.)

SEC. 10.

Witnesses may not be unreasonably detained. A person may not be imprisoned in a civil action for debt or tort, or in peacetime for a militia fine.
(Sec. 10 added Nov. 5, 1974, by Prop. 7. Res.Ch. 90, 1974.)

SEC. 11.

Habeas corpus may not be suspended unless required by public safety in cases of rebellion or invasion.
(Sec. 11 added Nov. 5, 1974, by Prop. 7. Res.Ch. 90, 1974.)

SEC. 12.

A person shall be released on bail by sufficient sureties, except for:
(a) Capital crimes when the facts are evident or the presumption great;
(b) Felony offenses involving acts of violence on another person, or felony sexual assault offenses on another person, when the facts are evident or the presumption great and the court finds based upon clear and convincing evidence that there is a substantial likelihood the person's release would result in great bodily harm to others; or

(c) Felony offenses when the facts are evident or the presumption great and the court finds based on clear and convincing evidence that the person has threatened another with great bodily harm and that there is a substantial likelihood that the person would carry out the threat if released.

Excessive bail may not be required. In fixing the amount of bail, the court shall take into consideration the seriousness of the offense charged, the previous criminal record of the defendant, and the probability of his or her appearing at the trial or hearing of the case.

A person may be released on his or her own recognizance in the court's discretion.

(Sec. 12 amended Nov. 8, 1994, by Prop. 189. Res.Ch. 95, 1994.)

SEC. 13.

The right of the people to be secure in their persons, houses, papers, and effects against unreasonable seizures and searches may not be violated; and a warrant may not issue except on probable cause, supported by oath or affirmation, particularly describing the place to be searched and the persons and things to be seized.

(Sec. 13 added Nov. 5, 1974, by Prop. 7. Res.Ch. 90, 1974.)

SEC. 14.

Felonies shall be prosecuted as provided by law, either by indictment or, after examination and commitment by a magistrate, by information.

A person charged with a felony by complaint subscribed under penalty of perjury and on file in a court in the county where the felony is triable shall be taken without unnecessary delay before a magistrate of that court. The magistrate shall immediately give the defendant a copy of the complaint, inform the defendant of the defendant's right to counsel, allow the defendant a reasonable time to send for counsel, and on the defendant's request read the complaint to the defendant. On the defendant's request the magistrate shall require a peace officer to transmit within the county where the court is located a message to counsel named by defendant.

A person unable to understand English who is charged with a crime has a right to an interpreter throughout the proceedings.

(Sec. 14 added Nov. 5, 1974, by Prop. 7. Res.Ch. 90, 1974.)

SEC. 14.1.

If a felony is prosecuted by indictment, there shall be no postindictment preliminary hearing.

(Sec. 14.1 added June 5, 1990, by Prop. 115. Initiative measure.)

SEC. 15.

The defendant in a criminal cause has the right to a speedy public trial, to compel attendance of witnesses in the defendant's behalf, to have the assistance of counsel for the defendant's defense, to be personally present with counsel, and to be confronted with the witnesses against the defendant. The Legislature may provide for the deposition of a witness in the presence of the defendant and the defendant's counsel.

Persons may not twice be put in jeopardy for the same offense, be compelled in a criminal cause to be a witness against themselves, or be deprived of life, liberty, or property without due process of law.

(Sec. 15 added Nov. 5, 1974, by Prop. 7. Res.Ch. 90, 1974.)

SEC. 16.

Trial by jury is an inviolate right and shall be secured to all, but in a civil cause three-fourths of the jury may render a verdict. A jury may be waived in a criminal cause by the consent of both parties expressed in open court by the defendant and the defendant's counsel. In a civil cause a jury may be waived by the consent of the parties expressed as prescribed by statute.

In civil causes the jury shall consist of 12 persons or a lesser number agreed on by the parties in open court. In civil causes other than causes within the appellate jurisdiction of the court of appeal the Legislature may provide that the jury shall consist of eight persons or a lesser number agreed on by the parties in open court.

In criminal actions in which a felony is charged, the jury shall consist of 12 persons. In criminal actions in which a misdemeanor is charged, the jury shall consist of 12 persons or a lesser number agreed on by the parties in open court.

(Sec. 16 amended June 2, 1998, by Prop. 220. Res.Ch. 36, 1996.)

SEC. 17.

Cruel or unusual punishment may not be inflicted or excessive fines imposed.

(Sec. 17 added Nov. 5, 1974, by Prop. 7. Res.Ch. 90, 1974.)

SEC. 18.

Treason against the State consists only in levying war against it, adhering to its enemies, or giving them aid and comfort. A person may not be convicted of treason except on the evidence of two witnesses to the same overt act or by confession in open court.

(Sec. 18 added Nov. 5, 1974, by Prop. 7. Res.Ch. 90, 1974.)

SEC. 19.

(a) Private property may be taken or damaged for a public use and only when just compensation, ascertained by a jury unless waived, has first been paid to, or into court for, the owner. The Legislature may provide for possession by the condemnor following commencement of eminent domain proceedings upon deposit in court and prompt release to the owner of money determined by the court to be the probable amount of just compensation.

(b) The State and local governments are prohibited from acquiring by eminent domain an owner-occupied residence for the purpose of conveying it to a private person.

(c) Subdivision (b) of this section does not apply when State or local government exercises the power of eminent domain for the purpose of protecting public health and safety; preventing serious, repeated criminal activity; responding to an emergency; or remedying environmental contamination that poses a threat to public health and safety.

(d) Subdivision (b) of this section does not apply when State or local government exercises the power of eminent domain for the purpose of acquiring private property for a public work or improvement.

(e) For the purpose of this section:

1. "Conveyance" means a transfer of real property whether by sale, lease, gift, franchise, or otherwise.

2. "Local government" means any city, including a charter city, county, city and county, school district, special district, authority, regional entity, redevelopment agency, or any other political subdivision within the State.

3. "Owner-occupied residence" means real property that is improved with a single-family residence such as a detached home, condominium, or townhouse and that is the owner or owners' principal place of residence for at least one year prior to the State or local government's initial written offer to purchase the property. Owner-occupied residence also includes a residential dwelling unit attached to or detached from such a single-family residence which provides complete independent living facilities for one or more persons.

4. "Person" means any individual or association, or any business entity, including, but not limited to, a partnership, corporation, or limited liability company.

5. "Public work or improvement" means facilities or infrastructure for the delivery of public services such as education, police, fire protection, parks, recreation, emergency medical, public health, libraries, flood protection, streets or highways, public transit, railroad, airports and seaports; utility, common carrier or other similar projects such as energy-related, communication-related, water-related and wastewater-related facilities or infrastructure; projects identified by a State or local government for recovery from natural disasters; and private uses incidental to, or necessary for, the public work or improvement.

6. "State" means the State of California and any of its agencies or departments.

(Sec. 19 amended June 3, 2008, by Prop. 99. Initiative measure.)

SEC. 20.

Noncitizens have the same property rights as citizens.
(Sec. 20 added Nov. 5, 1974, by Prop. 7. Res.Ch. 90, 1974.)

SEC. 21.

Property owned before marriage or acquired during marriage by gift, will, or inheritance is separate property.
(Sec. 21 renumbered from Sec. 8 (of Art. 20) on Nov. 5, 1974, by Prop. 7. Res.Ch. 90, 1974.)

SEC. 22.

The right to vote or hold office may not be conditioned by a property qualification.
(Sec. 22 added Nov. 5, 1974, by Prop. 7. Res.Ch. 90, 1974.)

SEC. 23.

One or more grand juries shall be drawn and summoned at least once a year in each county.
(Sec. 23 added Nov. 5, 1974, by Prop. 7. Res.Ch. 90, 1974.)

SEC. 24.

Rights guaranteed by this Constitution are not dependent on those guaranteed by the United States Constitution.

In criminal cases the rights of a defendant to equal protection of the laws, to due process of law, to the assistance of counsel, to be personally present with counsel, to a speedy and public trial, to compel the attendance of witnesses, to confront the witnesses against him or her, to be free from unreasonable searches and seizures, to privacy, to not be compelled to be a witness against himself or herself, to not be placed twice in jeopardy for the same offense, and to not suffer the imposition of cruel or unusual punishment, shall be construed by the courts of this State in a manner consistent with the Constitution of the United States. This Constitution shall not be construed by the courts to afford greater rights to criminal defendants than those afforded by the Constitution of the United States, nor shall it be construed to afford greater rights to minors in juvenile proceedings on criminal causes than those afforded by the Constitution of the United States.

This declaration of rights may not be construed to impair or deny others retained by the people.
(Sec. 24 amended June 5, 1990, by Prop. 115. Initiative measure.)

Section 25.

The people shall have the right to fish upon and from the public lands of the State and in the waters thereof, excepting upon lands set aside for fish hatcheries, and no land owned by the State shall ever be sold or transferred without reserving in the people the absolute right to fish thereupon; and no law shall ever be passed making it a crime for the people to enter upon the public lands within this State for the purpose of fishing in any water containing fish that have been planted therein by the State; provided, that the legislature may by statute, provide for the season when and the conditions under which the different species of fish may be taken.

(Sec. 25 added Nov. 8, 1910, by A.C.A. 14. Res.Ch. 44, 1909.)

SEC. 26.

The provisions of this Constitution are mandatory and prohibitory, unless by express words they are declared to be otherwise.

(Sec. 26 renumbered from Sec. 28 on June 8, 1976, by Prop. 14. Res.Ch. 5, 1976.)

SEC. 27.

All statutes of this State in effect on February 17, 1972, requiring, authorizing, imposing, or relating to the death penalty are in full force and effect, subject to legislative amendment or repeal by statute, initiative, or referendum.
The death penalty provided for under those statutes shall not be deemed to be, or to constitute, the infliction of cruel or unusual punishments within the meaning of Article 1, Section 6 nor shall such punishment for such offenses be deemed to contravene any other provision of this constitution.

(Sec. 27 added Nov. 7, 1972, by Prop. 17. Initiative measure.)

SEC. 28.

(a) The People of the State of California find and declare all of the following:

(1) Criminal activity has a serious impact on the citizens of California. The rights of victims of crime and their families in criminal prosecutions are a subject of grave statewide concern.

(2) Victims of crime are entitled to have the criminal justice system view criminal acts as serious threats to the safety and welfare of the people of California. The enactment of comprehensive provisions and laws ensuring a bill of rights for victims of crime, including safeguards in the criminal justice system fully protecting those rights and ensuring that crime victims are treated with respect and dignity, is a matter of high public importance. California's victims of crime are largely dependent upon the proper functioning of government, upon the criminal justice system and upon the expeditious enforcement of the rights of victims of crime described herein, in order to protect the public safety and to secure justice when the public safety has been compromised by criminal activity.

(3) The rights of victims pervade the criminal justice system. These rights include personally held and enforceable rights described in paragraphs (1) through (17) of subdivision (b).

(4) The rights of victims also include broader shared collective rights that are held in common with all of the People of the State of California and that are enforceable through the enactment of laws and through good-faith efforts and actions of California's elected, appointed, and publicly employed officials. These rights encompass the expectation shared with all of the people of California that persons who commit felonious acts causing injury to innocent victims will be appropriately and thoroughly investigated, appropriately detained in custody, brought before the courts of California even if arrested outside the State, tried by the courts in a timely manner, sentenced, and sufficiently punished so that the public safety is protected and encouraged as a goal of highest importance.

(5) Victims of crime have a collectively shared right to expect that persons convicted of committing criminal acts are sufficiently punished in both the manner and the length

of the sentences imposed by the courts of the State of California. This right includes the right to expect that the punitive and deterrent effect of custodial sentences imposed by the courts will not be undercut or diminished by the granting of rights and privileges to prisoners that are not required by any provision of the United States Constitution or by the laws of this State to be granted to any person incarcerated in a penal or other custodial facility in this State as a punishment or correction for the commission of a crime.

(6) Victims of crime are entitled to finality in their criminal cases. Lengthy appeals and other post-judgment proceedings that challenge criminal convictions, frequent and difficult parole hearings that threaten to release criminal offenders, and the ongoing threat that the sentences of criminal wrongdoers will be reduced, prolong the suffering of crime victims for many years after the crimes themselves have been perpetrated. This prolonged suffering of crime victims and their families must come to an end.

(7) Finally, the People find and declare that the right to public safety extends to public and private primary, elementary, junior high, and senior high school, and community college, California State University, University of California, and private college and university campuses, where students and staff have the right to be safe and secure in their persons.

(8) To accomplish the goals it is necessary that the laws of California relating to the criminal justice process be amended in order to protect the legitimate rights of victims of crime.

(b) In order to preserve and protect a victim's rights to justice and due process, a victim shall be entitled to the following rights:

(1) To be treated with fairness and respect for his or her privacy and dignity, and to be free from intimidation, harassment, and abuse, throughout the criminal or juvenile justice process.

(2) To be reasonably protected from the defendant and persons acting on behalf of the defendant.

(3) To have the safety of the victim and the victim's family considered in fixing the amount of bail and release conditions for the defendant.

(4) To prevent the disclosure of confidential information or records to the defendant, the defendant's attorney, or any other person acting on behalf of the defendant, which could be used to locate or harass the victim or the victim's family or which disclose confidential communications made in the course of medical or counseling treatment, or which are otherwise privileged or confidential by law.

(5) To refuse an interview, deposition, or discovery request by the defendant, the defendant's attorney, or any other person acting on behalf of the defendant, and to set reasonable conditions on the conduct of any such interview to which the victim consents.

(6) To reasonable notice of and to reasonably confer with the prosecuting agency, upon request, regarding, the arrest of the defendant if known by the prosecutor, the charges filed, the determination whether to extradite the defendant, and, upon request, to be notified of and informed before any pretrial disposition of the case.

(7) To reasonable notice of all public proceedings, including delinquency proceedings, upon request, at which the defendant and the prosecutor are entitled to be present and of all parole or other post-conviction release proceedings, and to be present at all such proceedings.

(8) To be heard, upon request, at any proceeding, including any delinquency proceeding, involving a post-arrest release decision, plea, sentencing, post-conviction release decision, or any proceeding in which a right of the victim is at issue.

(9) To a speedy trial and a prompt and final conclusion of the case and any related post-judgment proceedings.

(10) To provide information to a probation department official conducting a pre-sentence investigation concerning the impact of the offense on the victim and the victim's family and any sentencing recommendations before the sentencing of the defendant.

(11) To receive, upon request, the pre-sentence report when available to the defendant, except for those portions made confidential by law.

(12) To be informed, upon request, of the conviction, sentence, place and time of incarceration, or other disposition of the defendant, the scheduled release date of the defendant, and the release of or the escape by the defendant from custody.

(13) To restitution.

(A) It is the unequivocal intention of the People of the State of California that all persons who suffer losses as a result of criminal activity shall have the right to seek and secure restitution from the persons convicted of the crimes causing the losses they suffer.

(B) Restitution shall be ordered from the convicted wrongdoer in every case, regardless of the sentence or disposition imposed, in which a crime victim suffers a loss.

(C) All monetary payments, monies, and property collected from any person who has been ordered to make restitution shall be first applied to pay the amounts ordered as restitution to the victim.

(14) To the prompt return of property when no longer needed as evidence.

(15) To be informed of all parole procedures, to participate in the parole process, to provide information to the parole authority to be considered before the parole of the offender, and to be notified, upon request, of the parole or other release of the offender.

(16) To have the safety of the victim, the victim's family, and the general public considered before any parole or other post-judgment release decision is made.

(17) To be informed of the rights enumerated in paragraphs (1) through (16).

(c) (1) A victim, the retained attorney of a victim, a lawful representative of the victim, or the prosecuting attorney upon request of the victim, may enforce the rights enumerated in subdivision (b) in any trial or appellate court with jurisdiction over the case as a matter of right. The court shall act promptly on such a request.

(2) This section does not create any cause of action for compensation or damages against the State, any political subdivision of the State, any officer, employee, or agent of the State or of any of its political subdivisions, or any officer or employee of the court.

(d) The granting of these rights to victims shall not be construed to deny or disparage other rights possessed by victims. The court in its discretion may extend the right to be heard at sentencing to any person harmed by the defendant. The parole authority shall extend the right to be heard at a parole hearing to any person harmed by the offender.

(e) As used in this section, a "victim" is a person who suffers direct or threatened physical, psychological, or financial harm as a result of the commission or attempted commission of a crime or delinquent act. The term "victim" also includes the person's spouse, parents, children, siblings, or guardian, and includes a lawful representative of a crime victim who is deceased, a minor, or physically or psychologically incapacitated. The term "victim" does not include a person in custody for an offense, the accused, or a person whom the court finds would not act in the best interests of a minor victim.

(f) In addition to the enumerated rights provided in subdivision (b) that are personally enforceable by victims as provided in subdivision (c), victims of crime have additional rights that are shared with all of the People of the State of California. These collectively held rights include, but are not limited to, the following:

(1) Right to Safe Schools.All students and staff of public primary, elementary, junior high, and senior high schools, and community colleges, colleges, and universities have the inalienable right to attend campuses which are safe, secure and peaceful.

(2) Right to Truth-in-Evidence.Except as provided by statute hereafter enacted by a two-thirds vote of the membership in each house of the Legislature, relevant evidence shall not be excluded in any criminal proceeding, including pretrial and post conviction motions and hearings, or in any trial or hearing of a juvenile for a criminal offense, whether heard in juvenile or adult court. Nothing in this section shall affect any existing statutory rule of evidence relating to privilege or hearsay, or Evidence Code Sections 352, 782 or 1103. Nothing in this section shall affect any existing statutory or constitutional right of the press.

(3) Public Safety Bail.A person may be released on bail by sufficient sureties, except for capital crimes when the facts are evident or the presumption great. Excessive bail may not be required. In setting, reducing or denying bail, the judge or magistrate shall take into consideration the protection of the public, the safety of the victim, the seriousness of the offense charged, the previous criminal record of the defendant, and the probability of his or her appearing at the trial or hearing of the case. Public safety and the safety of the victim shall be the primary considerations.

A person may be released on his or her own recognizance in the court's discretion, subject to the same factors considered in setting bail.

Before any person arrested for a serious felony may be released on bail, a hearing may be held before the magistrate or judge, and the prosecuting attorney and the victim shall be given notice and reasonable opportunity to be heard on the matter.

When a judge or magistrate grants or denies bail or release on a person's own recognizance, the reasons for that decision shall be stated in the record and included in the court's minutes.

(4) Use of Prior Convictions.Any prior felony conviction of any person in any criminal proceeding, whether adult or juvenile, shall subsequently be used without limitation for purposes of impeachment or enhancement of sentence in any criminal proceeding. When a prior felony conviction is an element of any felony offense, it shall be proven to the trier of fact in open court.

(5) Truth in Sentencing.Sentences that are individually imposed upon convicted criminal wrongdoers based upon the facts and circumstances surrounding their cases shall be carried out in compliance with the courts' sentencing orders, and shall not be substantially diminished by early release policies intended to alleviate overcrowding in custodial facilities. The legislative branch shall ensure sufficient funding to adequately house inmates for the full terms of their sentences, except for statutorily authorized credits which reduce those sentences.

(6) Reform of the parole process.The current process for parole hearings is excessive, especially in cases in which the defendant has been convicted of murder. The parole hearing process must be reformed for the benefit of crime victims.

(g) As used in this article, the term "serious felony" is any crime defined in subdivision (c) of Section 1192.7 of the Penal Code, or any successor statute.

(Sec. 28 amended Nov. 4, 2008, by Prop. 9. Initiative measure.)

SEC. 29.

In a criminal case, the people of the State of California have the right to due process of law and to a speedy and public trial.

(Sec. 29 added June 5, 1990, by Prop. 115. Initiative measure.)

SEC. 30.

(a) This Constitution shall not be construed by the courts to prohibit the joining of criminal cases as prescribed by the Legislature or by the people through the initiative process.

(b) In order to protect victims and witnesses in criminal cases, hearsay evidence shall be admissible at preliminary hearings, as prescribed by the Legislature or by the people through the initiative process.

(c) In order to provide for fair and speedy trials, discovery in criminal cases shall be reciprocal in nature, as prescribed by the Legislature or by the people through the initiative process.

(Sec. 30 added June 5, 1990, by Prop. 115. Initiative measure.)

SEC. 31.

(a) The State shall not discriminate against, or grant preferential treatment to, any individual or group on the basis of race, sex, color, ethnicity, or national origin in the operation of public employment, public education, or public contracting.

(b) This section shall apply only to action taken after the section's effective date.

(c) Nothing in this section shall be interpreted as prohibiting bona fide qualifications based on sex which are reasonably necessary to the normal operation of public employment, public education, or public contracting.

(d) Nothing in this section shall be interpreted as invalidating any court order or consent decree which is in force as of the effective date of this section.

(e) Nothing in this section shall be interpreted as prohibiting action which must be taken to establish or maintain eligibility for any federal program, where ineligibility would result in a loss of federal funds to the State.

(f) For the purposes of this section, "State" shall include, but not necessarily be limited to, the State itself, any city, county, city and county, public university system, including the University of California, community college district, school district, special district, or any other political subdivision or governmental instrumentality of or within the State.

(g) The remedies available for violations of this section shall be the same, regardless of the injured party's race, sex, color, ethnicity, or national origin, as are otherwise available for violations of then-existing California antidiscrimination law.

(h) This section shall be self-executing. If any part or parts of this section are found to be in conflict with federal law or the United States Constitution, the section shall be implemented to the maximum extent that federal law and the United States Constitution permit. Any provision held invalid shall be severable from the remaining portions of this section.

(Sec. 31 added Nov. 5, 1996, by Prop. 209. Initiative measure.)

SEC. 32.

(a) The following provisions are hereby enacted to enhance public safety, improve rehabilitation, and avoid the release of prisoners by federal court order, notwithstanding anything in this article or any other provision of law:

(1) Parole Consideration: Any person convicted of a nonviolent felony offense and sentenced to state prison shall be eligible for parole consideration after completing the full term for his or her primary offense.

(A) For purposes of this section only, the full term for the primary offense means the longest term of imprisonment imposed by the court for any offense, excluding the imposition of an enhancement, consecutive sentence, or alternative sentence.

(2) Credit Earning: The Department of Corrections and Rehabilitation shall have authority to award credits earned for good behavior and approved rehabilitative or educational achievements.

(b) The Department of Corrections and Rehabilitation shall adopt regulations in furtherance of these provisions, and the Secretary of the Department of Corrections and Rehabilitation shall certify that these regulations protect and enhance public safety.

(Sec. 32 added Nov. 8, 2016, by Prop. 57. Initiative measure.)

ARTICLE II VOTING, INITIATIVE AND REFERENDUM, AND RECALL

[SECTION 1 - SEC. 20]

(Heading of Article 2 amended June 8, 1976, by Prop. 14. Res.Ch. 5, 1976.)

SECTION 1.

All political power is inherent in the people. Government is instituted for their protection, security, and benefit, and they have the right to alter or reform it when the public good may require.

(Sec. 1 renumbered from Sec. 26 (of Art. 1) on June 8, 1976, by Prop. 14. Res.Ch. 5, 1976.)

SEC. 2.

(a) A United States citizen 18 years of age and resident in this State may vote.

(b) An elector disqualified from voting while serving a state or federal prison term, as described in Section 4, shall have their right to vote restored upon the completion of their prison term.

(Sec. 2 amended Nov. 3, 2020, by Prop. 17. Res.Ch. 24, 2020. Effective December 16, 2020.)

SEC. 2.5.

A voter who casts a vote in an election in accordance with the laws of this State shall have that vote counted.

(Sec. 2.5 added March 5, 2002, by Prop. 43. Res.Ch. 114, 2001.)

SEC. 3.

The Legislature shall define residence and provide for registration and free elections.
(Sec. 3 renumbered from Sec. 2 on June 8, 1976, by Prop. 14. Res.Ch. 5, 1976.)

SEC. 4.

The Legislature shall prohibit improper practices that affect elections and shall provide for the disqualification of electors while mentally incompetent or serving a state or federal prison term for the conviction of a felony.
(Sec. 4 amended Nov. 3, 2020, by Prop. 17. Res.Ch. 24, 2020. Effective December 16, 2020.)

SEC. 5.

(a) A voter-nomination primary election shall be conducted to select the candidates for congressional and state elective offices in California. All voters may vote at a voter-nominated primary election for any candidate for congressional and state elective office without regard to the political party preference disclosed by the candidate or the voter, provided that the voter is otherwise qualified to vote for candidates for the office in question. The candidates who are the top two vote-getters at a voter-nominated primary election for a congressional or state elective office shall, regardless of party preference, compete in the ensuing general election.
(b) Except as otherwise provided by Section 6, a candidate for a congressional or state elective office may have his or her political party preference, or lack of political party preference, indicated upon the ballot for the office in the manner provided by statute. A political party or party central committee shall not nominate a candidate for any congressional or state elective office at the voter-

nominated primary. This subdivision shall not be interpreted to prohibit a political party or party central committee from endorsing, supporting, or opposing any candidate for a congressional or state elective office. A political party or party central committee shall not have the right to have its preferred candidate participate in the general election for a voter-nominated office other than a candidate who is one of the two highest vote-getters at the primary election, as provided in subdivision (a).

(c) The Legislature shall provide for partisan elections for presidential candidates, and political party and party central committees, including an open presidential primary whereby the candidates on the ballot are those found by the Secretary of State to be recognized candidates throughout the nation or throughout California for the office of President of the United States, and those whose names are placed on the ballot by petition, but excluding any candidate who has withdrawn by filing an affidavit of noncandidacy.

(d) A political party that participated in a primary election for a partisan office pursuant to subdivision (c) has the right to participate in the general election for that office and shall not be denied the ability to place on the general election ballot the candidate who received, at the primary election, the highest vote among that party's candidates.

(Sec. 5 amended June 8, 2010, by Prop. 14. Res.Ch. 2, 2009. Operative Jan. 1, 2011.)

SEC. 6.

(a) All judicial, school, county, and city offices, including the Superintendent of Public Instruction, shall be nonpartisan.

(b) A political party or party central committee shall not nominate a candidate for nonpartisan office, and the candidate's party preference shall not be included on the ballot for the nonpartisan office.

(Sec. 6 amended June 8, 2010, by Prop. 14. Res.Ch. 2, 2009. Operative Jan. 1, 2011.)

SEC. 7.

Voting shall be secret.
(Sec. 7 renumbered from Sec. 6 on June 8, 1976, by Prop. 14. Res.Ch. 5, 1976.)

SEC. 8.

(a) The initiative is the power of the electors to propose statutes and amendments to the Constitution and to adopt or reject them.

(b) An initiative measure may be proposed by presenting to the Secretary of State a petition that sets forth the text of the proposed statute or amendment to the Constitution and is certified to have been signed by electors equal in number to 5 percent in the case of a statute, and 8 percent in the case of an amendment to the Constitution, of the votes for all candidates for Governor at the last gubernatorial election.

(c) The Secretary of State shall then submit the measure at the next general election held at least 131 days after it qualifies or at any special statewide election held prior to that general election. The Governor may call a special statewide election for the measure.

(d) An initiative measure embracing more than one subject may not be submitted to the electors or have any effect.

(e) An initiative measure may not include or exclude any political subdivision of the State from the application or effect of its provisions based upon approval or disapproval of the initiative measure, or based upon the casting of a specified percentage of votes in favor of the measure, by the electors of that political subdivision.

(f) An initiative measure may not contain alternative or cumulative provisions wherein one or more of those provisions would become law depending upon the casting of a specified percentage of votes for or against the measure.

(Subdivisions (e) and (f) added June 2, 1998, by Prop. 219. Res.Ch. 34, 1996. Other Source: Entire Sec. 8 was renumbered from Sec. 22 (of Art. 4) on June 8, 1976, by Prop. 14; Res.Ch. 5, 1976.)

SEC. 9.

(a) The referendum is the power of the electors to approve or reject statutes or parts of statutes except urgency statutes, statutes calling elections, and statutes providing for tax levies or appropriations for usual current expenses of the State.

(b) A referendum measure may be proposed by presenting to the Secretary of State, within 90 days after the enactment date of the statute, a petition certified to have been signed by electors equal in number to 5 percent of the votes for all candidates for Governor at the last gubernatorial election, asking that the statute or part of it be submitted to the electors. In the case of a statute enacted by a bill passed by the Legislature on or before the date the Legislature adjourns for a joint recess to reconvene in the second calendar year of the biennium of the legislative session, and in the possession of the Governor after that date, the petition may not be presented on or after January 1 next following the enactment date unless a copy of the petition is submitted to the Attorney General pursuant to subdivision (d) of Section 10 of Article II before January 1.

(c) The Secretary of State shall then submit the measure at the next general election held at least 31 days after it qualifies or at a special statewide election held prior to that general election. The Governor may call a special statewide election for the measure.

(Sec. 9 amended June 5, 1990, by Prop. 109. Res.Ch. 74, 1988.)

SEC. 10.

(a) An initiative statute or referendum approved by a majority of votes cast thereon takes effect on the fifth day after the Secretary of State files the statement of the vote for the election at which the measure is voted on, but the measure may provide that it becomes operative after its effective date. If a referendum petition is filed against a part of a statute, the remainder of the statute shall not be delayed from going into effect.

(b) If provisions of two or more measures approved at the same election conflict, the provisions of the measure receiving the highest number of affirmative votes shall prevail.

(c) The Legislature may amend or repeal a referendum statute. The Legislature may amend or repeal an initiative statute by another statute that becomes effective only when approved by the electors unless the initiative statute permits amendment or repeal without the electors' approval.

(d) Before circulation of an initiative or referendum petition for signatures, a copy shall be submitted to the Attorney General who shall prepare a title and summary of the measure as provided by law.

(e) The Legislature shall provide for the manner in which a petition shall be circulated, presented, and certified, and the manner in which a measure shall be submitted to the electors.

(Sec. 10 amended June 5, 2018, by Prop. 71. Res.Ch. 190, 2017.)

SEC. 11.

(a) Initiative and referendum powers may be exercised by the electors of each city or county under procedures that the Legislature shall provide. Except as provided in subdivisions (b) and (c), this section does not affect a city having a charter.

(b) A city or county initiative measure may not include or exclude any part of the city or county from the application or effect of its provisions based upon approval or disapproval of the initiative measure, or based upon the casting of a specified percentage of votes in favor of the measure, by the electors of the city or county or any part thereof.

(c) A city or county initiative measure may not contain alternative or cumulative provisions wherein one or more of those provisions would become law depending upon the casting of a specified percentage of votes for or against the measure.

(Sec. 11 amended June 2, 1998, by Prop. 219. Res.Ch. 34, 1996.)

SEC. 12.

No amendment to the Constitution, and no statute proposed to the electors by the Legislature or by initiative, that names any individual to hold any office, or names or identifies any private corporation to perform any function or to have any power or duty, may be submitted to the electors or have any effect.

(Sec. 12 renumbered from Sec. 26 (of Art. 4) on June 8, 1976, by Prop. 14. Res.Ch. 5, 1976.)

SEC. 13.

Recall is the power of the electors to remove an elective officer.

(Sec. 13 added June 8, 1976, by Prop. 14. Res.Ch. 5, 1976.)

SEC. 14.

(a) Recall of a state officer is initiated by delivering to the Secretary of State a petition alleging reason for recall. Sufficiency of reason is not reviewable. Proponents have 160 days to file signed petitions.

(b) A petition to recall a statewide officer must be signed by electors equal in number to 12 percent of the last vote for the office, with signatures from each of 5 counties equal in number to 1 percent of the last vote for the office in the county. Signatures to recall Senators, members of the Assembly, members of the Board of Equalization, and judges of courts of appeal and trial courts must equal in number 20 percent of the last vote for the office.

(c) The Secretary of State shall maintain a continuous count of the signatures certified to that office.

(Sec. 14 added June 8, 1976, by Prop. 14. Res.Ch. 5, 1976, and Res.Ch. 24, Amdt. 3.)

SEC. 15.

(a) An election to determine whether to recall an officer and, if appropriate, to elect a successor shall be called by the Governor and held not less than 60 days nor more than 80 days from the date of certification of sufficient signatures.

(b) A recall election may be conducted within 180 days from the date of certification of sufficient signatures in order that the election may be consolidated with the next regularly scheduled election occurring wholly or partially within the same jurisdiction in which the recall election is held, if the number of voters eligible to vote at that next regularly scheduled election equal at least 50 percent of all the voters eligible to vote at the recall election.

(c) If the majority vote on the question is to recall, the officer is removed and, if there is a candidate, the candidate who receives a plurality is the successor. The officer may not be a candidate, nor shall there be any candidacy for an office filled pursuant to subdivision (d) of Section 16 of Article VI.

(Sec. 15 amended Nov. 8, 1994, by Prop. 183. Res.Ch. 59, 1994.)

SEC. 16.

The Legislature shall provide for circulation, filing, and certification of petitions, nomination of candidates, and the recall election.

(Sec. 16 added June 8, 1976, by Prop. 14. Res.Ch. 5, 1976.)

SEC. 17.

If recall of the Governor or Secretary of State is initiated, the recall duties of that office shall be performed by the Lieutenant Governor or Controller, respectively.
(Sec. 17 added June 8, 1976, by Prop. 14. Res.Ch. 5, 1976.)

SEC. 18.

A state officer who is not recalled shall be reimbursed by the State for the officer's recall election expenses legally and personally incurred. Another recall may not be initiated against the officer until six months after the election.
(Sec. 18 added June 8, 1976, by Prop. 14. Res.Ch. 5, 1976, and Res.Ch. 24, Amdts. 4 and 5.)

SEC. 19.

The Legislature shall provide for recall of local officers. This section does not affect counties and cities whose charters provide for recall.
(Sec. 19 added June 8, 1976, by Prop. 14. Res.Ch. 5, 1976.)

SEC. 20.

Terms of elective offices provided for by this Constitution, other than Members of the Legislature, commence on the Monday after January 1 following election. The election shall be held in the last even-numbered year before the term expires.
(Sec. 20 added June 8, 1976, by Prop. 14. Res.Ch. 5, 1976.)

ARTICLE III STATE OF CALIFORNIA

[SEC. 1 - SEC. 9]

(Article 3 added Nov. 7, 1972, by Prop. 6. Res.Ch. 120, 1972.)

SEC. 1.

The State of California is an inseparable part of the United States of America, and the United States Constitution is the supreme law of the land.

(Sec. 1 added Nov. 7, 1972, by Prop. 6. Res.Ch. 120, 1972.)

SEC. 2.

The boundaries of the State are those stated in the Constitution of 1849 as modified pursuant to statute. Sacramento is the capital of California.

(Sec. 2 added Nov. 7, 1972, by Prop. 6. Res.Ch. 120, 1972.)

SEC. 3.

The powers of state government are legislative, executive, and judicial. Persons charged with the exercise of one power may not exercise either of the others except as permitted by this Constitution.

(Sec. 3 added Nov. 7, 1972, by Prop. 6. Res.Ch. 120, 1972.)

SEC. 3.5.

An administrative agency, including an administrative agency created by the Constitution or an initiative statute, has no power:

(a) To declare a statute unenforceable, or refuse to enforce a statute, on the basis of it being unconstitutional unless an appellate court has made a determination that such statute is unconstitutional;

(b) To declare a statute unconstitutional;

(c) To declare a statute unenforceable, or to refuse to enforce a statute on the basis that federal law or federal regulations prohibit the enforcement of such statute unless an appellate court has made a determination that the enforcement of such statute is prohibited by federal law or federal regulations.

(Sec. 3.5 added June 6, 1978, by Prop. 5. Res.Ch. 48, 1977.)

SEC. 4.

(a) Except as provided in subdivision (b), salaries of elected state officers may not be reduced during their term of office. Laws that set these salaries are appropriations.

(b) Beginning on January 1, 1981, the base salary of a judge of a court of record shall equal the annual salary payable as of July 1, 1980, for that office had the judge been elected in 1978. The Legislature may prescribe increases in those salaries during a term of office, and it may terminate prospective increases in those salaries at any time during a term of office, but it shall not reduce the salary of a judge during a term of office below the highest level paid during that term of office. Laws setting the salaries of judges shall not constitute an obligation of contract pursuant to Section 9 of Article I or any other provision of law.

(Sec. 4 amended Nov. 4, 1980, by Prop. 11. Res.Ch. 77, 1980.)

SEC. 5.

Suits may be brought against the State in such manner and in such courts as shall be directed by law.

(Sec. 5 added Nov. 7, 1972, by Prop. 6. Res.Ch. 120, 1972.)

SEC. 6.

(a) Purpose.
English is the common language of the people of the United States of America and the State of California. This section is intended to preserve, protect and strengthen the English language, and not to supersede any of the rights guaranteed to the people by this Constitution.
(b) English as the Official Language of California.
English is the official language of the State of California.
(c) Enforcement.
The Legislature shall enforce this section by appropriate legislation. The Legislature and officials of the State of California shall take all steps necessary to insure that the role of English as the common language of the State of California is preserved and enhanced. The Legislature shall make no law which diminishes or ignores the role of English as the common language of the State of California.
(d) Personal Right of Action and Jurisdiction of Courts.
Any person who is a resident of or doing business in the State of California shall have standing to sue the State of California to enforce this section, and the Courts of record of the State of California shall have jurisdiction to hear cases brought to enforce this section. The Legislature may provide reasonable and appropriate limitations on the time and manner of suits brought under this section.
(Sec. 6 added Nov. 4, 1986, by Prop. 63. Initiative measure.)

Sec. 7.

(a) The retirement allowance for any person, all of whose credited service in the Legislators' Retirement System was rendered or was deemed to have been rendered as an elective officer of the State whose office is provided for by the California Constitution, other than a judge and other than a Member of the Senate or Assembly, and all or any part of whose retirement allowance is calculated on the basis of the compensation payable to the officer holding the office which the member last held prior to retirement, or for the survivor or beneficiary of such a person, shall not be increased or affected in any manner by changes on or after November 5, 1986, in the compensation payable to the officer holding the office which the member last held prior to retirement.

(b) This section shall apply to any person, survivor, or beneficiary described in subdivision (a) who receives, or is receiving, from the Legislators' Retirement System a retirement allowance on or after November 5, 1986, all or any part of which allowance is calculated on the basis of the compensation payable to the officer holding the office which the member last held prior to retirement.

(c) It is the intent of the people, in adopting this section, to restrict retirement allowances to amounts reasonably to be expected by certain members and retired members of the Legislators' Retirement System and to preserve the basic character of earned retirement benefits while prohibiting windfalls and unforeseen advantages which have no relation to the real theory and objective of a sound retirement system. It is not the intent of this section to deny any member, retired member, survivor, or beneficiary a reasonable retirement allowance. Thus, this section shall not be construed as a repudiation of a debt nor the impairment of a contract for a substantial and reasonable retirement allowance from the Legislators' Retirement System.

(d) The people and the Legislature hereby find and declare that the dramatic increase in the retirement allowances of persons described in subdivision (a) which would otherwise result when the compensation for those offices increases on November 5, 1986, or January 5, 1987, are not benefits which could have reasonably been expected. The people and the Legislature further find and declare that the Legislature did not intend to provide in its scheme of compensation for those offices such windfall benefits.

(Sec. 7 added Nov. 4, 1986, by Prop. 57. Res.Ch. 57, 1986.)

SEC. 8.

(a) The California Citizens Compensation Commission is hereby created and shall consist of seven members appointed by the Governor. The commission shall establish the annual salary and the medical, dental, insurance, and other similar benefits of state officers.

(b) The commission shall consist of the following persons:

(1) Three public members, one of whom has expertise in the area of compensation, such as an economist, market researcher, or personnel manager; one of whom is a member of a nonprofit public interest organization; and one of whom is representative of the general population and may include, among others, a retiree, homemaker, or person of median income. No person appointed pursuant to this paragraph may, during the 12 months prior to his or her appointment, have held public office, either elective or appointive, have been a candidate for elective public office, or have been a lobbyist, as defined by the Political Reform Act of 1974.

(2) Two members who have experience in the business community, one of whom is an executive of a corporation incorporated in this State which ranks among the largest private sector employers in the State based on the number of employees employed by the corporation in this State and one of whom is an owner of a small business in this State.

(3) Two members, each of whom is an officer or member of a labor organization.

(c) The Governor shall strive insofar as practicable to provide a balanced representation of the geographic, gender, racial, and ethnic diversity of the State in appointing commission members.

(d) The Governor shall appoint commission members and designate a chairperson for the commission not later than 30 days after the effective date of this section. The terms of two of the initial appointees shall expire on December 31, 1992, two on December 31, 1994, and three on December 31, 1996, as determined by the Governor. Thereafter, the term of each member shall be six years. Within 15 days of any vacancy, the Governor shall appoint a person to serve the unexpired portion of the term.

(e) No current or former officer or employee of this State is eligible for appointment to the commission.

(f) Public notice shall be given of all meetings of the commission, and the meetings shall be open to the public.

(g) On or before December 3, 1990, the commission shall, by a single resolution adopted by a majority of the membership of the commission, establish the annual salary and the medical, dental, insurance, and other similar benefits of state officers. The annual salary and benefits specified in that resolution shall be effective on and after December 3, 1990.

Thereafter, at or before the end of each fiscal year, the commission shall, by a resolution adopted by a majority of the membership of the commission, adjust the medical, dental, insurance, and other similar benefits of state officers. The benefits specified in the resolution shall be effective on and after the first Monday of the next December.

Thereafter, at or before the end of each fiscal year, the commission shall adjust the annual salary of state officers by a resolution adopted by a majority of the membership of the commission. The annual salary specified in the resolution shall be effective on and after the first Monday of the next December, except that a resolution shall not be adopted or take effect in any year that increases the annual salary of any state officer if, on or before the immediately preceding June 1, the Director of Finance certifies to the commission, based on estimates for the current fiscal year, that there will be a negative balance on June 30 of the current fiscal year in the Special Fund for Economic Uncertainties in an amount equal to, or greater than, 1 percent of estimated General Fund revenues.

(h) In establishing or adjusting the annual salary and the medical, dental, insurance, and other similar benefits, the commission shall consider all of the following:

(1) The amount of time directly or indirectly related to the performance of the duties, functions, and services of a state officer.

(2) The amount of the annual salary and the medical, dental, insurance, and other similar benefits for other elected and appointed officers and officials in this State

with comparable responsibilities, the judiciary, and, to the extent practicable, the private sector, recognizing, however, that state officers do not receive, and do not expect to receive, compensation at the same levels as individuals in the private sector with comparable experience and responsibilities.

(3) The responsibility and scope of authority of the entity in which the state officer serves.

(4) Whether the Director of Finance estimates that there will be a negative balance in the Special Fund for Economic Uncertainties in an amount equal to or greater than 1 percent of estimated General Fund revenues in the current fiscal year.

(i) Until a resolution establishing or adjusting the annual salary and the medical, dental, insurance, and other similar benefits for state officers takes effect, each state officer shall continue to receive the same annual salary and the medical, dental, insurance, and other similar benefits received previously.

(j) All commission members shall receive their actual and necessary expenses, including travel expenses, incurred in the performance of their duties. Each member shall be compensated at the same rate as members, other than the chairperson, of the Fair Political Practices Commission, or its successor, for each day engaged in official duties, not to exceed 45 days per year.

(k) It is the intent of the Legislature that the creation of the commission should not generate new state costs for staff and services. The Department of Personnel Administration, the Board of Administration of the Public Employees' Retirement System, or other appropriate agencies, or their successors, shall furnish, from existing resources, staff and services to the commission as needed for the performance of its duties.

(l) "State officer," as used in this section, means the Governor, Lieutenant Governor, Attorney General, Controller, Insurance Commissioner, Secretary of State, Superintendent of Public Instruction, Treasurer, member of the State Board of Equalization, and Member of the Legislature.

(Sec. 8 amended May 19, 2009, by Prop. 1F. Res.Ch. 3, 2009.)

SEC. 9.

The proceeds from the sale of surplus state property occurring on or after the effective date of this section, and any proceeds from the previous sale of surplus state property that have not been expended or encumbered as of that date, shall be used to pay the principal and interest on bonds issued pursuant to the Economic Recovery Bond Act authorized at the March 2, 2004, statewide primary election. Once the principal and interest on those bonds are fully paid, the proceeds from the sale of surplus state property shall be deposited into the Special Fund for Economic Uncertainties, or any successor fund. For purposes of this section, surplus state property does not include property purchased with revenues described in Article XIX or any other special fund moneys.

(Sec. 9 added Nov. 2, 2004, by Prop. 60A. Res.Ch. 103, 2004.)

ARTICLE IV LEGISLATIVE
[SEC. 1 - SEC. 28]

(Heading of Article 4 amended Nov. 8, 1966, by Prop. 1-a. Res.Ch. 139, 1966 1st Ex. Sess.)

SEC. 1.

The legislative power of this State is vested in the California Legislature which consists of the Senate and Assembly, but the people reserve to themselves the powers of initiative and referendum.

(Sec. 1 added Nov. 8, 1966, by Prop. 1-a. Res.Ch. 139, 1966 1st Ex. Sess.)

SEC. 1.5.

The people find and declare that the Founding Fathers established a system of representative government based upon free, fair, and competitive elections. The increased concentration of political power in the hands of incumbent representatives has made our electoral system less free, less competitive, and less representative.

The ability of legislators to serve unlimited number of terms, to establish their own retirement system, and to pay for staff and support services at state expense contribute heavily to the extremely high number of incumbents who are reelected. These unfair incumbent advantages discourage qualified candidates from seeking public office and create a class of career politicians, instead of the citizen representatives envisioned by the Founding Fathers. These career politicians become representatives of the bureaucracy, rather than of the people whom they are elected to represent.

To restore a free and democratic system of fair elections, and to encourage qualified candidates to seek public office, the people find and declare that the powers of incumbency must be limited. Retirement benefits must be restricted, state-financed incumbent staff and support services limited, and limitations placed upon the number of terms which may be served.

(Sec. 1.5 added Nov. 6, 1990, by Prop. 140. Initiative measure.)

SEC. 2.

(a) (1) The Senate has a membership of 40 Senators elected for 4-year terms, 20 to begin every 2 years.

(2) The Assembly has a membership of 80 members elected for 2-year terms.

(3) The terms of a Senator or a Member of the Assembly shall commence on the first Monday in December next following her or his election.

(4) During her or his lifetime a person may serve no more than 12 years in the Senate, the Assembly, or both, in any combination of terms. This subdivision shall apply only to those Members of the Senate or the Assembly who are first elected to the Legislature after the effective date of this subdivision and who have not previously served in the Senate or Assembly. Members of the Senate or Assembly who were elected before the effective date of this subdivision may serve only the number of terms allowed at the time of the last election before the effective date of this subdivision.

(b) Election of members of the Assembly shall be on the first Tuesday after the first Monday in November of even-numbered years unless otherwise prescribed by the Legislature. Senators shall be elected at the same time and places as members of the Assembly.

(c) A person is ineligible to be a member of the Legislature unless the person is an elector and has been a resident of the legislative district for one year, and a citizen of the United States and a resident of California for 3 years, immediately preceding the election, and service of the full term of office to which the person is seeking to be elected would not exceed the maximum years of service permitted by subdivision (a) of this section.

(d) When a vacancy occurs in the Legislature the Governor immediately shall call an election to fill the vacancy.
(Sec. 2 amended June 5, 2012, by Prop. 28. Initiative measure.)

SEC. 3.

(a) The Legislature shall convene in regular session at noon on the first Monday in December of each even-numbered year and each house shall immediately organize. Each session of the Legislature shall adjourn sine die by operation of the Constitution at midnight on November 30 of the following even-numbered year.
(b) On extraordinary occasions the Governor by proclamation may cause the Legislature to assemble in special session. When so assembled it has power to legislate only on subjects specified in the proclamation but may provide for expenses and other matters incidental to the session.
(Sec. 3 amended June 8, 1976, by Prop. 14. Res.Ch. 5, 1976.)

SEC. 4.

(a) To eliminate any appearance of a conflict with the proper discharge of his or her duties and responsibilities, no Member of the Legislature may knowingly receive any salary, wages, commissions, or other similar earned income from a lobbyist or lobbying firm, as defined by the Political Reform Act of 1974, or from a person who, during the previous 12 months, has been under a contract with the Legislature. The Legislature shall enact laws that define earned income. However, earned income does not include any community property interest in the income of a spouse. Any Member who knowingly receives any salary, wages, commissions, or other similar earned income from a lobbyist employer, as defined by the Political Reform Act of 1974, may not, for a period of one year following its receipt, vote upon or make, participate in making, or in any way attempt to use his or her official position to influence an action or decision before the Legislature, other than an action or decision involving a bill described in subdivision (c) of Section 12 of this article, which he or she knows, or has reason to know, would have a direct and significant financial impact on the lobbyist employer and would not impact the public generally or a significant segment of the public in a similar manner. As used in this subdivision, "public generally" includes an industry, trade, or profession.

(b) Travel and living expenses for Members of the Legislature in connection with their official duties shall be prescribed by statute passed by rollcall vote entered in the journal, two-thirds of the membership of each house concurring. A Member may not receive travel and living expenses during the times that the Legislature is in recess for more than three calendar days, unless the Member is traveling to or from, or is in attendance at, any meeting of a committee of which he or she is a member, or a meeting, conference, or other legislative function or responsibility as authorized by the rules of the house of which he or she is a member, which is held at a location at least 20 miles from his or her place of residence.

(c) The Legislature may not provide retirement benefits based on any portion of a monthly salary in excess of five hundred dollars ($500) paid to any Member of the Legislature unless the Member receives the greater amount while serving as a Member in the Legislature. The Legislature may, prior to their retirement, limit the retirement benefits payable to Members of the Legislature who serve during or after the term commencing in 1967.

When computing the retirement allowance of a Member who serves in the Legislature during the term commencing in 1967 or later, allowance may be made for increases in cost of living if so provided by statute, but only with respect to increases in the cost of living occurring after retirement of the Member. However, the Legislature may provide that no Member shall be deprived of a cost of living adjustment based on a monthly salary of five hundred dollars ($500) which has accrued prior to the

commencement of the 1967 Regular Session of the Legislature.
(Sec. 4 amended June 5, 1990, by Prop. 112. Res.Ch. 167, 1989.)

SEC. 4.5.

Notwithstanding any other provision of this Constitution or existing law, a person elected to or serving in the Legislature on or after November 1, 1990, shall participate in the Federal Social Security (Retirement, Disability, Health Insurance) Program and the State shall pay only the employer's share of the contribution necessary to such participation. No other pension or retirement benefit shall accrue as a result of service in the Legislature, such service not being intended as a career occupation. This Section shall not be construed to abrogate or diminish any vested pension or retirement benefit which may have accrued under an existing law to a person holding or having held office in the Legislature, but upon adoption of this Act no further entitlement to nor vesting in any existing program shall accrue to any such person, other than Social Security to the extent herein provided.
(Sec. 4.5 added Nov. 6, 1990, by Prop. 140. Initiative measure.)

SEC. 5.

(a) (1) Each house of the Legislature shall judge the qualifications and elections of its Members and, by rollcall vote entered in the journal, two-thirds of the membership concurring, may expel a Member.
(2) (A) Each house may suspend a Member by motion or resolution adopted by rollcall vote entered in the journal, two-thirds of the membership concurring. The motion or resolution shall contain findings and declarations setting forth the basis for the suspension. Notwithstanding any other provision of this Constitution, the house may deem the salary and benefits of the Member to be forfeited for all

or part of the period of the suspension by express provision of the motion or resolution.

(B) A Member suspended pursuant to this paragraph shall not exercise any of the rights, privileges, duties, or powers of his or her office, or utilize any resources of the Legislature, during the period the suspension is in effect.

(C) The suspension of a Member pursuant to this paragraph shall remain in effect until the date specified in the motion or resolution or, if no date is specified, the date a subsequent motion or resolution terminating the suspension is adopted by rollcall vote entered in the journal, two-thirds of the membership of the house concurring.

(b) No Member of the Legislature may accept any honorarium. The Legislature shall enact laws that implement this subdivision.

(c) The Legislature shall enact laws that ban or strictly limit the acceptance of a gift by a Member of the Legislature from any source if the acceptance of the gift might create a conflict of interest.

(d) No Member of the Legislature may knowingly accept any compensation for appearing, agreeing to appear, or taking any other action on behalf of another person before any state government board or agency. If a Member knowingly accepts any compensation for appearing, agreeing to appear, or taking any other action on behalf of another person before any local government board or agency, the Member may not, for a period of one year following the acceptance of the compensation, vote upon or make, participate in making, or in any way attempt to use his or her official position to influence an action or decision before the Legislature, other than an action or decision involving a bill described in subdivision (c) of Section 12, which he or she knows, or has reason to know, would have a direct and significant financial impact on that person and would not impact the public generally or a significant segment of the public in a similar manner. As used in this subdivision, "public generally" includes an industry, trade, or profession. However, a Member may engage in activities involving a board or agency which are strictly on his or her own behalf, appear in the capacity of an attorney before any court or the Workers' Compensation Appeals Board, or act as an advocate without compensation or make an inquiry for information on behalf of a person before a board or agency. This subdivision does not prohibit any action of a partnership or firm of which the Member is a member if the Member does not share directly or indirectly in the fee, less any expenses attributable to that fee, resulting from that action.

(e) The Legislature shall enact laws that prohibit a Member of the Legislature whose term of office commences on or after December 3, 1990, from lobbying, for compensation, as governed by the Political Reform Act of 1974, before the Legislature for 12 months after leaving office.

(f) The Legislature shall enact new laws, and strengthen the enforcement of existing laws, prohibiting Members of the Legislature from engaging in activities or having interests which conflict with the proper discharge of their duties and responsibilities. However, the people reserve to themselves the power to implement this requirement pursuant to Article II.

(Sec. 5 amended June 7, 2016, by Prop. 50. Res.Ch. 127, 2014.)

SEC. 6.

For the purpose of choosing members of the Legislature, the State shall be divided into 40 Senatorial and 80 Assembly districts to be called Senatorial and Assembly Districts. Each Senatorial district shall choose one Senator and each Assembly district shall choose one member of the Assembly.

(Sec. 6 added June 3, 1980, by Prop. 6. Res.Ch. 78, 1978.)

SEC. 7.

(a) Each house shall choose its officers and adopt rules for its proceedings. A majority of the membership constitutes a quorum, but a smaller number may recess from day to day and compel the attendance of absent members.

(b) Each house shall keep and publish a journal of its proceedings. The rollcall vote of the members on a question shall be taken and entered in the journal at the request of 3 members present.

(c) (1) Except as provided in paragraph (3), the proceedings of each house and the committees thereof shall be open and public. The right to attend open and public proceedings includes the right of any person to record by audio or video means any and all parts of the proceedings and to broadcast or otherwise transmit them; provided that the Legislature may adopt reasonable rules pursuant to paragraph (5) regulating the placement and use of the equipment for recording or broadcasting the proceedings for the sole purpose of minimizing disruption of the proceedings. Any aggrieved party shall have standing to challenge said rules in an action for declaratory and injunctive relief, and the Legislature shall have the burden of demonstrating that the rule is reasonable.

(2) Commencing on January 1 of the second calendar year following the adoption of this paragraph, the Legislature shall also cause audiovisual recordings to be made of all proceedings subject to paragraph (1) in their entirety, shall make such recordings public through the Internet within 24 hours after the proceedings have been recessed or adjourned for the day, and shall maintain an archive of said recordings, which shall be accessible to the public through the Internet and downloadable for a period of no less than 20 years as specified by statute.

(3) Notwithstanding paragraphs (1) and (2), closed sessions may be held solely for any of the following purposes:

(A) To consider the appointment, employment, evaluation of performance, or dismissal of a public officer or employee, to consider or hear complaints or charges brought against a Member of the Legislature or other public officer or employee, or to establish the classification or compensation of an employee of the Legislature.

(B) To consider matters affecting the safety and security of Members of the Legislature or its employees or the safety and security of any buildings and grounds used by the Legislature.

(C) To confer with, or receive advice from, its legal counsel regarding pending or reasonably anticipated, or whether to initiate, litigation when discussion in open session would not protect the interests of the house or committee regarding the litigation.

(4) A caucus of the Members of the Senate, the Members of the Assembly, or the Members of both houses, which is composed of the members of the same political party, may meet in closed session.

(5) The Legislature shall implement this subdivision by concurrent resolution adopted by rollcall vote entered in the journal, two-thirds of the membership of each house concurring, or by statute, and in the case of a closed session held pursuant to paragraph (3), shall prescribe that reasonable notice of the closed session and the purpose of the closed session shall be provided to the public. If there is a conflict between a concurrent resolution and statute, the last adopted or enacted shall prevail.

(d) Neither house without the consent of the other may recess for more than 10 days or to any other place.

(Sec. 7 amended Nov. 8, 2016, by Prop. 54. Initiative measure.)

SEC. 7.5.

In the fiscal year immediately following the adoption of this Act, the total aggregate expenditures of the Legislature for the compensation of members and employees of, and the operating expenses and equipment for, the Legislature may not exceed an amount equal to nine hundred fifty thousand dollars ($950,000) per member for that fiscal year or 80 percent of the amount of money expended for those purposes in the preceding fiscal year, whichever is less. For each fiscal year thereafter, the total aggregate expenditures may not exceed an amount equal to that expended for those purposes in the preceding fiscal year, adjusted and compounded by an amount equal to the

percentage increase in the appropriations limit for the State established pursuant to Article XIII B.
(Sec. 7.5 added Nov. 6, 1990, by Prop. 140. Initiative measure.)

SEC. 8.

(a) At regular sessions no bill other than the budget bill may be heard or acted on by committee or either house until the 31st day after the bill is introduced unless the house dispenses with this requirement by rollcall vote entered in the journal, three fourths of the membership concurring.

(b) (1) The Legislature may make no law except by statute and may enact no statute except by bill. No bill may be passed unless it is read by title on 3 days in each house except that the house may dispense with this requirement by rollcall vote entered in the journal, two thirds of the membership concurring.

(2) No bill may be passed or ultimately become a statute unless the bill with any amendments has been printed, distributed to the members, and published on the Internet, in its final form, for at least 72 hours before the vote, except that this notice period may be waived if the Governor has submitted to the Legislature a written statement that dispensing with this notice period for that bill is necessary to address a state of emergency, as defined in paragraph (2) of subdivision (c) of Section 3 of Article XIII B, that has been declared by the Governor, and the house considering the bill thereafter dispenses with the notice period for that bill by a separate rollcall vote entered in the journal, two thirds of the membership concurring, prior to the vote on the bill.

(3) No bill may be passed unless, by rollcall vote entered in the journal, a majority of the membership of each house concurs.

(c) (1) Except as provided in paragraphs (2) and (3) of this subdivision, a statute enacted at a regular session shall go into effect on January 1 next following a 90-day period from the date of enactment of the statute and a statute enacted at a special session shall go into effect on the 91st day after adjournment of the special session at which the bill was passed.

(2) A statute, other than a statute establishing or changing boundaries of any legislative, congressional, or other election district, enacted by a bill passed by the Legislature on or before the date the Legislature adjourns for a joint recess to reconvene in the second calendar year of the biennium of the legislative session, and in the possession of the Governor after that date, shall go into effect on January 1 next following the enactment date of the statute unless, before January 1, a copy of a referendum petition affecting the statute is submitted to the Attorney General pursuant to subdivision (d) of Section 10 of Article II, in which event the statute shall go into effect on the 91st day after the enactment date unless the petition has been presented to the Secretary of State pursuant to subdivision (b) of Section 9 of Article II.

(3) Statutes calling elections, statutes providing for tax levies or appropriations for the usual current expenses of the State, and urgency statutes shall go into effect immediately upon their enactment.

(d) Urgency statutes are those necessary for immediate preservation of the public peace, health, or safety. A statement of facts constituting the necessity shall be set forth in one section of the bill. In each house the section and the bill shall be passed separately, each by rollcall vote entered in the journal, two thirds of the membership concurring. An urgency statute may not create or abolish any office or change the salary, term, or duties of any office, or grant any franchise or special privilege, or create any vested right or interest.

(Sec. 8 amended Nov. 8, 2016, by Prop. 54. Initiative measure.)

SEC. 8.5.

An act amending an initiative statute, an act providing for the issuance of bonds, or a constitutional amendment proposed by the Legislature and submitted to the voters for approval may not do either of the following:

(a) Include or exclude any political subdivision of the State from the application or effect of its provisions based upon approval or disapproval of the measure, or based upon the casting of a specified percentage of votes in favor of the measure, by the electors of that political subdivision.

(b) Contain alternative or cumulative provisions wherein one or more of those provisions would become law depending upon the casting of a specified percentage of votes for or against the measure.

(Sec. 8.5 added June 2, 1998, by Prop. 219. Res.Ch. 34, 1996.)

SEC. 9.

A statute shall embrace but one subject, which shall be expressed in its title. If a statute embraces a subject not expressed in its title, only the part not expressed is void. A statute may not be amended by reference to its title. A section of a statute may not be amended unless the section is re-enacted as amended.

(Sec. 9 added Nov. 8, 1966, by Prop. 1-a. Res.Ch. 139, 1966 1st Ex. Sess.)

SEC. 10.

(a) Each bill passed by the Legislature shall be presented to the Governor. It becomes a statute if it is signed by the Governor. The Governor may veto it by returning it with any objections to the house of origin, which shall enter the objections in the journal and proceed to reconsider it. If each house then passes the bill by rollcall vote entered in the journal, two-thirds of the membership concurring, it becomes a statute.

(b) (1) Any bill, other than a bill which would establish or change boundaries of any legislative, congressional, or other election district, passed by the Legislature on or before the date the Legislature adjourns for a joint recess to reconvene in the second calendar year of the biennium of the legislative session, and in the possession of the Governor after that date, that is not returned within 30 days after that date becomes a statute.

(2) Any bill passed by the Legislature before September 1 of the second calendar year of the biennium of the legislative session and in the possession of the Governor on or after September 1 that is not returned on or before September 30 of that year becomes a statute.

(3) Any other bill presented to the Governor that is not returned within 12 days becomes a statute.

(4) If the Legislature by adjournment of a special session prevents the return of a bill with the veto message, the bill becomes a statute unless the Governor vetoes the bill within 12 days after it is presented by depositing it and the veto message in the office of the Secretary of State.

(5) If the 12th day of the period within which the Governor is required to perform an act pursuant to paragraph (3) or (4) of this subdivision is a Saturday, Sunday, or holiday, the period is extended to the next day that is not a Saturday, Sunday, or holiday.

(c) Any bill introduced during the first year of the biennium of the legislative session that has not been passed by the house of origin by January 31 of the second calendar year of the biennium may no longer be acted on by the house. No bill may be passed by either house on or after September 1 of an even-numbered year except statutes calling elections, statutes providing for tax levies or appropriations for the usual current expenses of the State, and urgency statutes, and bills passed after being vetoed by the Governor.

(d) The Legislature may not present any bill to the Governor after November 15 of the second calendar year of the biennium of the legislative session.

(e) The Governor may reduce or eliminate one or more items of appropriation while approving other portions of a bill. The Governor shall append to the bill a statement of the items reduced or eliminated with the reasons for the action. The Governor shall transmit to the house originating the bill a copy of the statement and reasons. Items reduced or eliminated shall be separately reconsidered and may be passed over the Governor's veto in the same manner as bills.

(f) (1) If, following the enactment of the budget bill for the 2004–05 fiscal year or any subsequent fiscal year, the Governor determines that, for that fiscal year, General Fund revenues will decline substantially below the estimate of General Fund revenues upon which the budget bill for that fiscal year, as enacted, was based, or General Fund expenditures will increase substantially above that estimate of General Fund revenues, or both, the Governor may issue a proclamation declaring a fiscal emergency and shall thereupon cause the Legislature to assemble in special session for this purpose. The proclamation shall identify the nature of the fiscal emergency and shall be submitted by the Governor to the Legislature, accompanied by proposed legislation to address the fiscal emergency.

(2) If the Legislature fails to pass and send to the Governor a bill or bills to address the fiscal emergency by the 45th day following the issuance of the proclamation, the Legislature may not act on any other bill, nor may the Legislature adjourn for a joint recess, until that bill or those bills have been passed and sent to the Governor.

(3) A bill addressing the fiscal emergency declared pursuant to this section shall contain a statement to that effect.

(Sec. 10 amended March 2, 2004, by Prop. 58. Res.Ch. 1, 2003-04 5th Ex. Sess.)

SEC. 11.

The Legislature or either house may by resolution provide for the selection of committees necessary for the conduct of its business, including committees to ascertain facts and make recommendations to the Legislature on a subject within the scope of legislative control.

(Sec. 11 amended Nov. 7, 1972, by Prop. 4. Res.Ch. 81, 1972.)

SEC. 12.

(a) Within the first 10 days of each calendar year, the Governor shall submit to the Legislature, with an explanatory message, a budget for the ensuing fiscal year containing itemized statements for recommended state expenditures and estimated state revenues. If recommended expenditures exceed estimated revenues, the Governor shall recommend the sources from which the additional revenues should be provided.

(b) The Governor and the Governor-elect may require a state agency, officer or employee to furnish whatever information is deemed necessary to prepare the budget.

(c) (1) The budget shall be accompanied by a budget bill itemizing recommended expenditures.

(2) The budget bill shall be introduced immediately in each house by the persons chairing the committees that consider the budget.

(3) The Legislature shall pass the budget bill by midnight on June 15 of each year.

(4) Until the budget bill has been enacted, the Legislature shall not send to the Governor for consideration any bill appropriating funds for expenditure during the fiscal year for which the budget bill is to be enacted, except emergency bills recommended by the Governor or appropriations for the salaries and expenses of the Legislature.

(d) No bill except the budget bill may contain more than one item of appropriation, and that for one certain, expressed purpose. Appropriations from the General Fund of the State, except appropriations for the public schools and appropriations in the budget bill and in other bills providing for appropriations related to the budget bill, are void unless passed in each house by rollcall vote entered in the journal, two-thirds of the membership concurring.

(e) (1) Notwithstanding any other provision of law or of this Constitution, the budget bill and other bills providing for appropriations related to the budget bill may be passed in each house by rollcall vote entered in the journal, a majority of the membership concurring, to take effect immediately upon being signed by the Governor or upon a date specified in the legislation. Nothing in this subdivision shall affect the vote requirement for appropriations for the public schools contained in subdivision (d) of this section and in subdivision (b) of Section 8 of this article.

(2) For purposes of this section, "other bills providing for appropriations related to the budget bill" shall consist only of bills identified as related to the budget in the budget bill passed by the Legislature.

(f) The Legislature may control the submission, approval, and enforcement of budgets and the filing of claims for all state agencies.

(g) For the 2004–05 fiscal year, or any subsequent fiscal year, the Legislature may not send to the Governor for consideration, nor may the Governor sign into law, a budget bill that would appropriate from the General Fund, for that fiscal year, a total amount that, when combined with all appropriations from the General Fund for that fiscal year made as of the date of the budget bill's passage, and the amount of any General Fund moneys transferred to the Budget Stabilization Account for that fiscal year pursuant to Section 20 of Article XVI, exceeds General Fund revenues for that fiscal year estimated as of the date of the budget bill's passage. That estimate of General Fund revenues shall be set forth in the budget bill passed by the Legislature.

(h) Notwithstanding any other provision of law or of this Constitution, including subdivision (c) of this section, Section 4 of this article, and Sections 4 and 8 of Article III, in any year in which the budget bill is not passed by the Legislature by midnight on June 15, there shall be no appropriation from the current budget or future budget to pay any salary or reimbursement for travel or living expenses for Members of the Legislature during any regular or special session for the period from midnight on June 15 until the day that the budget bill is presented to the Governor. No salary or reimbursement for travel or living expenses forfeited pursuant to this subdivision shall be paid retroactively.

(Sec. 12 amended Nov. 2, 2010, by Prop. 25. Initiative measure.)

SEC. 12.5.

Within 10 days following the submission of a budget pursuant to subdivision (a) of Section 12, following the proposed adjustments to the Governor's Budget required by subdivision (e) of Section 13308 of the Government Code or a successor statute, and following the enactment of the budget bill, or as soon as feasible thereafter, the Director of Finance shall submit to the Legislature both of the following:

(a) Estimates of General Fund revenues for the ensuing fiscal year and for the three fiscal years thereafter.

(b) Estimates of General Fund expenditures for the ensuing fiscal year and for the three fiscal years thereafter.

(Sec. 12.5 added Nov. 4, 2014, by Prop. 2. Res.Ch. 1, 2013-14 2nd Ex. Sess.)

SEC. 13.

A member of the Legislature may not, during the term for which the member is elected, hold any office or employment under the State other than an elective office.

(Sec. 13 amended Nov. 5, 1974, by Prop. 11. Res.Ch. 96, 1974.)

SEC. 14.

A member of the Legislature is not subject to civil process during a session of the Legislature or for 5 days before and after a session.

(Sec. 14 added Nov. 8, 1966, by Prop. 1-a. Res.Ch. 139, 1966 1st Ex. Sess.)

SEC. 15.

A person who seeks to influence the vote or action of a member of the Legislature in the member's legislative capacity by bribery, promise of reward, intimidation, or other dishonest means, or a member of the Legislature so influenced, is guilty of a felony.

(Sec. 15 amended Nov. 5, 1974, by Prop. 11. Res.Ch. 96, 1974.)

SEC. 16.

(a) All laws of a general nature have uniform operation.
(b) A local or special statute is invalid in any case if a general statute can be made applicable.
(Sec. 16 amended Nov. 5, 1974, by Prop. 7. Res.Ch. 90, 1974.)

SEC. 17.

The Legislature has no power to grant, or to authorize a city, county, or other public body to grant, extra compensation or extra allowance to a public officer, public employee, or contractor after service has been rendered or a contract has been entered into and performed in whole or in part, or to authorize the payment of a claim against the State or a city, county, or other public body under an agreement made without authority of law.
(Sec. 17 added Nov. 8, 1966, by Prop. 1-a. Res.Ch. 139, 1966 1st Ex. Sess.)

SEC. 18.

(a) The Assembly has the sole power of impeachment. Impeachments shall be tried by the Senate. A person may not be convicted unless, by rollcall vote entered in the journal, two thirds of the membership of the Senate concurs.
(b) State officers elected on a statewide basis, members of the State Board of Equalization, and judges of state courts are subject to impeachment for misconduct in office. Judgment may extend only to removal from office and disqualification to hold any office under the State, but the person convicted or acquitted remains subject to criminal punishment according to law.
(Sec. 18 added Nov. 8, 1966, by Prop. 1-a. Res.Ch. 139, 1966 1st Ex. Sess.)

SEC. 19.

(a) The Legislature has no power to authorize lotteries, and shall prohibit the sale of lottery tickets in the State.

(b) The Legislature may provide for the regulation of horse races and horse race meetings and wagering on the results.

(c) Notwithstanding subdivision (a), the Legislature by statute may authorize cities and counties to provide for bingo games, but only for charitable purposes.

(d) Notwithstanding subdivision (a), there is authorized the establishment of a California State Lottery.

(e) The Legislature has no power to authorize, and shall prohibit, casinos of the type currently operating in Nevada and New Jersey.

(f) Notwithstanding subdivisions (a) and (e), and any other provision of state law, the Governor is authorized to negotiate and conclude compacts, subject to ratification by the Legislature, for the operation of slot machines and for the conduct of lottery games and banking and percentage card games by federally recognized Indian tribes on Indian lands in California in accordance with federal law. Accordingly, slot machines, lottery games, and banking and percentage card games are hereby permitted to be conducted and operated on tribal lands subject to those compacts.

(f) Notwithstanding subdivision (a), the Legislature may authorize private, nonprofit, eligible organizations, as defined by the Legislature, to conduct raffles as a funding mechanism to provide support for their own or another private, nonprofit, eligible organization's beneficial and charitable works, provided that (1) at least 90 percent of the gross receipts from the raffle go directly to beneficial or charitable purposes in California, and (2) any person who receives compensation in connection with the operation of a raffle is an employee of the private nonprofit organization that is conducting the raffle. The Legislature, two-thirds of the membership of each house concurring, may amend the percentage of gross receipts required by this subdivision to

be dedicated to beneficial or charitable purposes by means of a statute that is signed by the Governor.
(Sec. 19 amended March 7, 2000, by Prop. 1A (Res.Ch. 142, 1999) and Prop. 17 (Res.Ch. 123, 1999).)

SEC. 20.

(a) The Legislature may provide for division of the State into fish and game districts and may protect fish and game in districts or parts of districts.
(b) There is a Fish and Game Commission of 5 members appointed by the Governor and approved by the Senate, a majority of the membership concurring, for 6-year terms and until their successors are appointed and qualified. Appointment to fill a vacancy is for the unexpired portion of the term. The Legislature may delegate to the commission such powers relating to the protection and propagation of fish and game as the Legislature sees fit. A member of the commission may be removed by concurrent resolution adopted by each house, a majority of the membership concurring.
(Sec. 20 added Nov. 8, 1966, by Prop. 1-a. Res.Ch. 139, 1966 1st Ex. Sess.)

SEC. 21.

To meet the needs resulting from war-caused or enemy-caused disaster in California, the Legislature may provide for:
(a) Filling the offices of members of the Legislature should at least one fifth of the membership of either house be killed, missing, or disabled, until they are able to perform their duties or successors are elected.
(b) Filling the office of Governor should the Governor be killed, missing, or disabled, until the Governor or the successor designated in this Constitution is able to perform the duties of the office of Governor or a successor is elected.

(c) Convening the Legislature.
(d) Holding elections to fill offices that are elective under this Constitution and that are either vacant or occupied by persons not elected thereto.
(e) Selecting a temporary seat of state or county government.
(Sec. 21 amended Nov. 5, 1974, by Prop. 11. Res.Ch. 96, 1974.)

SEC. 22.

It is the right of the people to hold their legislators accountable. To assist the people in exercising this right, at the convening of each regular session of the Legislature, the President pro Tempore of the Senate, the Speaker of the Assembly, and the minority leader of each house shall report to their house the goals and objectives of that house during that session and, at the close of each regular session, the progress made toward meeting those goals and objectives.
(Sec. 22 added June 5, 1990, by Prop. 112. Res.Ch. 167, 1989.)

SEC. 28.

(a) Notwithstanding any other provision of this Constitution, no bill shall take effect as an urgency statute if it authorizes or contains an appropriation for either (1) the alteration or modification of the color, detail, design, structure or fixtures of the historically restored areas of the first, second, and third floors and the exterior of the west wing of the State Capitol from that existing upon the completion of the project of restoration or rehabilitation of the building conducted pursuant to Section 9124 of the Government Code as such section read upon the effective date of this section, or (2) the purchase of furniture of different design to replace that restored, replicated, or designed to conform to the historic period of the historically restored areas specified above, including the legislators' chairs and desks in the Senate and Assembly Chambers.

(b) No expenditures shall be made in payment for any of the purposes described in subdivision (a) of this section unless funds are appropriated expressly for such purposes.

(c) This section shall not apply to appropriations or expenditures for ordinary repair and maintenance of the State Capitol building, fixtures and furniture.

(Sec. 28 added June 3, 1980, by Prop. 3. Res.Ch. 56, 1978.)

ARTICLE V EXECUTIVE
[SECTION 1 - SEC. 14]

(Article 5 added Nov. 8, 1966, by Prop. 1-a. Res.Ch. 139, 1966 1st Ex. Sess.)

SECTION 1.

The supreme executive power of this State is vested in the Governor. The Governor shall see that the law is faithfully executed.
(Sec. 1 amended Nov. 5, 1974, by Prop. 11. Res.Ch. 96, 1974.)

SEC. 2.

The Governor shall be elected every fourth year at the same time and places as members of the Assembly and hold office from the Monday after January 1 following the election until a successor qualifies. The Governor shall be an elector who has been a citizen of the United States and a resident of this State for 5 years immediately preceding the Governor's election. The Governor may not hold other public office. No Governor may serve more than 2 terms.
(Sec. 2 amended Nov. 6, 1990, by Prop. 140. Initiative measure.)

SEC. 3.

The Governor shall report to the Legislature each calendar year on the condition of the State and may make recommendations.
(Sec. 3 amended Nov. 7, 1972, by Prop. 4. Res.Ch. 81, 1972.)

SEC. 4.

The Governor may require executive officers and agencies and their employees to furnish information relating to their duties.

(Sec. 4 added Nov. 8, 1966, by Prop. 1-a. Res.Ch. 139, 1966 1st Ex. Sess.)

SEC. 5.

(a) Unless the law otherwise provides, the Governor may fill a vacancy in office by appointment until a successor qualifies.

(b) Whenever there is a vacancy in the office of the Superintendent of Public Instruction, the Lieutenant Governor, Secretary of State, Controller, Treasurer, or Attorney General, or on the State Board of Equalization, the Governor shall nominate a person to fill the vacancy who shall take office upon confirmation by a majority of the membership of the Senate and a majority of the membership of the Assembly and who shall hold office for the balance of the unexpired term. In the event the nominee is neither confirmed nor refused confirmation by both the Senate and the Assembly within 90 days of the submission of the nomination, the nominee shall take office as if he or she had been confirmed by a majority of the Senate and Assembly; provided, that if such 90-day period ends during a recess of the Legislature, the period shall be extended until the sixth day following the day on which the Legislature reconvenes.

(Sec. 5 amended Nov. 2, 1976, by Prop. 9. Res.Ch. 58, 1976.)

SEC. 6.

Authority may be provided by statute for the Governor to assign and reorganize functions among executive officers and agencies and their employees, other than elective officers and agencies administered by elective officers.

(Sec. 6 added Nov. 8, 1966, by Prop. 1-a. Res.Ch. 139, 1966 1st Ex. Sess.)

SEC. 7.

The Governor is commander in chief of a militia that shall be provided by statute. The Governor may call it forth to execute the law.

(Sec. 7 amended Nov. 5, 1974, by Prop. 11. Res.Ch. 96, 1974.)

SEC. 8.

(a) Subject to application procedures provided by statute, the Governor, on conditions the Governor deems proper, may grant a reprieve, pardon, and commutation, after sentence, except in case of impeachment. The Governor shall report to the Legislature each reprieve, pardon, and commutation granted, stating the pertinent facts and the reasons for granting it. The Governor may not grant a pardon or commutation to a person twice convicted of a felony except on recommendation of the Supreme Court, 4 judges concurring.

(b) No decision of the parole authority of this State with respect to the granting, denial, revocation, or suspension of parole of a person sentenced to an indeterminate term upon conviction of murder shall become effective for a period of 30 days, during which the Governor may review the decision subject to procedures provided by statute. The Governor may only affirm, modify, or reverse the decision of the parole authority on the basis of the same factors which the parole authority is required to consider. The Governor shall report to the Legislature each parole decision affirmed, modified, or reversed, stating the pertinent facts and reasons for the action.

(Sec. 8 amended Nov. 8, 1988, by Prop. 89. Res.Ch. 63, 1988.)

SEC. 9.

The Lieutenant Governor shall have the same qualifications as the Governor. The Lieutenant Governor is President of the Senate but has only a casting vote.
(Sec. 9 amended Nov. 5, 1974, by Prop. 11. Res.Ch. 96, 1974.)

SEC. 10.

The Lieutenant Governor shall become Governor when a vacancy occurs in the office of Governor.

The Lieutenant Governor shall act as Governor during the impeachment, absence from the State, or other temporary disability of the Governor or of a Governor-elect who fails to take office.

The Legislature shall provide an order of precedence after the Lieutenant Governor for succession to the office of Governor and for the temporary exercise of the Governor's functions.

The Supreme Court has exclusive jurisdiction to determine all questions arising under this section.

Standing to raise questions of vacancy or temporary disability is vested exclusively in a body provided by statute.
(Sec. 10 amended Nov. 5, 1974, by Prop. 11. Res.Ch. 96, 1974.)

SEC. 11.

The Lieutenant Governor, Attorney General, Controller, Secretary of State, and Treasurer shall be elected at the same time and places and for the same term as the Governor. No Lieutenant Governor, Attorney General, Controller, Secretary of State, or Treasurer may serve in the same office for more than 2 terms.
(Sec. 11 amended Nov. 6, 1990, by Prop. 140. Initiative measure.)

SEC. 13.

Subject to the powers and duties of the Governor, the Attorney General shall be the chief law officer of the State. It shall be the duty of the Attorney General to see that the laws of the State are uniformly and adequately enforced. The Attorney General shall have direct supervision over every district attorney and sheriff and over such other law enforcement officers as may be designated by law, in all matters pertaining to the duties of their respective offices, and may require any of said officers to make reports concerning the investigation, detection, prosecution, and punishment of crime in their respective jurisdictions as to the Attorney General may seem advisable. Whenever in the opinion of the Attorney General any law of the State is not being adequately enforced in any county, it shall be the duty of the Attorney General to prosecute any violations of law of which the superior court shall have jurisdiction, and in such cases the Attorney General shall have all the powers of a district attorney. When required by the public interest or directed by the Governor, the Attorney General shall assist any district attorney in the discharge of the duties of that office.

(Sec. 13 amended Nov. 5, 1974, by Prop. 11. Res.Ch. 96, 1974.)

SEC. 14.

(a) To eliminate any appearance of a conflict with the proper discharge of his or her duties and responsibilities, no state officer may knowingly receive any salary, wages, commissions, or other similar earned income from a lobbyist or lobbying firm, as defined by the Political Reform Act of 1974, or from a person who, during the previous 12 months, has been under a contract with the state agency under the jurisdiction of the state officer. The Legislature shall enact laws that define earned income. However, earned income does not include any community property interest in the income of a spouse. Any state officer who knowingly receives any salary, wages, commissions, or other similar earned income from a lobbyist employer, as defined by the Political Reform Act of 1974, may not, for a period of one year following its receipt, vote upon or make, participate in making, or in any way attempt to use his or her official position to influence an action or decision before the agency for which the state officer serves, other than an action or decision involving a bill described in subdivision (c) of Section 12 of Article IV, which he or she knows, or has reason to know, would have a direct and significant financial impact on the lobbyist employer and would not impact the public generally or a significant segment of the public in a similar manner. As used in this subdivision, "public generally" includes an industry, trade, or profession.

(b) No state officer may accept any honorarium. The Legislature shall enact laws that implement this subdivision.

(c) The Legislature shall enact laws that ban or strictly limit the acceptance of a gift by a state officer from any source if the acceptance of the gift might create a conflict of interest.

(d) No state officer may knowingly accept any compensation for appearing, agreeing to appear, or taking any other action on behalf of another person before any state government board or agency. If a state officer knowingly accepts any compensation for appearing, agreeing to appear, or taking any other action on behalf of another person before any local government board or agency, the state officer may not, for a period of one year following the acceptance of the compensation, make, participate in making, or in any way attempt to use his or her official position to influence an action or decision before the state agency for which the state officer serves, other than an action or decision involving a bill described in subdivision (c) of Section 12 of Article IV, which he or she knows, or has reason to know, would have a direct and significant financial impact on that person and would not impact the public generally or a significant segment of the public in a similar manner. As used in this subdivision, "public generally" includes an industry, trade, or profession. However, a state officer may engage in activities involving a board or agency which are strictly on his or her own behalf, appear in the capacity of an attorney before any court or the Workers' Compensation Appeals Board, or act as an advocate without compensation or make an inquiry for information on behalf of a person before a board or agency. This subdivision does not prohibit any action of a partnership or firm of which the state officer is a member if the state officer does not share directly or indirectly in the fee, less any expenses attributable to that fee, resulting from that action.

(e) The Legislature shall enact laws that prohibit a state officer, or a secretary of an agency or director of a department appointed by the Governor, who has not resigned or retired from state service prior to January 7, 1991, from lobbying, for compensation, as governed by the Political Reform Act of 1974, before the executive branch of state government for 12 months after leaving office.

(f) "State officer," as used in this section, means the Governor, Lieutenant Governor, Attorney General, Controller, Insurance Commissioner, Secretary of State, Superintendent of Public Instruction, Treasurer, and member of the State Board of Equalization.

(Sec. 14 added June 5, 1990, by Prop. 112. Res.Ch. 167, 1989. Subd. (b) operative Dec. 3, 1990.)

ARTICLE VI JUDICIAL

[SEC. 1 - SEC. 22]

(Article 6 added Nov. 8, 1966, by Prop. 1-a. Res.Ch. 139, 1966 1st Ex. Sess.)

SEC. 1.

The judicial power of this State is vested in the Supreme Court, courts of appeal, and superior courts, all of which are courts of record.

(Sec. 1 amended Nov. 5, 2002, by Prop. 48. Res.Ch. 88, 2002.)

SEC. 2.

The Supreme Court consists of the Chief Justice of California and 6 associate justices. The Chief Justice may convene the court at any time. Concurrence of 4 judges present at the argument is necessary for a judgment.

An acting Chief Justice shall perform all functions of the Chief Justice when the Chief Justice is absent or unable to act. The Chief Justice or, if the Chief Justice fails to do so, the court shall select an associate justice as acting Chief Justice.

(Sec. 2 amended Nov. 5, 1974, by Prop. 11. Res.Ch. 96, 1974.)

SEC. 3.

The Legislature shall divide the State into districts each containing a court of appeal with one or more divisions. Each division consists of a presiding justice and 2 or more associate justices. It has the power of a court of appeal and shall conduct itself as a 3-judge court. Concurrence of 2 judges present at the argument is necessary for a judgment.

An acting presiding justice shall perform all functions of the presiding justice when the presiding justice is absent or unable to act. The presiding justice or, if the presiding justice fails to do so, the Chief Justice shall select an associate justice of that division as acting presiding justice.
(Sec. 3 amended Nov. 5, 1974, by Prop. 11. Res.Ch. 96, 1974.)

SEC. 4.

In each county there is a superior court of one or more judges. The Legislature shall prescribe the number of judges and provide for the officers and employees of each superior court. If the governing body of each affected county concurs, the Legislature may provide that one or more judges serve more than one superior court.
In each superior court there is an appellate division. The Chief Justice shall assign judges to the appellate division for specified terms pursuant to rules, not inconsistent with statute, adopted by the Judicial Council to promote the independence of the appellate division.
(Sec. 4 amended June 2, 1998, by Prop. 220. Res.Ch. 36, 1996.)

SEC. 6.

(a) The Judicial Council consists of the Chief Justice and one other judge of the Supreme Court, three judges of courts of appeal, 10 judges of superior courts, two nonvoting court administrators, and any other nonvoting members as determined by the voting membership of the council, each appointed by the Chief Justice for a three-year term pursuant to procedures established by the council; four members of the State Bar appointed by its governing body for three-year terms; and one member of each house of the Legislature appointed as provided by the house.
(b) Council membership terminates if a member ceases to hold the position that qualified the member for

appointment. A vacancy shall be filled by the appointing power for the remainder of the term.

(c) The council may appoint an Administrative Director of the Courts, who serves at its pleasure and performs functions delegated by the council or the Chief Justice, other than adopting rules of court administration, practice and procedure.

(d) To improve the administration of justice the council shall survey judicial business and make recommendations to the courts, make recommendations annually to the Governor and Legislature, adopt rules for court administration, practice and procedure, and perform other functions prescribed by statute. The rules adopted shall not be inconsistent with statute.

(e) The Chief Justice shall seek to expedite judicial business and to equalize the work of judges. The Chief Justice may provide for the assignment of any judge to another court but only with the judge's consent if the court is of lower jurisdiction. A retired judge who consents may be assigned to any court.

(f) Judges shall report to the council as the Chief Justice directs concerning the condition of judicial business in their courts. They shall cooperate with the council and hold court as assigned.

(Sec. 6 amended Nov. 5, 2002, by Prop. 48. Res.Ch. 88, 2002.)

SEC. 7.

The Commission on Judicial Appointments consists of the Chief Justice, the Attorney General, and the presiding justice of the court of appeal of the affected district or, if there are 2 or more presiding justices, the one who has presided longest or, when a nomination or appointment to the Supreme Court is to be considered, the presiding justice who has presided longest on any court of appeal.

(Sec. 7 added Nov. 8, 1966, by Prop. 1-a. Res.Ch. 139, 1966 1st Ex. Sess.)

SEC. 8.

(a) The Commission on Judicial Performance consists of one judge of a court of appeal and two judges of superior courts, each appointed by the Supreme Court; two members of the State Bar of California who have practiced law in this State for 10 years, each appointed by the Governor; and six citizens who are not judges, retired judges, or members of the State Bar of California, two of whom shall be appointed by the Governor, two by the Senate Committee on Rules, and two by the Speaker of the Assembly. Except as provided in subdivisions (b) and (c), all terms are for four years. No member shall serve more than two four-year terms, or for more than a total of 10 years if appointed to fill a vacancy.

(b) Commission membership terminates if a member ceases to hold the position that qualified the member for appointment. A vacancy shall be filled by the appointing power for the remainder of the term. A member whose term has expired may continue to serve until the vacancy has been filled by the appointing power. Appointing powers may appoint members who are already serving on the commission prior to March 1, 1995, to a single two-year term, but may not appoint them to an additional term thereafter.

(c) To create staggered terms among the members of the Commission on Judicial Performance, the following members shall be appointed, as follows:

(1) Two members appointed by the Supreme Court to a term commencing March 1, 1995, shall each serve a term of two years and may be reappointed to one full term.

(2) One attorney appointed by the Governor to a term commencing March 1, 1995, shall serve a term of two years and may be reappointed to one full term.

(3) One citizen member appointed by the Governor to a term commencing March 1, 1995, shall serve a term of two years and may be reappointed to one full term.

(4) One member appointed by the Senate Committee on Rules to a term commencing March 1, 1995, shall serve a

term of two years and may be reappointed to one full term.

(5) One member appointed by the Speaker of the Assembly to a term commencing March 1, 1995, shall serve a term of two years and may be reappointed to one full term.

(6) All other members shall be appointed to full four-year terms commencing March 1, 1995.

(Sec. 8 amended Nov. 5, 2002, by Prop. 48. Res.Ch. 88, 2002.)

SEC. 9.

The State Bar of California is a public corporation. Every person admitted and licensed to practice law in this State is and shall be a member of the State Bar except while holding office as a judge of a court of record.

(Sec. 9 added Nov. 8, 1966, by Prop. 1-a. Res.Ch. 139, 1966 1st Ex. Sess.)

SEC. 10.

The Supreme Court, courts of appeal, superior courts, and their judges have original jurisdiction in habeas corpus proceedings. Those courts also have original jurisdiction in proceedings for extraordinary relief in the nature of mandamus, certiorari, and prohibition. The appellate division of the superior court has original jurisdiction in proceedings for extraordinary relief in the nature of mandamus, certiorari, and prohibition directed to the superior court in causes subject to its appellate jurisdiction. Superior courts have original jurisdiction in all other causes.

The court may make any comment on the evidence and the testimony and credibility of any witness as in its opinion is necessary for the proper determination of the cause.

(Sec. 10 amended Nov. 5, 2002, by Prop. 48. Res.Ch. 88, 2002.)

SEC. 11.

(a) The Supreme Court has appellate jurisdiction when judgment of death has been pronounced. With that exception courts of appeal have appellate jurisdiction when superior courts have original jurisdiction in causes of a type within the appellate jurisdiction of the courts of appeal on June 30, 1995, and in other causes prescribed by statute. When appellate jurisdiction in civil causes is determined by the amount in controversy, the Legislature may change the appellate jurisdiction of the courts of appeal by changing the jurisdictional amount in controversy.

(b) Except as provided in subdivision (a), the appellate division of the superior court has appellate jurisdiction in causes prescribed by statute.

(c) The Legislature may permit courts exercising appellate jurisdiction to take evidence and make findings of fact when jury trial is waived or not a matter of right.

(Sec. 11 amended June 2, 1998, by Prop. 220. Res.Ch. 36, 1996.)

SEC. 12.

(a) The Supreme Court may, before decision, transfer to itself a cause in a court of appeal. It may, before decision, transfer a cause from itself to a court of appeal or from one court of appeal or division to another. The court to which a cause is transferred has jurisdiction.

(b) The Supreme Court may review the decision of a court of appeal in any cause.

(c) The Judicial Council shall provide, by rules of court, for the time and procedure for transfer and for review, including, among other things, provisions for the time and procedure for transfer with instructions, for review of all or part of a decision, and for remand as improvidently granted.

(d) This section shall not apply to an appeal involving a judgment of death.

(Sec. 12 amended Nov. 6, 1984, by Prop. 32. Res.Ch. 64, 1984. Operative May 6, 1985.)

SEC. 13.

No judgment shall be set aside, or new trial granted, in any cause, on the ground of misdirection of the jury, or of the improper admission or rejection of evidence, or for any error as to any matter of pleading, or for any error as to any matter of procedure, unless, after an examination of the entire cause, including the evidence, the court shall be of the opinion that the error complained of has resulted in a miscarriage of justice.

(Sec. 13 added Nov. 8, 1966, by Prop. 1-a. Res.Ch. 139, 1966 1st Ex. Sess.)

SEC. 14.

The Legislature shall provide for the prompt publication of such opinions of the Supreme Court and courts of appeal as the Supreme Court deems appropriate, and those opinions shall be available for publication by any person. Decisions of the Supreme Court and courts of appeal that determine causes shall be in writing with reasons stated.

(Sec. 14 added Nov. 8, 1966, by Prop. 1-a. Res.Ch. 139, 1966 1st Ex. Sess.)

SEC. 15.

A person is ineligible to be a judge of a court of record unless for 10 years immediately preceding selection, the person has been a member of the State Bar or served as a judge of a court of record in this State.

(Sec. 15 amended Nov. 5, 2002, by Prop. 48. Res.Ch. 88, 2002.)

SEC. 16.

(a) Judges of the Supreme Court shall be elected at large and judges of courts of appeal shall be elected in their districts at general elections at the same time and places as the Governor. Their terms are 12 years beginning the Monday after January 1 following their election, except that a judge elected to an unexpired term serves the remainder of the term. In creating a new court of appeal district or division the Legislature shall provide that the first elective terms are 4, 8, and 12 years.

(b) Judges of superior courts shall be elected in their counties at general elections except as otherwise necessary to meet the requirements of federal law. In the latter case the Legislature, by two-thirds vote of the membership of each house thereof, with the advice of judges within the affected court, may provide for their election by the system prescribed in subdivision (d), or by any other arrangement. The Legislature may provide that an unopposed incumbent's name not appear on the ballot.

(c) Terms of judges of superior courts are six years beginning the Monday after January 1 following their election. A vacancy shall be filled by election to a full term at the next general election after the second January 1 following the vacancy, but the Governor shall appoint a person to fill the vacancy temporarily until the elected judge's term begins.

(d) (1) Within 30 days before August 16 preceding the expiration of the judge's term, a judge of the Supreme Court or a court of appeal may file a declaration of candidacy to succeed to the office presently held by the judge. If the declaration is not filed, the Governor before September 16 shall nominate a candidate. At the next general election, only the candidate so declared or nominated may appear on the ballot, which shall present the question whether the candidate shall be elected. The candidate shall be elected upon receiving a majority of the votes on the question. A candidate not elected may not be appointed to that court but later may be nominated and elected.

(2) The Governor shall fill vacancies in those courts by appointment. An appointee holds office until the Monday after January 1 following the first general election at which

the appointee had the right to become a candidate or until an elected judge qualifies. A nomination or appointment by the Governor is effective when confirmed by the Commission on Judicial Appointments.

(3) Electors of a county, by majority of those voting and in a manner the Legislature shall provide, may make this system of selection applicable to judges of superior courts.

(Sec. 16 amended Nov. 5, 2002, by Prop. 48. Res.Ch. 88, 2002.)

SEC. 17.

A judge of a court of record may not practice law and during the term for which the judge was selected is ineligible for public employment or public office other than judicial employment or judicial office, except a judge of a court of record may accept a part-time teaching position that is outside the normal hours of his or her judicial position and that does not interfere with the regular performance of his or her judicial duties while holding office. A judge of a trial court of record may, however, become eligible for election to other public office by taking a leave of absence without pay prior to filing a declaration of candidacy. Acceptance of the public office is a resignation from the office of judge.

A judicial officer may not receive fines or fees for personal use.

A judicial officer may not earn retirement service credit from a public teaching position while holding judicial office.

(Sec. 17 amended Nov. 8, 1988, by Prop. 94. Res.Ch. 70, 1988.)

SEC. 18.

(a) A judge is disqualified from acting as a judge, without loss of salary, while there is pending (1) an indictment or an information charging the judge in the United States with a crime punishable as a felony under California or federal law, or (2) a petition to the Supreme Court to review a determination by the Commission on Judicial Performance to remove or retire a judge.

(b) The Commission on Judicial Performance may disqualify a judge from acting as a judge, without loss of salary, upon notice of formal proceedings by the commission charging the judge with judicial misconduct or disability.

(c) The Commission on Judicial Performance shall suspend a judge from office without salary when in the United States the judge pleads guilty or no contest or is found guilty of a crime punishable as a felony under California or federal law or of any other crime that involves moral turpitude under that law. If the conviction is reversed, suspension terminates, and the judge shall be paid the salary for the judicial office held by the judge for the period of suspension. If the judge is suspended and the conviction becomes final, the Commission on Judicial Performance shall remove the judge from office.

(d) Except as provided in subdivision (f), the Commission on Judicial Performance may (1) retire a judge for disability that seriously interferes with the performance of the judge's duties and is or is likely to become permanent, or (2) censure a judge or former judge or remove a judge for action occurring not more than 6 years prior to the commencement of the judge's current term or of the former judge's last term that constitutes willful misconduct in office, persistent failure or inability to perform the judge's duties, habitual intemperance in the use of intoxicants or drugs, or conduct prejudicial to the administration of justice that brings the judicial office into disrepute, or (3) publicly or privately admonish a judge or former judge found to have engaged in an improper action or dereliction of duty. The commission may also bar a former judge who has been censured from receiving an assignment, appointment, or reference of work from any California state court. Upon petition by the judge or former judge, the Supreme Court may, in its discretion, grant review of a determination by the commission to retire, remove, censure, admonish, or disqualify pursuant to subdivision (b) a judge or former judge. When the Supreme Court reviews a determination of the commission, it may make an independent review of the record. If the

Supreme Court has not acted within 120 days after granting the petition, the decision of the commission shall be final.

(e) A judge retired by the commission shall be considered to have retired voluntarily. A judge removed by the commission is ineligible for judicial office, including receiving an assignment, appointment, or reference of work from any California state court, and pending further order of the court is suspended from practicing law in this State. The State Bar may institute appropriate attorney disciplinary proceedings against any judge who retires or resigns from office with judicial disciplinary charges pending.

(f) A determination by the Commission on Judicial Performance to admonish or censure a judge or former judge of the Supreme Court or remove or retire a judge of the Supreme Court shall be reviewed by a tribunal of 7 court of appeal judges selected by lot.

(g) No court, except the Supreme Court, shall have jurisdiction in a civil action or other legal proceeding of any sort brought against the commission by a judge. Any request for injunctive relief or other provisional remedy shall be granted or denied within 90 days of the filing of the request for relief. A failure to comply with the time requirements of this section does not affect the validity of commission proceedings.

(h) Members of the commission, the commission staff, and the examiners and investigators employed by the commission shall be absolutely immune from suit for all conduct at any time in the course of their official duties. No civil action may be maintained against a person, or adverse employment action taken against a person, by any employer, public or private, based on statements presented by the person to the commission.

(i) The Commission on Judicial Performance shall make rules implementing this section, including, but not limited to, the following:

(1) The commission shall make rules for the investigation of judges. The commission may provide for the confidentiality of complaints to and investigations by the commission.

(2) The commission shall make rules for formal proceedings against judges when there is cause to believe there is a disability or wrongdoing within the meaning of subdivision (d).

(j) When the commission institutes formal proceedings, the notice of charges, the answer, and all subsequent papers and proceedings shall be open to the public for all formal proceedings instituted after February 28, 1995.

(k) The commission may make explanatory statements.

(l) The budget of the commission shall be separate from the budget of any other state agency or court.

(m) The Supreme Court shall make rules for the conduct of judges, both on and off the bench, and for judicial candidates in the conduct of their campaigns. These rules shall be referred to as the Code of Judicial Ethics.

(Sec. 18 amended Nov. 8, 1994, by Prop. 190. Res.Ch. 111, 1994. Operative March 1, 1995.)

SEC. 18.1.

The Commission on Judicial Performance shall exercise discretionary jurisdiction with regard to the oversight and discipline of subordinate judicial officers, according to the same standards, and subject to review upon petition to the Supreme Court, as specified in Section 18.

No person who has been found unfit to serve as a subordinate judicial officer after a hearing before the Commission on Judicial Performance shall have the requisite status to serve as a subordinate judicial officer.

This section does not diminish or eliminate the responsibility of a court to exercise initial jurisdiction to discipline or dismiss a subordinate judicial officer as its employee.

(Sec. 18.1 added June 2, 1998, by Prop. 221. Res.Ch. 54, 1996.)

SEC. 18.5.

(a) Upon request, the Commission on Judicial Performance shall provide to the Governor of any State of the Union the text of any private admonishment, advisory letter, or other disciplinary action together with any information that the Commission on Judicial Performance deems necessary to a full understanding of the commission's action, with respect to any applicant whom the Governor of any State of the Union indicates is under consideration for any judicial appointment.

(b) Upon request, the Commission on Judicial Performance shall provide the President of the United States the text of any private admonishment, advisory letter, or other disciplinary action together with any information that the Commission on Judicial Performance deems necessary to a full understanding of the commission's action, with respect to any applicant whom the President indicates is under consideration for any federal judicial appointment.

(c) Upon request, the Commission on Judicial Performance shall provide the Commission on Judicial Appointments the text of any private admonishment, advisory letter, or other disciplinary action together with any information that the Commission on Judicial Performance deems necessary to a full understanding of the commission action, with respect to any applicant whom the Commission on Judicial Appointments indicates is under consideration for any judicial appointment.

(d) All information released under this section shall remain confidential and privileged.

(e) Notwithstanding subdivision (d), any information released pursuant to this section shall also be provided to the applicant about whom the information was requested.

(f) "Private admonishment" refers to a disciplinary action against a judge by the Commission on Judicial Performance as authorized by subdivision (c) of Section 18 of Article VI, as amended November 8, 1988.

(Sec. 18.5 added Nov. 8, 1994, by Prop. 190. Res.Ch. 111, 1994. Operative March 1, 1995.)

SEC. 19.

The Legislature shall prescribe compensation for judges of courts of record.

A judge of a court of record may not receive the salary for the judicial office held by the judge while any cause before the judge remains pending and undetermined for 90 days after it has been submitted for decision.

(Sec. 19 amended Nov. 5, 1974, by Prop. 11. Res.Ch. 96, 1974.)

SEC. 20.

The Legislature shall provide for retirement, with reasonable allowance, of judges of courts of record for age or disability.

(Sec. 20 added Nov. 8, 1966, by Prop. 1-a. Res.Ch. 139, 1966 1st Ex. Sess.)

SEC. 21.

On stipulation of the parties litigant the court may order a cause to be tried by a temporary judge who is a member of the State Bar, sworn and empowered to act until final determination of the cause.

(Sec. 21 added Nov. 8, 1966, by Prop. 1-a. Res.Ch. 139, 1966 1st Ex. Sess.)

SEC. 22.

The Legislature may provide for the appointment by trial courts of record of officers such as commissioners to perform subordinate judicial duties.

(Sec. 22 added Nov. 8, 1966, by Prop. 1-a. Res.Ch. 139, 1966 1st Ex. Sess.)

ARTICLE VII PUBLIC OFFICERS AND EMPLOYEES

[SECTION 1 - SEC. 11]

(Article 7 added June 8, 1976, by Prop. 14. Res.Ch. 5, 1976.)

SECTION 1.

(a) The civil service includes every officer and employee of the State except as otherwise provided in this Constitution.
(b) In the civil service permanent appointment and promotion shall be made under a general system based on merit ascertained by competitive examination.
(Sec. 1 added June 8, 1976, by Prop. 14. Res.Ch. 5, 1976.)

SEC. 2.

(a) There is a Personnel Board of 5 members appointed by the Governor and approved by the Senate, a majority of the membership concurring, for 10-year terms and until their successors are appointed and qualified. Appointment to fill a vacancy is for the unexpired portion of the term. A member may be removed by concurrent resolution adopted by each house, two-thirds of the membership of each house concurring.
(b) The board annually shall elect one of its members as presiding officer.
(c) The board shall appoint and prescribe compensation for an executive officer who shall be a member of the civil service but not a member of the board.
(Sec. 2 added June 8, 1976, by Prop. 14. Res.Ch. 5, 1976.)

SEC. 3.

(a) The board shall enforce the civil service statutes and, by majority vote of all its members, shall prescribe probationary periods and classifications, adopt other rules authorized by statute, and review disciplinary actions.

(b) The executive officer shall administer the civil service statutes under rules of the board.

(Sec. 3 added June 8, 1976, by Prop. 14. Res.Ch. 5, 1976.)

SEC. 4.

The following are exempt from civil service:

(a) Officers and employees appointed or employed by the Legislature, either house, or legislative committees.

(b) Officers and employees appointed or employed by councils, commissions or public corporations in the judicial branch or by a court of record or officer thereof.

(c) Officers elected by the people and a deputy and an employee selected by each elected officer.

(d) Members of boards and commissions.

(e) A deputy or employee selected by each board or commission either appointed by the Governor or authorized by statute.

(f) State officers directly appointed by the Governor with or without the consent or confirmation of the Senate and the employees of the Governor's office, and the employees of the Lieutenant Governor's office directly appointed or employed by the Lieutenant Governor.

(g) A deputy or employee selected by each officer, except members of boards and commissions, exempted under Section 4(f).

(h) Officers and employees of the University of California and the California State Colleges.

(i) The teaching staff of schools under the jurisdiction of the Department of Education or the Superintendent of Public Instruction.

(j) Member, inmate, and patient help in state homes, charitable or correctional institutions, and state facilities for mentally ill or retarded persons.

(k) Members of the militia while engaged in military service.

(l) Officers and employees of district agricultural associations employed less than 6 months in a calendar year.

(m) In addition to positions exempted by other provisions of this section, the Attorney General may appoint or employ six deputies or employees, the Public Utilities Commission may appoint or employ one deputy or employee, and the Legislative Counsel may appoint or employ two deputies or employees.

(Sec. 4 added June 8, 1976, by Prop. 14. Res.Ch. 5, 1976.)

SEC. 5.

A temporary appointment may be made to a position for which there is no employment list. No person may serve in one or more positions under temporary appointment longer than 9 months in 12 consecutive months.

(Sec. 5 added June 8, 1976, by Prop. 14. Res.Ch. 5, 1976.)

SEC. 6.

(a) The Legislature may provide preferences for veterans and their surviving spouses.

(b) The board by special rule may permit persons in exempt positions, brought under civil service by constitutional provision, to qualify to continue in their positions.

(c) When the State undertakes work previously performed by a county, city, public district of this State or by a federal department or agency, the board by special rule shall provide for persons who previously performed this work to qualify to continue in their positions in the state civil service subject to such minimum standards as may be established by statute.

(Sec. 6 added June 8, 1976, by Prop. 14. Res.Ch. 5, 1976.)

SEC. 7.

A person holding a lucrative office under the United States or other power may not hold a civil office of profit. A local officer or postmaster whose compensation does not exceed 500 dollars per year or an officer in the militia or a member of a reserve component of the armed forces of the United States except where on active federal duty for more than 30 days in any year is not a holder of a lucrative office, nor is the holding of a civil office of profit affected by this military service.

(Sec. 7 added June 8, 1976, by Prop. 14. Res.Ch. 5, 1976.)

SEC. 8.

(a) Every person shall be disqualified from holding any office of profit in this State who shall have been convicted of having given or offered a bribe to procure personal election or appointment.

(b) Laws shall be made to exclude persons convicted of bribery, perjury, forgery, malfeasance in office, or other high crimes from office or serving on juries. The privilege of free suffrage shall be supported by laws regulating elections and prohibiting, under adequate penalties, all undue influence thereon from power, bribery, tumult, or other improper practice.

(Sec. 8 added June 8, 1976, by Prop. 14. Res.Ch. 5, 1976.)

SEC. 9.

Notwithstanding any other provision of this Constitution, no person or organization which advocates the overthrow of the Government of the United States or the State by force or violence or other unlawful means or who advocates the support of a foreign government against the United States in the event of hostilities shall:

(a) Hold any office or employment under this State, including but not limited to the University of California, or with any county, city or county, city, district, political subdivision, authority, board, bureau, commission or other public agency of this State; or

(b) Receive any exemption from any tax imposed by this State or any county, city or county, city, district, political subdivision, authority, board, bureau, commission or other public agency of this State.

The Legislature shall enact such laws as may be necessary to enforce the provisions of this section.

(Sec. 9 added June 8, 1976, by Prop. 14. Res.Ch. 5, 1976.)

SEC. 10.

(a) No person who is found liable in a civil action for making libelous or slanderous statements against an opposing candidate during the course of an election campaign for any federal, statewide, Board of Equalization, or legislative office or for any county, city and county, city, district, or any other local elective office shall retain the seat to which he or she is elected, where it is established that the libel or slander was a major contributing cause in the defeat of an opposing candidate.

A libelous or slanderous statement shall be deemed to have been made by a person within the meaning of this section if that person actually made the statement or if the person actually or constructively assented to, authorized, or ratified the statement.

"Federal office," as used in this section means the office of United States Senator and Member of the House of Representatives; and to the extent that the provisions of this section do not conflict with any provision of federal law, it is intended that candidates seeking the office of United States Senator or Member of the House of Representatives comply with this section.

(b) In order to determine whether libelous or slanderous statements were a major contributing cause in the defeat of an opposing candidate, the trier of fact shall make a separate, distinct finding on that issue. If the trier of fact finds that libel or slander was a major contributing cause in the defeat of an opposing candidate and that the libelous or slanderous statement was made with knowledge that it was false or with reckless disregard of whether it was false or true, the person holding office shall be disqualified from or shall forfeit that office as provided in subdivision (d). The findings required by this section shall be in writing and shall be incorporated as part of the judgment.

(c) In a case where a person is disqualified from holding office or is required to forfeit an office under subdivisions (a) and (b), that disqualification or forfeiture shall create a vacancy in office, which vacancy shall be filled in the manner provided by law for the filling of a vacancy in that particular office.

(d) Once the judgment of liability is entered by the trial court and the time for filing a notice of appeal has expired, or all possibility of direct attack in the courts of this State has been finally exhausted, the person shall be disqualified from or shall forfeit the office involved in that election and shall have no authority to exercise the powers or perform the duties of the office.

(e) This section shall apply to libelous or slanderous statements made on or after the effective date of this section.

(Sec. 10 added June 5, 1984, by Prop. 20. Res.Ch. 181, 1982.)

SEC. 11.

(a) The Legislators' Retirement System shall not pay any unmodified retirement allowance or its actuarial equivalent to any person who on or after January 1, 1987, entered for the first time any state office for which membership in the Legislators' Retirement System was elective or to any beneficiary or survivor of such a person, which exceeds the higher of (1) the salary receivable by the person currently serving in the office in which the retired person served or (2) the highest salary that was received by the retired person while serving in that office.

(b) The Judges' Retirement System shall not pay any unmodified retirement allowance or its actuarial equivalent to any person who on or after January 1, 1987, entered for the first time any judicial office subject to the Judges' Retirement System or to any beneficiary or survivor of such a person, which exceeds the higher of (1) the salary receivable by the person currently serving in the judicial office in which the retired person served or (2) the highest salary that was received by the retired person while serving in that judicial office.

(c) The Legislature may define the terms used in this section.

(d) If any part of this measure or the application to any person or circumstance is held invalid, the invalidity shall not affect other provisions or applications which reasonably can be given effect without the invalid provision or application.

(Sec. 11 amended (by adding subd. (d)) Nov. 6, 1990, by Prop. 140. Initiative measure.)

ARTICLE IX EDUCATION
[SECTION 1 - SEC. 16]

(Article 9 adopted 1879.)

SECTION 1.

A general diffusion of knowledge and intelligence being essential to the preservation of the rights and liberties of the people, the Legislature shall encourage by all suitable means the promotion of intellectual, scientific, moral, and agricultural improvement.

(Sec. 1 adopted 1879.)

SEC. 2.

A Superintendent of Public Instruction shall be elected by the qualified electors of the State at each gubernatorial election. The Superintendent of Public Instruction shall enter upon the duties of the office on the first Monday after the first day of January next succeeding each gubernatorial election. No Superintendent of Public Instruction may serve more than 2 terms.

(Sec. 2 amended Nov. 6, 1990, by Prop. 140. Initiative measure.)

SEC. 2.1.

The State Board of Education, on nomination of the Superintendent of Public Instruction, shall appoint one Deputy Superintendent of Public Instruction and three Associate Superintendents of Public Instruction who shall be exempt from state civil service and whose terms of office shall be four years.

This section shall not be construed as prohibiting the appointment, in accordance with law, of additional

Associate Superintendents of Public Instruction subject to state civil service.
(Sec. 2.1 added Nov. 5, 1946, by Prop. 9. Res.Ch. 161, 1945.)

SEC. 3.

A Superintendent of Schools for each county may be elected by the qualified electors thereof at each gubernatorial election or may be appointed by the county board of education, and the manner of the selection shall be determined by a majority vote of the electors of the county voting on the question; provided, that two or more counties may, by an election conducted pursuant to Section 3.2 of this article, unite for the purpose of electing or appointing one joint superintendent for the counties so uniting.
(Sec. 3 amended Nov. 2, 1976, by Prop. 8. Res.Ch. 57, 1976.)

SEC. 3.1.

(a) Notwithstanding any provision of this Constitution to the contrary, the Legislature shall prescribe the qualifications required of county superintendents of schools, and for these purposes shall classify the several counties in the State.
(b) Notwithstanding any provision of this Constitution to the contrary, the county board of education or joint county board of education, as the case may be, shall fix the salary of the county superintendent of schools or the joint county superintendent of schools, respectively.
(Sec. 3.1 amended Nov. 2, 1976, by Prop. 8. Res.Ch. 57, 1976.)

SEC. 3.2.

Notwithstanding any provision of this Constitution to the contrary, any two or more chartered counties, or nonchartered counties, or any combination thereof, may, by a majority vote of the electors of each such county voting on the proposition at an election called for that purpose in each such county, establish one joint board of education and one joint county superintendent of schools for the counties so uniting. A joint county board of education and a joint county superintendent of schools shall be governed by the general statutes and shall not be governed by the provisions of any county charter.

(Sec. 3.2 added Nov. 2, 1976, by Prop. 8. Res.Ch. 57, 1976.)

SEC. 3.3.

Except as provided in Section 3.2 of this article, it shall be competent to provide in any charter framed for a county under any provision of this Constitution, or by the amendment of any such charter, for the election of the members of the county board of education of such county and for their qualifications and terms of office.

(Sec. 3.3 amended Nov. 2, 1976, by Prop. 8. Res.Ch. 57, 1976.)

SEC. 5.

The Legislature shall provide for a system of common schools by which a free school shall be kept up and supported in each district at least six months in every year, after the first year in which a school has been established.

(Sec. 5 adopted 1879.)

SEC. 6.

Each person, other than a substitute employee, employed by a school district as a teacher or in any other position requiring certification qualifications shall be paid a salary which shall be at the rate of an annual salary of not less than twenty-four hundred dollars ($2,400) for a person serving full time, as defined by law.

The Public School System shall include all kindergarten schools, elementary schools, secondary schools, technical schools, and state colleges, established in accordance with law and, in addition, the school districts and the other agencies authorized to maintain them. No school or college or any other part of the Public School System shall be, directly or indirectly, transferred from the Public School System or placed under the jurisdiction of any authority other than one included within the Public School System.

The Legislature shall add to the State School Fund such other means from the revenues of the State as shall provide in said fund for apportionment in each fiscal year, an amount not less than one hundred eighty dollars ($180) per pupil in average daily attendance in the kindergarten schools, elementary schools, secondary schools, and technical schools in the Public School System during the next preceding fiscal year.

The entire State School Fund shall be apportioned in each fiscal year in such manner as the Legislature may provide, through the school districts and other agencies maintaining such schools, for the support of, and aid to, kindergarten schools, elementary schools, secondary schools, and technical schools except that there shall be apportioned to each school district in each fiscal year not less than one hundred twenty dollars ($120) per pupil in average daily attendance in the district during the next preceding fiscal year and except that the amount apportioned to each school district in each fiscal year shall be not less than twenty-four hundred dollars ($2,400).

Solely with respect to any retirement system provided for in the charter of any county or city and county pursuant to the provisions of which the contributions of, and benefits to, certificated employees of a school district who are members of such system are based upon the proportion of the salaries of such certificated employees contributed by said county or city and county, all amounts apportioned to said county or city and county, or to school districts therein, pursuant to the provisions of this section shall be considered as though derived from county or city and

county school taxes for the support of county and city and county government and not money provided by the State within the meaning of this section.
(Sec. 6 amended Nov. 5, 1974, by Prop. 8. Res.Ch. 70, 1974.)

SEC. 6½.

Nothing in this constitution contained shall forbid the formation of districts for school purposes situate in more than one county or the issuance of bonds by such districts under such general laws as have been or may hereafter be prescribed by the legislature; and the officers mentioned in such laws shall be authorized to levy and assess such taxes and perform all such other acts as may be prescribed therein for the purpose of paying such bonds and carrying out the other powers conferred upon such districts; provided, that all such bonds shall be issued subject to the limitations prescribed in section eighteen of article eleven hereof.
(Sec. 6½ added Nov. 7, 1922, by Prop. 26. Res.Ch. 46, 1921.)

SEC. 7.

The Legislature shall provide for the appointment or election of the State Board of Education and a board of education in each county or for the election of a joint county board of education for two or more counties.
(Sec. 7 amended Nov. 2, 1976, by Prop. 8. Res.Ch. 57, 1976.)

SEC. 7.5.

The State Board of Education shall adopt textbooks for use in grades one through eight throughout the State, to be furnished without cost as provided by statute.
(Sec. 7.5 added June 2, 1970, by Prop. 6. Res.Ch. 358, 1969.)

SEC. 8.

No public money shall ever be appropriated for the support of any sectarian or denominational school, or any school not under the exclusive control of the officers of the public schools; nor shall any sectarian or denominational doctrine be taught, or instruction thereon be permitted, directly or indirectly, in any of the common schools of this State.
(Sec. 8 adopted 1879.)

SEC. 9.

(a) The University of California shall constitute a public trust, to be administered by the existing corporation known as "The Regents of the University of California," with full powers of organization and government, subject only to such legislative control as may be necessary to insure the security of its funds and compliance with the terms of the endowments of the university and such competitive bidding procedures as may be made applicable to the university by statute for the letting of construction contracts, sales of real property, and purchasing of materials, goods, and services. Said corporation shall be in form a board composed of seven ex officio members, which shall be: the Governor, the Lieutenant Governor, the Speaker of the Assembly, the Superintendent of Public Instruction, the president and the vice president of the alumni association of the university and the acting president of the university, and 18 appointive members appointed by the Governor and approved by the Senate, a majority of the membership concurring; provided, however that the present appointive members shall hold office until the expiration of their present terms.
(b) The terms of the members appointed prior to November 5, 1974, shall be 16 years; the terms of two appointive members to expire as heretofore on March 1st of every even-numbered calendar year, and two members shall be appointed for terms commencing on March 1,

1976, and on March 1 of each year thereafter; provided that no such appointments shall be made for terms to commencé on March 1, 1979, or on March 1 of each fourth year thereafter, to the end that no appointment to the regents for a newly commencing term shall be made during the first year of any gubernatorial term of office. The terms of the members appointed for terms commencing on and after March 1, 1976, shall be 12 years. During the period of transition until the time when the appointive membership is comprised exclusively of persons serving for terms of 12 years, the total number of appointive members may exceed the numbers specified in the preceeding paragraph.

In case of any vacancy, the term of office of the appointee to fill such vacancy, who shall be appointed by the Governor and approved by the Senate, a majority of the membership concurring, shall be for the balance of the term for which such vacancy exists.

(c) The members of the board may, in their discretion, following procedures established by them and after consultation with representatives of faculty and students of the university, including appropriate officers of the academic senate and student governments, appoint to the board either or both of the following persons as members with all rights of participation: a member of the faculty at a campus of the university or of another institution of higher education; a person enrolled as a student at a campus of the university for each regular academic term during his service as a member of the board. Any person so appointed shall serve for not less than one year commencing on July 1.

(d) Regents shall be able persons broadly reflective of the economic, cultural, and social diversity of the State, including ethnic minorities and women. However, it is not intended that formulas or specific ratios be applied in the selection of regents.

(e) In the selection of the Regents, the Governor shall consult an advisory committee composed as follows: The Speaker of the Assembly and two public members appointed by the Speaker, the President Pro Tempore of the Senate and two public members appointed by the

Rules Committee of the Senate, two public members appointed by the Governor, the chairman of the regents of the university, an alumnus of the university chosen by the alumni association of the university, a student of the university chosen by the Council of Student Body Presidents, and a member of the faculty of the university chosen by the academic senate of the university. Public members shall serve for four years, except that one each of the initially appointed members selected by the Speaker of the Assembly, the President Pro Tempore of the Senate, and the Governor shall be appointed to serve for two years; student, alumni, and faculty members shall serve for one year and may not be regents of the university at the time of their service on the advisory committee.

(f) The Regents of the University of California shall be vested with the legal title and the management and disposition of the property of the university and of property held for its benefit and shall have the power to take and hold, either by purchase or by donation, or gift, testamentary or otherwise, or in any other manner, without restriction, all real and personal property for the benefit of the university or incidentally to its conduct; provided, however, that sales of university real property shall be subject to such competitive bidding procedures as may be provided by statute. Said corporation shall also have all the powers necessary or convenient for the effective administration of its trust, including the power to sue and to be sued, to use a seal, and to delegate to its committees or to the faculty of the university, or to others, such authority or functions as it may deem wise. The Regents shall receive all funds derived from the sale of lands pursuant to the act of Congress of July 2, 1862, and any subsequent acts amendatory thereof. The university shall be entirely independent of all political or sectarian influence and kept free therefrom in the appointment of its regents and in the administration of its affairs, and no person shall be debarred admission to any department of the university on account of race, religion, ethnic heritage, or sex.

(g) Meetings of the Regents of the University of California shall be public, with exceptions and notice requirements as may be provided by statute.

(Subdivisions (a) and (f) amended Nov. 2, 1976, by Prop. 4. Res.Ch. 35, 1976. Other Source: Entire Sec. 9 was last amended Nov. 5, 1974, by Prop. 4; Res.Ch. 85, 1974.)

SEC. 14.

The Legislature shall have power, by general law, to provide for the incorporation and organization of school districts, high school districts, and community college districts, of every kind and class, and may classify such districts.

The Legislature may authorize the governing boards of all school districts to initiate and carry on any programs, activities, or to otherwise act in any manner which is not in conflict with the laws and purposes for which school districts are established.

(Sec. 14 amended Nov. 7, 1972, by Prop. 5. Res.Ch. 95, 1972. Operative July 1, 1973.)

SEC. 16.

(a) It shall be competent, in all charters framed under the authority given by Section 5 of Article XI, to provide, in addition to those provisions allowable by this Constitution, and by the laws of the State for the manner in which, the times at which, and the terms for which the members of boards of education shall be elected or appointed, for their qualifications, compensation and removal, and for the number which shall constitute any one of such boards.

(b) Notwithstanding Section 3 of Article XI, when the boundaries of a school district or community college district extend beyond the limits of a city whose charter provides for any or all of the foregoing with respect to the members of its board of education, no charter amendment effecting a change in the manner in which, the times at which, or the terms for which the members of the board of education shall be elected or appointed, for their qualifications, compensation, or removal, or for the number which shall constitute such board, shall be adopted unless it is submitted to and approved by a majority of all the qualified electors of the school district or community college district voting on the question. Any such amendment, and any portion of a proposed charter or a revised charter which would establish or change any of the foregoing provisions respecting a board of education, shall be submitted to the electors of the school district or community college district as one or more separate questions. The failure of any such separate question to be approved shall have the result of continuing in effect the applicable existing law with respect to that board of education.

(Sec. 16 amended June 6, 1978, by Prop. 4. Res.Ch. 47, 1977.)

ARTICLE X WATER

[SECTION 1 - SEC. 7]

(Article 10 added June 8, 1976, by Prop. 14. Res.Ch. 5, 1976.)

SECTION 1.

The right of eminent domain is hereby declared to exist in the State to all frontages on the navigable waters of this State.

(Sec. 1 added June 8, 1976, by Prop. 14. Res.Ch. 5, 1976.)

SEC. 2.

It is hereby declared that because of the conditions prevailing in this State the general welfare requires that the water resources of the State be put to beneficial use to the fullest extent of which they are capable, and that the waste or unreasonable use or unreasonable method of use of water be prevented, and that the conservation of such waters is to be exercised with a view to the reasonable and beneficial use thereof in the interest of the people and for the public welfare. The right to water or to the use or flow of water in or from any natural stream or water course in this State is and shall be limited to such water as shall be reasonably required for the beneficial use to be served, and such right does not and shall not extend to the waste or unreasonable use or unreasonable method of use or unreasonable method of diversion of water. Riparian rights in a stream or water course attach to, but to no more than so much of the flow thereof as may be required or used consistently with this section, for the purposes for which such lands are, or may be made adaptable, in view of such reasonable and beneficial uses; provided, however, that nothing herein contained shall be construed as depriving any riparian owner of the reasonable use of water of the stream to which the owner's land is riparian under reasonable methods of diversion and use, or as depriving any appropriator of water to which the appropriator is lawfully entitled. This section shall be self-executing, and the Legislature may also enact laws in the furtherance of the policy in this section contained.

(Sec. 2 added June 8, 1976, by Prop. 14. Res.Ch. 5, 1976.)

SEC. 3.

All tidelands within two miles of any incorporated city, city and county, or town in this State, and fronting on the water of any harbor, estuary, bay, or inlet used for the purposes of navigation, shall be withheld from grant or sale to private persons, partnerships, or corporations; provided, however, that any such tidelands, reserved to the State solely for street purposes, which the Legislature finds and declares are not used for navigation purposes and are not necessary for such purposes may be sold to any town, city, county, city and county, municipal corporations, private persons, partnerships or corporations subject to such conditions as the Legislature determines are necessary to be imposed in connection with any such sales in order to protect the public interest.

(Sec. 3 added June 8, 1976, by Prop. 14. Res.Ch. 5, 1976.)

SEC. 4.

No individual, partnership, or corporation, claiming or possessing the frontage or tidal lands of a harbor, bay, inlet, estuary, or other navigable water in this State, shall be permitted to exclude the right of way to such water whenever it is required for any public purpose, nor to destroy or obstruct the free navigation of such water; and the Legislature shall enact such laws as will give the most liberal construction to this provision, so that access to the navigable waters of this State shall be always attainable for the people thereof.

(Sec. 4 added June 8, 1976, by Prop. 14. Res.Ch. 5, 1976.)

SEC. 5.

The use of all water now appropriated, or that may hereafter be appropriated, for sale, rental, or distribution, is hereby declared to be a public use, and subject to the regulation and control of the State, in the manner to be prescribed by law.

(Sec. 5 added June 8, 1976, by Prop. 14. Res.Ch. 5, 1976.)

SEC. 6.

The right to collect rates or compensation for the use of water supplied to any county, city and county, or town, or the inhabitants thereof, is a franchise, and cannot be exercised except by authority of and in the manner prescribed by law.

(Sec. 6 added June 8, 1976, by Prop. 14. Res.Ch. 5, 1976.)

SEC. 7.

Whenever any agency of government, local, state, or federal, hereafter acquires any interest in real property in this State, the acceptance of the interest shall constitute an agreement by the agency to conform to the laws of California as to the acquisition, control, use, and distribution of water with respect to the land so acquired.

(Sec. 7 added June 8, 1976, by Prop. 14. Res.Ch. 5, 1976.)

ARTICLE X A WATER RESOURCES DEVELOPMENT

[SECTION 1 - SEC. 8]

(Article 10A added Nov. 4, 1980, by Prop. 8. Res.Ch. 49, 1980.)

<u>SECTION 1.</u>

The people of the State hereby provide the following guarantees and protections in this article for water rights, water quality, and fish and wildlife resources.

(Sec. 1 added Nov. 4, 1980, by Prop. 8. Res.Ch. 49, 1980. No force or effect.)

<u>SEC. 2.</u>

No statute amending or repealing, or adding to, the provisions of the statute enacted by Senate Bill No. 200 of the 1979–80 Regular Session of the Legislature which specify (1) the manner in which the State will protect fish and wildlife resources in the Sacramento-San Joaquin Delta, Suisun Marsh, and San Francisco Bay system westerly of the delta; (2) the manner in which the State will protect existing water rights in the Sacramento-San Joaquin Delta; and (3) the manner in which the State will operate the State Water Resources Development System to comply with water quality standards and water quality control plans, shall become effective unless approved by the electors in the same manner as statutes amending initiative statutes are approved; except that the Legislature may, by statute passed in each house by roll call vote entered in the journal, two-thirds of the membership concurring, amend or repeal, or add to, these provisions if the statute does not in any manner reduce the protection of the delta or fish and wildlife.

(Sec. 2 added Nov. 4, 1980, by Prop. 8. Res.Ch. 49, 1980. No force or effect.)

<u>SEC. 3.</u>

No water shall be available for appropriation by storage in, or by direct diversion from, any of the components of the California Wild and Scenic Rivers System, as such system exists on January 1, 1981, where such appropriation is for export of water into another major hydrologic basin of the State, as defined in the Department of Water Resources Bulletin 160-74, unless such export is expressly authorized prior to such appropriation by: (a) an initiative statute approved by the electors, or (b) the Legislature, by statute passed in each house by roll call vote entered in the journal, two-thirds of the membership concurring.
(Sec. 3 added Nov. 4, 1980, by Prop. 8. Res.Ch. 49, 1980. No force or effect.)

<u>SEC. 4.</u>

No statute amending or repealing, or adding to, the provisions of Part 4.5 (commencing with Section 12200) of Division 6 of the Water Code (the Delta Protection Act) shall become effective unless approved by the electors in the same manner as statutes amending initiative statutes are approved; except that the Legislature may, by statute passed in each house by roll call vote entered in the journal, two-thirds of the membership concurring, amend or repeal, or add to, these provisions if the statute does not in any manner reduce the protection of the delta or fish and wildlife.
(Sec. 4 added Nov. 4, 1980, by Prop. 8. Res.Ch. 49, 1980. No force or effect.)

<u>SEC. 5.</u>

No public agency may utilize eminent domain proceedings to acquire water rights, which are held for uses within the Sacramento-San Joaquin Delta as defined in Section 12220 of the Water Code, or any contract rights for water or water quality maintenance in the Delta for the purpose of exporting such water from the Delta. This provision shall not be construed to prohibit the utilization of eminent domain proceedings for the purpose of acquiring land or any other rights necessary for the construction of water facilities, including, but not limited to, facilities authorized in Chapter 8 (commencing with Section 12930) of Part 6 of Division 6 of the Water Code.

(Sec. 5 added Nov. 4, 1980, by Prop. 8. Res.Ch. 49, 1980. No force or effect.)

SEC. 6.

(a) The venue of any of the following actions or proceedings brought in a superior court shall be Sacramento County:

(1) An action or proceeding to attack, review, set aside, void, or annul any provision of the statute enacted by Senate Bill No. 200 of the 1979–80 Regular Session of the Legislature.

(2) An action or proceeding to attack, review, set aside, void, or annul the determination made by the Director of Water Resources and the Director of Fish and Game pursuant to subdivision (a) of Section 11255 of the Water Code.

(3) An action or proceeding which would have the effect of attacking, reviewing, preventing, or substantially delaying the construction, operation, or maintenance of the peripheral canal unit described in subdivision (a) of Section 11255 of the Water Code.

(4) An action or proceeding to require the State Water Resources Development System to comply with subdivision (b) of Section 11460 of the Water Code.

(5) An action or proceeding to require the Department of Water Resources or its successor agency to comply with the permanent agreement specified in subdivision (a) of Section 11256 of the Water Code.

(6) An action or proceeding to require the Department of Water Resources or its successor agency to comply with

the provisions of the contracts entered into pursuant to Section 11456 of the Water Code.

(b) An action or proceeding described in paragraph (1) of subdivision (a) shall be commenced within one year after the effective date of the statute enacted by Senate Bill No. 200 of the 1979–80 Regular Session of the Legislature. Any other action or proceeding described in subdivision (a) shall be commenced within one year after the cause of action arises unless a shorter period is otherwise provided by statute.

(c) The superior court or a court of appeals shall give preference to the actions or proceedings described in this section over all civil actions or proceedings pending in the court. The superior court shall commence hearing any such action or proceeding within six months after the commencement of the action or proceeding, provided that any such hearing may be delayed by joint stipulation of the parties or at the discretion of the court for good cause shown. The provisions of this section shall supersede any provisions of law requiring courts to give preference to other civil actions or proceedings. The provisions of this subdivision may be enforced by mandamus.

(d) The Supreme Court shall, upon the request of any party, transfer to itself, before a decision in the court of appeal, any appeal or petition for extraordinary relief from an action or proceeding described in this section, unless the Supreme Court determines that the action or proceeding is unlikely to substantially affect (1) the construction, operation, or maintenance of the peripheral canal unit described in subdivision (a) of Section 11255 of the Water Code, (2) compliance with subdivision (b) of Section 11460 of the Water Code, (3) compliance with the permanent agreement specified in Section 11256 of the Water Code, or (4) compliance with the provisions of the contracts entered into pursuant to Section 11456 of the Water Code. The request for transfer shall receive preference on the Supreme Court's calendar. If the action or proceeding is transferred to the Supreme Court, the Supreme Court shall commence to hear the matter within six months of the transfer unless the parties by joint stipulation request additional time or the court, for good cause shown, grants additional time.

(e) The remedy prescribed by the court for an action or proceeding described in paragraph (4), (5), or (6) of subdivision (a) shall include, but need not be limited to, compliance with subdivision (b) of Section 11460 of the Water Code, the permanent agreement specified in Section 11256 of the Water Code, or the provisions of the contracts entered into pursuant to Section 11456 of the Water Code.

(f) The Board of Supervisors of the County of Sacramento may apply to the State Board of Control for actual costs imposed by the requirements of this section upon the county, and the State Board of Control shall pay such actual costs.

(g) Notwithstanding the provisions of this section, nothing in this Article shall be construed as prohibiting the Supreme Court from exercising the transfer authority contained in Article VI, Section 12 of the Constitution.

(Sec. 6 added Nov. 4, 1980, by Prop. 8. Res.Ch. 49, 1980. No force or effect.)

SEC. 7.

State agencies shall exercise their authorized powers in a manner consistent with the protections provided by this article.

(Sec. 7 added Nov. 4, 1980, by Prop. 8. Res.Ch. 49, 1980. No force or effect.)

SEC. 8.

This article shall have no force or effect unless Senate Bill No. 200 of the 1979–80 Regular Session of the Legislature is enacted and takes effect.

(Sec. 8 added Nov. 4, 1980, by Prop. 8. Res.Ch. 49, 1980. Note: SB 200 (Stats. 1980, Ch. 632) did not take effect and was rejected by referendum on June 8, 1982.)

ARTICLE X B MARINE RESOURCES PROTECTION ACT OF 1990

[SECTION 1 - SEC. 16]

(Article 10B added Nov. 6, 1990, by Prop. 132. Initiative measure.)

SECTION 1.

This article shall be known and may be cited as the Marine Resources Protection Act of 1990.

(Sec. 1 added Nov. 6, 1990, by Prop. 132. Initiative measure.)

SEC. 2.

(a) "District" means a fish and game district as defined in the Fish and Game Code by statute on January 1, 1990.

(b) Except as specifically provided in this article, all references to Fish and Game Code sections, articles, chapters, parts, and divisions are defined as those statutes in effect on January 1, 1990.

(c) "Ocean waters" means the waters of the Pacific Ocean regulated by the State.

(d) "Zone" means the Marine Resources Protection zone established pursuant to this article. The zone consists of the following:

(1) In waters less than 70 fathoms or within one mile, whichever is less, around the Channel Islands consisting of the Islands of San Miguel, Santa Rosa, Santa Cruz, Anacapa, San Nicolaus, Santa Barbara, Santa Catalina, and San Clemente.

(2) The area within three nautical miles offshore of the mainland coast, and the area within three nautical miles off any manmade breakwater, between a line extending due west from Point Arguello and a line extending due west from the Mexican border.

(3) In waters less than 35 fathoms between a line running 180 degrees true from Point Fermin and a line running 270 degrees true from the south jetty of Newport Harbor.

(Sec. 2 added Nov. 6, 1990, by Prop. 132. Initiative measure.)

SEC. 3.

(a) From January 1, 1991, to December 31, 1993, inclusive, gill nets or trammel nets may only be used in the zone pursuant to a nontransferable permit issued by the Department of Fish and Game pursuant to Section 5.

(b) On and after January 1, 1994, gill nets and trammel nets shall not be used in the zone.

(Sec. 3 added Nov. 6, 1990, by Prop. 132. Initiative measure.)

SEC. 4.

(a) Notwithstanding any other provision of law, gill nets and trammel nets may not be used to take any species of rockfish.

(b) In ocean waters north of Point Arguello on and after the effective date of this article, the use of gill nets and trammel nets shall be regulated by the provisions of Article 4 (commencing with Section 8660), Article 5 (commencing with Section 8680) and Article 6 (commencing with Section 8720) of Chapter 3 of Part 3 of Division 6 of the Fish and Game Code, or any regulation or order issued pursuant to these articles, in effect on January 1, 1990, except that as to Sections 8680, 8681, 8681.7, and 8682, and subdivisions (a) through (f), inclusive of Section 8681.5 of the Fish and Game Code, or any regulation or order issued pursuant to these sections, the provisions in effect on January 1, 1989, shall control where not in conflict with other provisions of this article, and shall be applicable to all ocean waters. Notwithstanding the provisions of this section, the Legislature shall not be precluded from imposing more restrictions on the use and/or possession of gill nets or trammel nets. The Director of the Department of Fish and Game shall not authorize the use of gill nets or trammel nets in any area where the use is not permitted even if the director makes specified findings.

(Sec. 4 added Nov. 6, 1990, by Prop. 132. Initiative measure.)

SEC. 5.

The Department of Fish and Game shall issue a permit to use a gill net or trammel net in the zone for the period specified in subdivision (a) of Section 3 to any applicant who meets both of the following requirements:

(a) Has a commercial fishing license issued pursuant to Sections 7850–7852.3 of the Fish and Game Code.

(b) Has a permit issued pursuant to Section 8681 of the Fish and Game Code and is presently the owner or operator of a vessel equipped with a gill net or trammel net.

(Sec. 5 added Nov. 6, 1990, by Prop. 132. Initiative measure.)

SEC. 6.

The Department of Fish and Game shall charge the following fees for permits issued pursuant to Section 5 pursuant to the following schedule:

Calendar Year	Fee
1991	$250
1992	500
1993	1,000

(Sec. 6 added Nov. 6, 1990, by Prop. 132. Initiative measure.)

SEC. 7.

(a) Within 90 days after the effective date of this section, every person who intends to seek the compensation provided in subdivision (b) shall notify the Department of Fish and Game, on forms provided by the department, of that intent. Any person who does not submit the form within that 90-day period shall not be compensated pursuant to subdivision (b). The department shall publish a list of all persons submitting the form within 120 days after the effective date of this section.

(b) After July 1, 1993, and before January 1, 1994, any person who holds a permit issued pursuant to Section 5 and operates in the zone may surrender that permit to the department and agree to permanently discontinue fishing with gill or trammel nets in the zone, for which he or she shall receive, beginning on July 1, 1993, a one time compensation which shall be based upon the average annual ex vessel value of the fish other than any species of rockfish landed by a fisherman, which were taken pursuant to a valid general gill net or trammel net permit issued pursuant to Sections 8681 and 8682 of the Fish and Game Code within the zone during the years 1983 to 1987, inclusive. The department shall verify those landings by reviewing logs and landing receipts submitted to it. Any person who is denied compensation by the department as a result of the department's failure to verify landings may appeal that decision to the Fish and Game Commission.

(c) The State Board of Control shall, prior to the disbursement of any funds, verify the eligibility of each person seeking compensation and the amount of the compensation to be provided in order to ensure compliance with this section.

(d) Unless the Legislature enacts any required enabling legislation to implement this section on or before July 1, 1993, no compensation shall be paid under this article.

(Sec. 7 added Nov. 6, 1990, by Prop. 132. Initiative measure.)

SEC. 8.

(a) There is hereby created the Marine Resources Protection Account in the Fish and Game Preservation Fund. On and after January 1, 1991, the Department of Fish and Game shall collect any and all fees required by this article. All fees received by the department pursuant to this article shall be deposited in the account and shall be expended or encumbered to compensate persons who surrender permits pursuant to Section 7 or to provide for administration of this article. All funds received by the department during any fiscal year pursuant to this article which are not expended during that fiscal year to compensate persons as set forth in Section 7 or to provide for administration of this article shall be carried over into the following fiscal year and shall be used only for those purposes. All interest accrued from the department's retention of fees received pursuant to this article shall be credited to the account. The accrued interest may only be expended for the purposes authorized by this article. The account shall continue in existence, and the requirement to pay fees under this article shall remain in effect, until the compensation provided in Section 7 has been fully funded or until January 1, 1995, whichever occurs first.

(b) An amount, not to exceed 15 percent of the total annual revenues deposited in the account excluding any interest accrued or any funds carried over from a prior fiscal year may be expended for the administration of this article.

(c) In addition to a valid California sportfishing license issued pursuant to Sections 7149, 7149.1 or 7149.2 of the Fish and Game Code and any applicable sport license stamp issued pursuant to the Fish and Game Code, a person taking fish from ocean waters south of a line extending due west from Point Arguello for sport purposes shall have permanently affixed to that person's sportfishing license a marine resources protection stamp which may be obtained from the department upon payment of a fee of three dollars ($3). This subdivision does not apply to any one-day fishing license.

(d) In addition to a valid California commercial passenger fishing boat license required by Section 7920 of the Fish and Game Code, the owner of any boat or vessel who, for profit, permits any person to fish from the boat or vessel in ocean waters south of a line extending due west from Point Arguello, shall obtain and permanently affix to the license a commercial marine resources protection stamp which may be obtained from the department upon payment of a fee of three dollars ($3).

(e) The department may accept contributions or donations from any person who wishes to donate money to be used for the compensation of commercial gill net and trammel net fishermen who surrender permits under this article.

(f) This section shall become inoperative on January 1, 1995.

(Sec. 8 added Nov. 6, 1990, by Prop. 132. Initiative measure. Inoperative Jan. 1, 1995.)

SEC. 9.

Any funds remaining in the Marine Resources Protection Account in the Fish and Game Preservation Fund on or after January 1, 1995, shall, with the approval of the Fish and Game Commission, be used to provide grants to colleges, universities and other bonafide scientific research groups to fund marine resource related scientific research within the ecological reserves established by Section 14 of this act.

(Sec. 9 added Nov. 6, 1990, by Prop. 132. Initiative measure.)

SEC. 10.

On or before December 31 of each year, the Director of Fish and Game shall prepare and submit a report to the Legislature regarding the implementation of this article including an accounting of all funds.

(Sec. 10 added Nov. 6, 1990, by Prop. 132. Initiative measure.)

SEC. 11.

It is unlawful for any person to take, possess, receive, transport, purchase, sell, barter, or process any fish obtained in violation of this article.
(Sec. 11 added Nov. 6, 1990, by Prop. 132. Initiative measure.)

SEC. 12.

To increase the State's scientific and biological information on the ocean fisheries of this State, the Department of Fish and Game shall establish a program whereby it can monitor and evaluate the daily landings of fish by commercial fishermen who are permitted under this article to take these fish. The cost of implementing this monitoring program shall be borne by the commercial fishing industry.
(Sec. 12 added Nov. 6, 1990, by Prop. 132. Initiative measure.)

SEC. 13.

(a) The penalty for a first violation of the provisions of Sections 3 and 4 of this article is a fine of not less than one thousand dollars ($1,000) and not more than five thousand dollars ($5,000) and a mandatory suspension of any license, permit or stamp to take, receive, transport, purchase, sell, barter or process fish for commercial purposes for six months. The penalty for a second or subsequent violation of the provisions of Sections 3 and 4 of this article is a fine of not less than two thousand five hundred dollars ($2,500) and not more than ten thousand dollars ($10,000) and a mandatory suspension of any license, permit or stamp to take, receive, transport, purchase, sell, barter, or process fish for commercial purposes for one year.
(b) Notwithstanding any other provisions of law, a violation of Section 8 of this article shall be deemed a violation of the provisions of Section 7145 of the Fish and Game Code

and the penalty for such violation shall be consistent with the provisions of Section 12002.2 of said code.

(c) If a person convicted of a violation of Section 3, 4, or 8 of this article is granted probation, the court shall impose as a term or condition of probation, in addition to any other term or condition of probation, that the person pay at least the minimum fine prescribed in this section.

(Sec. 13 added Nov. 6, 1990, by Prop. 132. Initiative measure.)

SEC. 14.

Prior to January 1, 1994, the Fish and Game Commission shall establish four new ecological reserves in ocean waters along the mainland coast. Each ecological reserve shall have a surface area of at least two square miles. The commission shall restrict the use of these ecological reserves to scientific research relating to the management and enhancement of marine resources.

(Sec. 14 added Nov. 6, 1990, by Prop. 132. Initiative measure.)

SEC. 15.

This article does not preempt or supersede any other closures to protect any other wildlife, including sea otters, whales, and shorebirds.

(Sec. 15 added Nov. 6, 1990, by Prop. 132. Initiative measure.)

SEC. 16.

If any provision of this article or the application thereof to any person or circumstances is held invalid, that invalidity shall not affect other provisions or applications of this article which can be given effect without the invalid provision or application, and to this end the provisions of this article are severable.

(Sec. 16 added Nov. 6, 1990, by Prop. 132. Initiative measure.)

ARTICLE XI LOCAL GOVERNMENT
[SEC. 1 - SEC. 15]

(Article 11 added June 2, 1970, by Prop. 2. Res.Ch. 331, 1969.)

SEC. 1.

(a) The State is divided into counties which are legal subdivisions of the State. The Legislature shall prescribe uniform procedure for county formation, consolidation, and boundary change. Formation or consolidation requires approval by a majority of electors voting on the question in each affected county. A boundary change requires approval by the governing body of each affected county. No county seat shall be removed unless two-thirds of the qualified electors of the county, voting on the proposition at a general election, shall vote in favor of such removal. A proposition of removal shall not be submitted in the same county more than once in four years.

(b) The Legislature shall provide for county powers, an elected county sheriff, an elected district attorney, an elected assessor, and an elected governing body in each county. Except as provided in subdivision (b) of Section 4 of this article, each governing body shall prescribe by ordinance the compensation of its members, but the ordinance prescribing such compensation shall be subject to referendum. The Legislature or the governing body may provide for other officers whose compensation shall be prescribed by the governing body. The governing body shall provide for the number, compensation, tenure, and appointment of employees.

(Sec. 1 amended June 7, 1988, by Prop. 66. Res.Ch. 1, 1988.)

SEC. 2.

(a) The Legislature shall prescribe uniform procedure for city formation and provide for city powers.

(b) Except with approval by a majority of its electors voting on the question, a city may not be annexed to or consolidated into another.

(Sec. 2 added June 2, 1970, by Prop. 2. Res.Ch. 331, 1969.)

SEC. 3.

(a) For its own government, a county or city may adopt a charter by majority vote of its electors voting on the question. The charter is effective when filed with the Secretary of State. A charter may be amended, revised, or repealed in the same manner. A charter, amendment, revision, or repeal thereof shall be published in the official state statutes. County charters adopted pursuant to this section shall supersede any existing charter and all laws inconsistent therewith. The provisions of a charter are the law of the State and have the force and effect of legislative enactments.

(b) The governing body or charter commission of a county or city may propose a charter or revision. Amendment or repeal may be proposed by initiative or by the governing body.

(c) An election to determine whether to draft or revise a charter and elect a charter commission may be required by initiative or by the governing body.

(d) If provisions of 2 or more measures approved at the same election conflict, those of the measure receiving the highest affirmative vote shall prevail.

(Subdivision (a) amended Nov. 5, 1974, by Prop. 2. Res.Ch. 81, 1974. Other Source: Entire Sec. 3 was added June 2, 1970, by Prop. 2; Res.Ch. 331, 1969.)

SEC. 4.

County charters shall provide for:

(a) A governing body of 5 or more members, elected (1) by district or, (2) at large, or (3) at large, with a requirement that they reside in a district. Charter counties are subject to statutes that relate to apportioning population of governing body districts.

(b) The compensation, terms, and removal of members of the governing body. If a county charter provides for the Legislature to prescribe the salary of the governing body, such compensation shall be prescribed by the governing body by ordinance.

(c) An elected sheriff, an elected district attorney, an elected assessor, other officers, their election or appointment, compensation, terms and removal.

(d) The performance of functions required by statute.

(e) The powers and duties of governing bodies and all other county officers, and for consolidation and segregation of county officers, and for the manner of filling all vacancies occurring therein.

(f) The fixing and regulation by governing bodies, by ordinance, of the appointment and number of assistants, deputies, clerks, attachés, and other persons to be employed, and for the prescribing and regulating by such bodies of the powers, duties, qualifications, and compensation of such persons, the times at which, and terms for which they shall be appointed, and the manner of their appointment and removal.

(g) Whenever any county has framed and adopted a charter, and the same shall have been approved by the Legislature as herein provided, the general laws adopted by the Legislature in pursuance of Section 1(b) of this article, shall, as to such county, be superseded by said charter as to matters for which, under this section it is competent to make provision in such charter, and for which provision is made therein, except as herein otherwise expressly provided.

(h) Charter counties shall have all the powers that are provided by this Constitution or by statute for counties.

(Sec. 4 amended June 7, 1988, by Prop. 66. Res.Ch. 1, 1988.)

SEC. 5.

(a) It shall be competent in any city charter to provide that the city governed thereunder may make and enforce all ordinances and regulations in respect to municipal affairs, subject only to restrictions and limitations provided in their several charters and in respect to other matters they shall be subject to general laws. City charters adopted pursuant to this Constitution shall supersede any existing charter, and with respect to municipal affairs shall supersede all laws inconsistent therewith.

(b) It shall be competent in all city charters to provide, in addition to those provisions allowable by this Constitution, and by the laws of the State for: (1) the constitution, regulation, and government of the city police force (2) subgovernment in all or part of a city (3) conduct of city elections and (4) plenary authority is hereby granted, subject only to the restrictions of this article, to provide therein or by amendment thereto, the manner in which, the method by which, the times at which, and the terms for which the several municipal officers and employees whose compensation is paid by the city shall be elected or appointed, and for their removal, and for their compensation, and for the number of deputies, clerks and other employees that each shall have, and for the compensation, method of appointment, qualifications, tenure of office and removal of such deputies, clerks and other employees.

(Sec. 5 added June 2, 1970, by Prop. 2. Res.Ch. 331, 1969.)

SEC. 6.

(a) A county and all cities within it may consolidate as a charter city and county as provided by statute.

(b) A charter city and county is a charter city and a charter county. Its charter city powers supersede conflicting charter county powers.

(Sec. 6 added June 2, 1970, by Prop. 2. Res.Ch. 331, 1969.)

SEC. 7.

A county or city may make and enforce within its limits all local, police, sanitary, and other ordinances and regulations not in conflict with general laws.
(Sec. 7 added June 2, 1970, by Prop. 2. Res.Ch. 331, 1969.)

SEC. 7.5.

(a) A city or county measure proposed by the legislative body of a city, charter city, county, or charter county and submitted to the voters for approval may not do either of the following:
(1) Include or exclude any part of the city, charter city, county, or charter county from the application or effect of its provisions based upon approval or disapproval of the city or county measure, or based upon the casting of a specified percentage of votes in favor of the measure, by the electors of the city, charter city, county, charter county, or any part thereof.
(2) Contain alternative or cumulative provisions wherein one or more of those provisions would become law depending upon the casting of a specified percentage of votes for or against the measure.
(b) "City or county measure," as used in this section, means an advisory question, proposed charter or charter amendment, ordinance, proposition for the issuance of bonds, or other question or proposition submitted to the voters of a city, or to the voters of a county at an election held throughout an entire single county.
(Sec. 7.5 added June 2, 1998, by Prop. 219. Res.Ch. 34, 1996.)

SEC. 8.

(a) The Legislature may provide that counties perform municipal functions at the request of cities within them.

(b) If provided by their respective charters, a county may agree with a city within it to assume and discharge specified municipal functions.

(Sec. 8 added June 2, 1970, by Prop. 2. Res.Ch. 331, 1969.)

SEC. 9.

(a) A municipal corporation may establish, purchase, and operate public works to furnish its inhabitants with light, water, power, heat, transportation, or means of communication. It may furnish those services outside its boundaries, except within another municipal corporation which furnishes the same service and does not consent.

(b) Persons or corporations may establish and operate works for supplying those services upon conditions and under regulations that the city may prescribe under its organic law.

(Sec. 9 added June 2, 1970, by Prop. 2. Res.Ch. 331, 1969.)

SEC. 10.

(a) A local government body may not grant extra compensation or extra allowance to a public officer, public employee, or contractor after service has been rendered or a contract has been entered into and performed in whole or in part, or pay a claim under an agreement made without authority of law.

(b) A city or county, including any chartered city or chartered county, or public district, may not require that its employees be residents of such city, county, or district; except that such employees may be required to reside within a reasonable and specific distance of their place of employment or other designated location.

(Sec. 10 amended June 8, 1976, by Prop. 14. Res.Ch. 5, 1976.)

SEC. 11.

(a) The Legislature may not delegate to a private person or body power to make, control, appropriate, supervise, or interfere with county or municipal corporation improvements, money, or property, or to levy taxes or assessments, or perform municipal functions.

(b) The Legislature may, however, provide for the deposit of public moneys in any bank in this State or in any savings and loan association in this State or any credit union in this State or in any federally insured industrial loan company in this State and for payment of interest, principal, and redemption premiums of public bonds and other evidence of public indebtedness by banks within or without this State. It may also provide for investment of public moneys in securities and the registration of bonds and other evidences of indebtedness by private persons or bodies, within or without this State, acting as trustees or fiscal agents.

(Sec. 11 amended Nov. 8, 1988, by Prop. 88. Res.Ch. 59, 1988.)

SEC. 12.

The Legislature may prescribe procedure for presentation, consideration, and enforcement of claims against counties, cities, their officers, agents, or employees.

(Sec. 12 added June 2, 1970, by Prop. 2. Res.Ch. 331, 1969.)

SEC. 13.

The provisions of Sections 1(b) (except for the second sentence), 3(a), 4, and 5 of this Article relating to matters affecting the distribution of powers between the Legislature and cities and counties, including matters affecting supersession, shall be construed as a restatement of all related provisions of the Constitution in effect immediately prior to the effective date of this amendment, and as making no substantive change.

The terms general law, general laws, and laws, as used in this Article, shall be construed as a continuation and restatement of those terms as used in the Constitution in effect immediately prior to the effective date of this amendment, and not as effecting a change in meaning.

(Sec. 13 added June 2, 1970, by Prop. 2. Res.Ch. 331, 1969.)

SEC. 14.

A local government formed after the effective date of this section, the boundaries of which include all or part of two or more counties, shall not levy a property tax unless such tax has been approved by a majority vote of the qualified voters of that local government voting on the issue of the tax.

(Sec. 14 added Nov. 2, 1976, by Prop. 10. Res.Ch. 59, 1976.)

SEC. 15.

(a) From the revenues derived from taxes imposed pursuant to the Vehicle License Fee Law (Part 5 (commencing with Section 10701) of Division 2 of the Revenue and Taxation Code), or its successor, other than fees on trailer coaches and mobilehomes, over and above the costs of collection and any refunds authorized by law, those revenues derived from that portion of the vehicle license fee rate that does not exceed 0.65 percent of the market value of the vehicle shall be allocated as follows:

(1) An amount shall be specified in the Vehicle License Fee Law, or the successor to that law, for deposit in the State Treasury to the credit of the Local Revenue Fund established in Chapter 6 (commencing with Section 17600) of Part 5 of Division 9 of the Welfare and Institutions Code, or its successor, if any, for allocation to cities, counties, and cities and counties as otherwise provided by law.

(2) The balance shall be allocated to cities, counties, and cities and counties as otherwise provided by law.

(b) If a statute enacted by the Legislature reduces the annual vehicle license fee below 0.65 percent of the market value of a vehicle, the Legislature shall, for each fiscal year for which that reduced fee applies, provide by statute for the allocation of an additional amount of money that is equal to the decrease, resulting from the fee reduction, in the total amount of revenues that are otherwise required to be deposited and allocated under subdivision (a) for that same fiscal year. That amount shall be allocated to cities, counties, and cities and counties in the same pro rata amounts and for the same purposes as are revenues subject to subdivision (a).

(Sec. 15 amended Nov. 2, 2004, by Prop. 1A. Res.Ch. 133, 2004.)

ARTICLE XII PUBLIC UTILITIES
[SECTION 1 - SEC. 9]

(Article 12 added Nov. 5, 1974, by Prop. 12. Res.Ch. 88, 1974.)

SECTION 1.

The Public Utilities Commission consists of 5 members appointed by the Governor and approved by the Senate, a majority of the membership concurring, for staggered 6-year terms. A vacancy is filled for the remainder of the term. The Legislature may remove a member for incompetence, neglect of duty, or corruption, two thirds of the membership of each house concurring.
(Sec. 1 added Nov. 5, 1974, by Prop. 12. Res.Ch. 88, 1974.)

SEC. 2.

Subject to statute and due process, the commission may establish its own procedures. Any commissioner as designated by the commission may hold a hearing or investigation or issue an order subject to commission approval.
(Sec. 2 added Nov. 5, 1974, by Prop. 12. Res.Ch. 88, 1974.)

SEC. 3.

Private corporations and persons that own, operate, control, or manage a line, plant, or system for the transportation of people or property, the transmission of telephone and telegraph messages, or the production, generation, transmission, or furnishing of heat, light, water, power, storage, or wharfage directly or indirectly to or for the public, and common carriers, are public utilities subject to control by the Legislature. The Legislature may

prescribe that additional classes of private corporations or other persons are public utilities.
(Sec. 3 added Nov. 5, 1974, by Prop. 12. Res.Ch. 88, 1974.)

SEC. 4.

The commission may fix rates and establish rules for the transportation of passengers and property by transportation companies, prohibit discrimination, and award reparation for the exaction of unreasonable, excessive, or discriminatory charges. A transportation company may not raise a rate or incidental charge except after a showing to and a decision by the commission that the increase is justified, and this decision shall not be subject to judicial review except as to whether confiscation of property will result.
(Sec. 4 added Nov. 5, 1974, by Prop. 12. Res.Ch. 88, 1974.)

SEC. 5.

The Legislature has plenary power, unlimited by the other provisions of this constitution but consistent with this article, to confer additional authority and jurisdiction upon the commission, to establish the manner and scope of review of commission action in a court of record, and to enable it to fix just compensation for utility property taken by eminent domain.
(Sec. 5 added Nov. 5, 1974, by Prop. 12. Res.Ch. 88, 1974.)

SEC. 6.

The commission may fix rates, establish rules, examine records, issue subpenas, administer oaths, take testimony, punish for contempt, and prescribe a uniform system of accounts for all public utilities subject to its jurisdiction.
(Sec. 6 added Nov. 5, 1974, by Prop. 12. Res.Ch. 88, 1974.)

SEC. 7.

A transportation company may not grant free passes or discounts to anyone holding an office in this State; and the acceptance of a pass or discount by a public officer, other than a Public Utilities Commissioner, shall work a forfeiture of that office. A Public Utilities Commissioner may not hold an official relation to nor have a financial interest in a person or corporation subject to regulation by the commission.
(Sec. 7 added Nov. 5, 1974, by Prop. 12. Res.Ch. 88, 1974.)

SEC. 8.

A city, county, or other public body may not regulate matters over which the Legislature grants regulatory power to the Commission. This section does not affect power over public utilities relating to the making and enforcement of police, sanitary, and other regulations concerning municipal affairs pursuant to a city charter existing on October 10, 1911, unless that power has been revoked by the city's electors, or the right of any city to grant franchises for public utilities or other businesses on terms, conditions, and in the manner prescribed by law.
(Sec. 8 added Nov. 5, 1974, by Prop. 12. Res.Ch. 88, 1974.)

SEC. 9.

The provisions of this article restate all related provisions of the Constitution in effect immediately prior to the effective date of this amendment and make no substantive change.
(Sec. 9 added Nov. 5, 1974, by Prop. 12. Res.Ch. 88, 1974.)

ARTICLE XIII TAXATION
[SEC. 1 - SEC. 36]

(Article 13 added Nov. 5, 1974, by Prop. 8. Res.Ch. 70, 1974.)

SEC. 1.

Unless otherwise provided by this Constitution or the laws of the United States:

(a) All property is taxable and shall be assessed at the same percentage of fair market value. When a value standard other than fair market value is prescribed by this Constitution or by statute authorized by this Constitution, the same percentage shall be applied to determine the assessed value. The value to which the percentage is applied, whether it be the fair market value or not, shall be known for property tax purposes as the full value.

(b) All property so assessed shall be taxed in proportion to its full value.

(Sec. 1 added Nov. 5, 1974, by Prop. 8. Res.Ch. 70, 1974.)

SEC. 2.

The Legislature may provide for property taxation of all forms of tangible personal property, shares of capital stock, evidences of indebtedness, and any legal or equitable interest therein not exempt under any other provision of this article. The Legislature, two-thirds of the membership of each house concurring, may classify such personal property for differential taxation or for exemption. The tax on any interest in notes, debentures, shares of capital stock, bonds, solvent credits, deeds of trust, or mortgages shall not exceed four-tenths of one percent of full value, and the tax per dollar of full value shall not be higher on personal property than on real property in the same taxing jurisdiction.

(Sec. 2 added Nov. 5, 1974, by Prop. 8. Res.Ch. 70, 1974.)

SEC. 3.

The following are exempt from property taxation:
(a) Property owned by the State.
(b) Property owned by a local government, except as otherwise provided in Section 11(a).
(c) Bonds issued by the State or a local government in the State.
(d) Property used for libraries and museums that are free and open to the public and property used exclusively for public schools, community colleges, state colleges, and state universities.
(e) Buildings, land, equipment, and securities used exclusively for educational purposes by a nonprofit institution of higher education.
(f) Buildings, land on which they are situated, and equipment used exclusively for religious worship.
(g) Property used or held exclusively for the permanent deposit of human dead or for the care and maintenance of the property or the dead, except when used or held for profit. This property is also exempt from special assessment.
(h) Growing crops.
(i) Fruit and nut trees until 4 years after the season in which they were planted in orchard form and grape vines until 3 years after the season in which they were planted in vineyard form.
(j) Immature forest trees planted on lands not previously bearing merchantable timber or planted or of natural growth on lands from which the merchantable original growth timber stand to the extent of 70 percent of all trees over 16 inches in diameter has been removed. Forest trees or timber shall be considered mature at such time after 40 years from the time of planting or removal of the original timber when so declared by a majority vote of a board consisting of a representative from the State Board of Forestry, a representative from the State Board of Equalization, and the assessor of the county in which the trees are located.

The Legislature may supersede the foregoing provisions with an alternative system or systems of taxing or exempting forest trees or timber, including a taxation system not based on property valuation. Any alternative system or systems shall provide for exemption of unharvested immature trees, shall encourage the continued use of timberlands for the production of trees for timber products, and shall provide for restricting the use of timberland to the production of timber products and compatible uses with provisions for taxation of timberland based on the restrictions. Nothing in this paragraph shall be construed to exclude timberland from the provisions of Section 8 of this article.

(k) $7,000 of the full value of a dwelling, as defined by the Legislature, when occupied by an owner as his principal residence, unless the dwelling is receiving another real property exemption. The Legislature may increase this exemption and may deny it if the owner received state or local aid to pay taxes either in whole or in part, and either directly or indirectly, on the dwelling.

No increase in this exemption above the amount of $7,000 shall be effective for any fiscal year unless the Legislature increases the rate of state taxes in an amount sufficient to provide the subventions required by Section 25.

If the Legislature increases the homeowners' property tax exemption, it shall provide increases in benefits to qualified renters, as defined by law, comparable to the average increase in benefits to homeowners, as calculated by the Legislature.

(l) Vessels of more than 50 tons burden in this State and engaged in the transportation of freight or passengers.

(m) Household furnishings and personal effects not held or used in connection with a trade, profession, or business.

(n) Any debt secured by land.

(o) Property in the amount of $1,000 of a claimant who—

(1) is serving in or has served in and has been discharged under honorable conditions from service in the United States Army, Navy, Air Force, Marine Corps, Coast Guard, or Revenue Marine (Revenue Cutter) Service; and—

(2) served either

(i) in time of war, or

(ii) in time of peace in a campaign or expedition for which a medal has been issued by Congress, or

(iii) in time of peace and because of a service-connected disability was released from active duty; and—

(3) resides in the State on the current lien date.

An unmarried person who owns property valued at $5,000 or more, or a married person, who, together with the spouse, owns property valued at $10,000 or more, is ineligible for this exemption.

If the claimant is married and does not own property eligible for the full amount of the exemption, property of the spouse shall be eligible for the unused balance of the exemption.

(p) Property in the amount of $1,000 of a claimant who—

(1) is the unmarried spouse of a deceased veteran who met the service requirement stated in paragraphs (1) and (2) of subsection 3(o), and

(2) does not own property in excess of $10,000, and

(3) is a resident of the State on the current lien date.

(q) Property in the amount of $1,000 of a claimant who—

(1) is the parent of a deceased veteran who met the service requirement stated in paragraphs (1) and (2) of subsection 3(o), and

(2) receives a pension because of the veteran's service, and

(3) is a resident of the State on the current lien date.

Either parent of a deceased veteran may claim this exemption.

An unmarried person who owns property valued at $5,000 or more, or a married person, who, together with the spouse, owns property valued at $10,000 or more, is ineligible for this exemption.

(r) No individual residing in the State on the effective date of this amendment who would have been eligible for the exemption provided by the previous section $1\frac{1}{4}$ of this article had it not been repealed shall lose eligibility for the exemption as a result of this amendment.

(Subdivisions (o), (p), and (q) amended Nov. 8, 1988, by Prop. 93. Res.Ch. 68, 1988. Other Sources: Entire Sec. 3 (except subdivision (k)) was added Nov. 5, 1974, by Prop. 8; Res.Ch. 70, 1974. Subdivision (k) was added Nov. 5, 1974, by Prop. 6; Res.Ch. 77, 1974, third resolved clause.)

SEC. 3.5.

In any year in which the assessment ratio is changed, the Legislature shall adjust the valuation of assessable property described in subdivisions (o), (p) and (q) of Section 3 of this article to maintain the same proportionate values of such property.
(Sec. 3.5 added Nov. 6, 1979, by Prop. 3. Res.Ch. 85, 1978.)

SEC. 4.

The Legislature may exempt from property taxation in whole or in part:
(a) The home of a person or a person's spouse, including an unmarried surviving spouse, if the person, because of injury incurred in military service, is blind in both eyes, has lost the use of 2 or more limbs, or is totally disabled, or if the person has, as a result of a service-connected injury or disease, died while on active duty in military service, unless the home is receiving another real property exemption.
(b) Property used exclusively for religious, hospital, or charitable purposes and owned or held in trust by corporations or other entities (1) that are organized and operating for those purposes, (2) that are nonprofit, and (3) no part of whose net earnings inures to the benefit of any private shareholder or individual.
(c) Property owned by the California School of Mechanical Arts, California Academy of Sciences, or Cogswell Polytechnical College, or held in trust for the Huntington Library and Art Gallery, or their successors.
(d) Real property not used for commercial purposes that is reasonably and necessarily required for parking vehicles of persons worshipping on land exempt by Section 3(f).
(Subdivision (a) amended Nov. 3, 1992, by Prop. 160. Res.Ch. 49, 1992. Other Source: Entire Sec. 4 was added Nov. 5, 1974, by Prop. 8; Res.Ch. 70, 1974.)

SEC. 5.

Exemptions granted or authorized by Sections 3(e), 3(f), and 4(b) apply to buildings under construction, land required for their convenient use, and equipment in them if the intended use would qualify the property for exemption.
(Sec. 5 added Nov. 5, 1974, by Prop. 8. Res.Ch. 70, 1974.)

SEC. 6.

The failure in any year to claim, in a manner required by the laws in effect at the time the claim is required to be made, an exemption or classification which reduces a property tax shall be deemed a waiver of the exemption or classification for that year.
(Sec. 6 added Nov. 5, 1974, by Prop. 8. Res.Ch. 70, 1974.)

SEC. 7.

The Legislature, two-thirds of the membership of each house concurring, may authorize county boards of supervisors to exempt real property having a full value so low that, if not exempt, the total taxes and applicable subventions on the property would amount to less than the cost of assessing and collecting them.
(Sec. 7 added Nov. 5, 1974, by Prop. 8. Res.Ch. 70, 1974.)

SEC. 8.

To promote the conservation, preservation and continued existence of open space lands, the Legislature may define open space land and shall provide that when this land is enforceably restricted, in a manner specified by the Legislature, to recreation, enjoyment of scenic beauty, use or conservation of natural resources, or production of food or fiber, it shall be valued for property tax purposes only on a basis that is consistent with its restrictions and uses.

To promote the preservation of property of historical significance, the Legislature may define such property and shall provide that when it is enforceably restricted, in a manner specified by the Legislature, it shall be valued for property tax purposes only on a basis that is consistent with its restrictions and uses.

(Second paragraph added June 8, 1976, by Prop. 7. Res.Ch. 198, 1974. Other Source: Entire Sec. 8 was added Nov. 5, 1974, by Prop. 8; Res.Ch. 70, 1974.)

SEC. 8.5.

The Legislature may provide by law for the manner in which a person of low or moderate income who is 62 years of age or older may postpone ad valorem property taxes on the dwelling owned and occupied by him or her as his or her principal place of residence. The Legislature may also provide by law for the manner in which a disabled person may postpone payment of ad valorem property taxes on the dwelling owned and occupied by him or her as his or her principal place of residence. The Legislature shall have plenary power to define all terms in this section.

The Legislature shall provide by law for subventions to counties, cities and counties, cities and districts in an amount equal to the amount of revenue lost by each by reason of the postponement of taxes and for the reimbursement to the State of subventions from the payment of postponed taxes. Provision shall be made for the inclusion of reimbursement for the payment of interest on, and any costs to the State incurred in connection with, the subventions.

(Sec. 8.5 amended Nov. 6, 1984, by Prop. 33. Res.Ch. 65, 1984.)

SEC. 9.

The Legislature may provide for the assessment for taxation only on the basis of use of a single-family dwelling, as defined by the Legislature, and so much of the land as is required for its convenient use and occupation, when the dwelling is occupied by an owner and located on land zoned exclusively for single-family dwellings or for agricultural purposes.
(Sec. 9 added Nov. 5, 1974, by Prop. 8. Res.Ch. 70, 1974.)

SEC. 10.

Real property in a parcel of 10 or more acres which, on the lien date and for 2 or more years immediately preceding, has been used exclusively for nonprofit golf course purposes shall be assessed for taxation on the basis of such use, plus any value attributable to mines, quarries, hydrocarbon substances, or other minerals in the property or the right to extract hydrocarbons or other minerals from the property.
(Sec. 10 added Nov. 5, 1974, by Prop. 8. Res.Ch. 70, 1974.)

SEC. 11.

(a) Lands owned by a local government that are outside its boundaries, including rights to use or divert water from surface or underground sources and any other interests in lands, are taxable if (1) they are located in Inyo or Mono County and (a) they were assessed for taxation to the local government in Inyo County as of the 1966 lien date, or in Mono County as of the 1967 lien date, whether or not the assessment was valid when made, or (b) they were acquired by the local government subsequent to that lien date and were assessed to a prior owner as of that lien date and each lien date thereafter, or (2) they are located outside Inyo or Mono County and were taxable when acquired by the local government. Improvements owned by a local government that are outside its boundaries are taxable if they were taxable when acquired or were constructed by the local government to replace improvements which were taxable when acquired.

(b) Taxable land belonging to a local government and located in Inyo County shall be assessed in any year subsequent to 1968 at the place where it was assessed as of the 1966 lien date and in an amount derived by multiplying its 1966 assessed value by the ratio of the statewide per capita assessed value of land as of the last lien date prior to the current lien date to $766, using civilian population only. Taxable land belonging to a local government and located in Mono County shall be assessed in any year subsequent to 1968 at the place where it was assessed as of the 1967 lien date and in an amount determined by the preceding formula except that the 1967 lien date, the 1967 assessed value, and the figure $856 shall be used in the formula. Taxable land belonging to a local government and located outside of Inyo and Mono counties shall be assessed at the place where located and in an amount that does not exceed the lower of (1) its fair market value times the prevailing percentage of fair market value at which other lands are assessed and (2) a figure derived in the manner specified in this Section for land located in Mono County.

If land acquired by a local government after the lien date of the base year specified in this Section was assessed in the base year as part of a larger parcel, the assessed value of the part in the base year shall be that fraction of the assessed value of the larger parcel that the area of the part is of the area of the larger parcel.

If a local government divests itself of ownership of land without water rights and this land was assessed in Inyo County as of the 1966 lien date or in Mono County as of the 1967 lien date, the divestment shall not diminish the quantity of water rights assessable and taxable at the place where assessed as of that lien date.

(c) In the event the Legislature changes the prevailing percentage of fair market value at which land is assessed for taxation, there shall be used in the computations required by Section 11(b) of this Article, for the first year for which the new percentage is applicable, in lieu of the statewide per capita assessed value of land as of the last lien date prior to the current lien date, the statewide per capita assessed value of land on the prior lien date times the ratio of the new prevailing percentage of fair market value to the previous prevailing percentage.

(d) If, after March 1954, a taxable improvement is replaced while owned by and in possession of a local government, the replacement improvement shall be assessed, as long as it is owned by a local government, as other improvements are except that the assessed value shall not exceed the product of (1) the percentage at which privately owned improvements are assessed times (2) the highest full value ever used for taxation of the improvement that has been replaced. For purposes of this calculation, the full value for any year prior to 1967 shall be conclusively presumed to be 4 times the assessed value in that year.

(e) No tax, charge, assessment, or levy of any character, other than those taxes authorized by Sections 11(a) to 11(d), inclusive, of this Article, shall be imposed upon one local government by another local government that is based or calculated upon the consumption or use of water outside the boundaries of the government imposing it.

(f) Any taxable interest of any character, other than a lease for agricultural purposes and an interest of a local government, in any land owned by a local government that is subject to taxation pursuant to Section 11(a) of this Article shall be taxed in the same manner as other taxable interests. The aggregate value of all the interests subject to taxation pursuant to Section 11(a), however, shall not exceed the value of all interests in the land less the taxable value of the interest of any local government ascertained as provided in Sections 11(a) to 11(e), inclusive, of this Article.

(g) Any assessment made pursuant to Sections 11(a) to 11(d), inclusive, of this Article shall be subject to review, equalization, and adjustment by the State Board of Equalization, but an adjustment shall conform to the provisions of these Sections.

(Sec. 11 added Nov. 5, 1974, by Prop. 8. Res.Ch. 70, 1974.)

SEC. 12.

(a) Except as provided in subdivision (b), taxes on personal property, possessory interests in land, and taxable improvements located on land exempt from taxation which are not a lien upon land sufficient in value to secure their payment shall be levied at the rates for the preceding tax year upon property of the same kind where the taxes were a lien upon land sufficient in value to secure their payment.

(b) In any year in which the assessment ratio is changed, the Legislature shall adjust the rate described in subdivision (a) to maintain equality between property on the secured and unsecured rolls.

(Sec. 12 amended Nov. 2, 1976, by Prop. 11. Res.Ch. 60, 1976.)

SEC. 13.

Land and improvements shall be separately assessed.

(Sec. 13 added Nov. 5, 1974, by Prop. 8. Res.Ch. 70, 1974.)

SEC. 14.

All property taxed by local government shall be assessed in the county, city, and district in which it is situated.

(Sec. 14 added Nov. 5, 1974, by Prop. 8. Res.Ch. 70, 1974.)

SEC. 15.

The Legislature may authorize local government to provide for the assessment or reassessment of taxable property physically damaged or destroyed after the lien date to which the assessment or reassessment relates.

(Sec. 15 added Nov. 5, 1974, by Prop. 8. Res.Ch. 70, 1974, third resolved clause.)

<u>SEC. 16.</u>

The county board of supervisors, or one or more assessment appeals boards created by the county board of supervisors, shall constitute the county board of equalization for a county. Two or more county boards of supervisors may jointly create one or more assessment appeals boards which shall constitute the county board of equalization for each of the participating counties.

Except as provided in subdivision (g) of Section 11, the county board of equalization, under such rules of notice as the county board may prescribe, shall equalize the values of all property on the local assessment roll by adjusting individual assessments.

County boards of supervisors shall fix the compensation for members of assessment appeals boards, furnish clerical and other assistance for those boards, adopt rules of notice and procedures for those boards as may be required to facilitate their work and to insure uniformity in the processing and decision of equalization petitions, and may provide for their discontinuance.

The Legislature shall provide for: (a) the number and qualifications of members of assessment appeals boards, the manner of selecting, appointing, and removing them, and the terms for which they serve, and (b) the procedure by which two or more county boards of supervisors may jointly create one or more assessment appeals boards.

(Sec. 16 added Nov. 5, 1974, by Prop. 8. Res.Ch. 70, 1974.)

<u>SEC. 17.</u>

The Board of Equalization consists of 5 voting members: the Controller and 4 members elected for 4-year terms at gubernatorial elections. The State shall be divided into four Board of Equalization districts with the voters of each district electing one member. No member may serve more than 2 terms.

(Sec. 17 amended Nov. 6, 1990, by Prop. 140. Initiative measure.)

SEC. 18.

The Board shall measure county assessment levels annually and shall bring those levels into conformity by adjusting entire secured local assessment rolls. In the event a property tax is levied by the State, however, the effects of unequalized local assessment levels, to the extent any remain after such adjustments, shall be corrected for purposes of distributing this tax by equalizing the assessment levels of locally and state-assessed properties and varying the rate of the state tax inversely with the counties' respective assessment levels.
(Sec. 18 added Nov. 5, 1974, by Prop. 8. Res.Ch. 70, 1974.)

SEC. 19.

The Board shall annually assess (1) pipelines, flumes, canals, ditches, and aqueducts lying within 2 or more counties and (2) property, except franchises, owned or used by regulated railway, telegraph, or telephone companies, car companies operating on railways in the State, and companies transmitting or selling gas or electricity. This property shall be subject to taxation to the same extent and in the same manner as other property.
No other tax or license charge may be imposed on these companies which differs from that imposed on mercantile, manufacturing, and other business corporations. This restriction does not release a utility company from payments agreed on or required by law for a special privilege or franchise granted by a government body.
The Legislature may authorize Board assessment of property owned or used by other public utilities.
The Board may delegate to a local assessor the duty to assess a property used but not owned by a state assessee on which the taxes are to be paid by a local assessee.
(Sec. 19 added Nov. 5, 1974, by Prop. 8. Res.Ch. 70, 1974.)

SEC. 20.

The Legislature may provide maximum property tax rates and bonding limits for local governments.
(Sec. 20 added Nov. 5, 1974, by Prop. 8. Res.Ch. 70, 1974.)

SEC. 21.

Within such limits as may be provided under Section 20 of this Article, the Legislature shall provide for an annual levy by county governing bodies of school district taxes sufficient to produce annual revenues for each district that the district's board determines are required for its schools and district functions.
(Sec. 21 added Nov. 5, 1974, by Prop. 8. Res.Ch. 70, 1974.)

SEC. 22.

Not more than 25 percent of the total appropriations from all funds of the State shall be raised by means of taxes on real and personal property according to the value thereof.
(Sec. 22 added Nov. 5, 1974, by Prop. 8. Res.Ch. 70, 1974.)

SEC. 23.

If state boundaries change, the Legislature shall determine how property affected shall be taxed.
(Sec. 23 added Nov. 5, 1974, by Prop. 8. Res.Ch. 70, 1974.)

SEC. 24.

(a) The Legislature may not impose taxes for local purposes but may authorize local governments to impose them.

(b) The Legislature may not reallocate, transfer, borrow, appropriate, restrict the use of, or otherwise use the proceeds of any tax imposed or levied by a local government solely for the local government's purposes.

(c) Money appropriated from state funds to a local government for its local purposes may be used as provided by law.

(d) Money subvened to a local government under Section 25 may be used for state or local purposes.

(Sec. 24 amended Nov. 2, 2010, by Prop. 22. Initiative measure.)

SEC. 25.

The Legislature shall provide, in the same fiscal year, reimbursements to each local government for revenue lost because of Section 3(k).

(Sec. 25 added Nov. 5, 1974, by Prop. 8. Res.Ch. 70, 1974.)

SEC. 25.5.

(a) On or after November 3, 2004, the Legislature shall not enact a statute to do any of the following:

(1) (A) Except as otherwise provided in subparagraph (B), modify the manner in which ad valorem property tax revenues are allocated in accordance with subdivision (a) of Section 1 of Article XIII A so as to reduce for any fiscal year the percentage of the total amount of ad valorem property tax revenues in a county that is allocated among all of the local agencies in that county below the percentage of the total amount of those revenues that would be allocated among those agencies for the same fiscal year under the statutes in effect on November 3, 2004. For purposes of this subparagraph, "percentage"

does not include any property tax revenues referenced in paragraph (2).

(B) In the 2009–10 fiscal year only, and except as otherwise provided in subparagraph (C), subparagraph (A) may be suspended for that fiscal year if all of the following conditions are met:

(i) The Governor issues a proclamation that declares that, due to a severe state fiscal hardship, the suspension of subparagraph (A) is necessary.

(ii) The Legislature enacts an urgency statute, pursuant to a bill passed in each house of the Legislature by rollcall vote entered in the journal, two-thirds of the membership concurring, that contains a suspension of subparagraph (A) for that fiscal year and does not contain any other provision.

(iii) No later than the effective date of the statute described in clause (ii), a statute is enacted that provides for the full repayment to local agencies of the total amount of revenue losses, including interest as provided by law, resulting from the modification of ad valorem property tax revenue allocations to local agencies. This full repayment shall be made not later than the end of the third fiscal year immediately following the fiscal year to which the modification applies.

(C) A suspension of subparagraph (A) shall not result in a total ad valorem property tax revenue loss to all local agencies within a county that exceeds 8 percent of the total amount of ad valorem property tax revenues that were allocated among all local agencies within that county for the fiscal year immediately preceding the fiscal year for which subparagraph (A) is suspended.

(2) (A) Except as otherwise provided in subparagraphs (B) and (C), restrict the authority of a city, county, or city and county to impose a tax rate under, or change the method of distributing revenues derived under, the Bradley-Burns Uniform Local Sales and Use Tax Law set forth in Part 1.5 (commencing with Section 7200) of Division 2 of the Revenue and Taxation Code, as that law read on November 3, 2004. The restriction imposed by this subparagraph also applies to the entitlement of a city, county, or city and county to the change in tax rate resulting from the end of

the revenue exchange period, as defined in Section 7203.1 of the Revenue and Taxation Code as that section read on November 3, 2004.

(B) The Legislature may change by statute the method of distributing the revenues derived under a use tax imposed pursuant to the Bradley-Burns Uniform Local Sales and Use Tax Law to allow the State to participate in an interstate compact or to comply with federal law.

(C) The Legislature may authorize by statute two or more specifically identified local agencies within a county, with the approval of the governing body of each of those agencies, to enter into a contract to exchange allocations of ad valorem property tax revenues for revenues derived from a tax rate imposed under the Bradley-Burns Uniform Local Sales and Use Tax Law. The exchange under this subparagraph of revenues derived from a tax rate imposed under that law shall not require voter approval for the continued imposition of any portion of an existing tax rate from which those revenues are derived.

(3) Except as otherwise provided in subparagraph (C) of paragraph (2), change for any fiscal year the pro rata shares in which ad valorem property tax revenues are allocated among local agencies in a county other than pursuant to a bill passed in each house of the Legislature by rollcall vote entered in the journal, two-thirds of the membership concurring. The Legislature shall not change the pro rata shares of ad valorem property tax pursuant to this paragraph, nor change the allocation of the revenues described in Section 15 of Article XI, to reimburse a local government when the Legislature or any state agency mandates a new program or higher level of service on that local government.

(4) Extend beyond the revenue exchange period, as defined in Section 7203.1 of the Revenue and Taxation Code as that section read on November 3, 2004, the suspension of the authority, set forth in that section on that date, of a city, county, or city and county to impose a sales and use tax rate under the Bradley-Burns Uniform Local Sales and Use Tax Law.

(5) Reduce, during any period in which the rate authority suspension described in paragraph (4) is operative, the

payments to a city, county, or city and county that are required by Section 97.68 of the Revenue and Taxation Code, as that section read on November 3, 2004.

(6) Restrict the authority of a local entity to impose a transactions and use tax rate in accordance with the Transactions and Use Tax Law (Part 1.6 (commencing with Section 7251) of Division 2 of the Revenue and Taxation Code), or change the method for distributing revenues derived under a transaction and use tax rate imposed under that law, as it read on November 3, 2004.

(7) Require a community redevelopment agency (A) to pay, remit, loan, or otherwise transfer, directly or indirectly, taxes on ad valorem real property and tangible personal property allocated to the agency pursuant to Section 16 of Article XVI to or for the benefit of the State, any agency of the State, or any jurisdiction; or (B) to use, restrict, or assign a particular purpose for such taxes for the benefit of the State, any agency of the State, or any jurisdiction, other than (i) for making payments to affected taxing agencies pursuant to Sections 33607.5 and 33607.7 of the Health and Safety Code or similar statutes requiring such payments, as those statutes read on January 1, 2008, or (ii) for the purpose of increasing, improving, and preserving the supply of low and moderate income housing available at affordable housing cost.

(b) For purposes of this section, the following definitions apply:

(1) "Ad valorem property tax revenues" means all revenues derived from the tax collected by a county under subdivision (a) of Section 1 of Article XIII A, regardless of any of this revenue being otherwise classified by statute.

(2) "Local agency" has the same meaning as specified in Section 95 of the Revenue and Taxation Code as that section read on November 3, 2004.

(3) "Jurisdiction" has the same meaning as specified in Section 95 of the Revenue and Taxation Code as that section read on November 3, 2004.

(Sec. 25.5 amended Nov. 2, 2010, by Prop. 22. Initiative measure.)

SEC. 26.

(a) Taxes on or measured by income may be imposed on persons, corporations, or other entities as prescribed by law.

(b) Interest on bonds issued by the State or a local government in the State is exempt from taxes on income.

(c) Income of a nonprofit educational institution of collegiate grade within the State of California is exempt from taxes on or measured by income if both of the following conditions are met:

(1) The income is not unrelated business income as defined by the Legislature.

(2) The income is used exclusively for educational purposes.

(d) A nonprofit organization that is exempted from taxation by Chapter 4 (commencing with Section 23701) of Part 11 of Division 2 of the Revenue and Taxation Code or Subchapter F (commencing with Section 501) of Chapter 1 of Subtitle A of the Internal Revenue Code of 1986, or the successor of either, is exempt from any business license tax or fee measured by income or gross receipts that is levied by a county or city, whether charter or general law, a city and county, a school district, a special district, or any other local agency.

(Sec. 26 amended June 7, 1994, by Prop. 176. Res.Ch. 67, 1993.)

SEC. 27.

The Legislature, a majority of the membership of each house concurring, may tax corporations, including state and national banks, and their franchises by any method not prohibited by this Constitution or the Constitution or laws of the United States. Unless otherwise provided by the Legislature, the tax on state and national banks shall be according to or measured by their net income and shall be in lieu of all other taxes and license fees upon banks or their shares, except taxes upon real property and vehicle registration and license fees.

(Sec. 27 amended June 8, 1976, by Prop. 5. Res.Ch. 126, 1975.)

SEC. 28.

(a) "Insurer," as used in this section, includes insurance companies or associations and reciprocal or interinsurance exchanges together with their corporate or other attorneys in fact considered as a single unit, and the State Compensation Insurance Fund. As used in this paragraph, "companies" includes persons, partnerships, joint stock associations, companies and corporations.

(b) An annual tax is hereby imposed on each insurer doing business in this State on the base, at the rates, and subject to the deductions from the tax hereinafter specified.

(c) In the case of an insurer not transacting title insurance in this State, the "basis of the annual tax" is, in respect to each year, the amount of gross premiums, less return premiums, received in such year by such insurer upon its business done in this State, other than premiums received for reinsurance and for ocean marine insurance.

In the case of an insurer transacting title insurance in this State, the "basis of the annual tax" is, in respect to each year, all income upon business done in this State, except:

(1) Interest and dividends.

(2) Rents from real property.

(3) Profits from the sale or other disposition of investments.

(4) Income from investments.

"Investments" as used in this subdivision includes property acquired by such insurer in the settlement or adjustment of claims against it but excludes investments in title plants and title records. Income derived directly or indirectly from the use of title plants and title records is included in the basis of the annual tax.

In the case of an insurer transacting title insurance in this State which has a trust department and does a trust business under the banking laws of this State, there shall be excluded from the basis of the annual tax imposed by this section, the income of, and from the assets of, such trust department and such trust business, if such income is taxed by this State or included in the measure of any tax imposed by this State.

(d) The rate of the tax to be applied to the basis of the annual tax in respect to each year is 2.35 percent.

(f) The tax imposed on insurers by this section is in lieu of all other taxes and licenses, state, county, and municipal, upon such insurers and their property, except:

(1) Taxes upon their real estate.

(2) That an insurer transacting title insurance in this State which has a trust department or does a trust business under the banking laws of this State is subject to taxation with respect to such trust department or trust business to the same extent and in the same manner as trust companies and the trust departments of banks doing business in this State.

(3) When by or pursuant to the laws of any other state or foreign country any taxes, licenses and other fees, in the aggregate, and any fines, penalties, deposit requirements or other material obligations, prohibitions or restrictions are or would be imposed upon California insurers, or upon the agents or representatives of such insurers, which are in excess of such taxes, licenses and other fees, in the aggregate, or which are in excess of the fines, penalties, deposit requirements or other obligations, prohibitions, or restrictions directly imposed upon similar insurers, or upon the agents or representatives of such insurers, of such other state or country under the statutes of this State; so long as such laws of such other state or country continue in force or are so applied, the same taxes, licenses and other fees, in the aggregate, or fines, penalties or deposit requirements or other material obligations, prohibitions, or restrictions, of whatever kind shall be imposed upon the insurers, or upon the agents or representatives of such insurers, of such other state or country doing business or seeking to do business in California. Any tax, license or other fee or other obligation imposed by any city, county, or other political subdivision or agency of such other state

or country on California insurers or their agents or representatives shall be deemed to be imposed by such state or country within the meaning of this paragraph (3) of subdivision (f).

The provisions of this paragraph (3) of subdivision (f) shall not apply as to personal income taxes, nor as to ad valorem taxes on real or personal property nor as to special purpose obligations or assessments heretofore imposed by another state or foreign country in connection with particular kinds of insurance, other than property insurance; except that deductions, from premium taxes or other taxes otherwise payable, allowed on account of real estate or personal property taxes paid shall be taken into consideration in determining the propriety and extent of retaliatory action under this paragraph (3) of subdivision (f).

For the purposes of this paragraph (3) of subdivision (f) the domicile of an alien insurer, other than insurers formed under the laws of Canada, shall be that state in which is located its principal place of business in the United States.

In the case of an insurer formed under the laws of Canada or a province thereof, its domicile shall be deemed to be that province in which its head office is situated.

The provisions of this paragraph (3) of subdivision (f) shall also be applicable to reciprocals or interinsurance exchanges and fraternal benefit societies.

(4) The tax on ocean marine insurance.

(5) Motor vehicle and other vehicle registration license fees and any other tax or license fee imposed by the State upon vehicles, motor vehicles or the operation thereof.

(6) That each corporate or other attorney in fact of a reciprocal or interinsurance exchange shall be subject to all taxes imposed upon corporations or others doing business in the State, other than taxes on income derived from its principal business as attorney in fact.

A corporate or other attorney in fact of each exchange shall annually compute the amount of tax that would be payable by it under prevailing law except for the provisions of this section, and any management fee due from each exchange to its corporate or other attorney in fact shall be reduced pro tanto by a sum equivalent to the amount so computed.

(g) Every insurer transacting the business of ocean marine insurance in this State shall annually pay to the State a tax measured by that proportion of the underwriting profit of such insurer from such insurance written in the United States, which the gross premiums of the insurer from such insurance written in this State bear to the gross premiums of the insurer from such insurance written within the United States, at the rate of 5 per centum, which tax shall be in lieu of all other taxes and licenses, state, county and municipal, upon such insurer, except taxes upon real estate, and such other taxes as may be assessed or levied against such insurer on account of any other class of insurance written by it. The Legislature shall define the terms "ocean marine insurance" and "underwriting profit," and shall provide for the assessment, levy, collection and enforcement of the ocean marine tax.

(h) The taxes provided for by this section shall be assessed by the State Board of Equalization.

(i) The Legislature, a majority of all the members elected to each of the two houses voting in favor thereof, may by law change the rate or rates of taxes herein imposed upon insurers.

(j) This section is not intended to and does not change the law as it has previously existed with respect to the meaning of the words "gross premiums, less return premiums, received" as used in this article.

(Subdivision (e) repealed and subdivision (g) amended June 8, 1976, by Prop. 6; Res.Ch. 116, 1975. Subdivision (i) amended June 8, 1976, by Prop. 5; Res.Ch. 126, 1975. Other Source: Entire Sec. 28 was added Nov. 5, 1974, by Prop. 8; Res.Ch. 70, 1974.)

SEC. 29.

(a) The Legislature may authorize counties, cities and counties, and cities to enter into contracts to apportion between them the revenue derived from any sales or use tax imposed by them that is collected for them by the

State. Before the contract becomes operative, it shall be authorized by a majority of those voting on the question in each jurisdiction at a general or direct primary election.

(b) Notwithstanding subdivision (a), on and after the operative date of this subdivision, counties, cities and counties, and cities may enter into contracts to apportion between them the revenue derived from any sales or use tax imposed by them pursuant to the Bradley-Burns Uniform Local Sales and Use Tax Law, or any successor provisions, that is collected for them by the State, if the ordinance or resolution proposing each contract is approved by a two-thirds vote of the governing body of each jurisdiction that is a party to the contract.

(Sec. 29 amended Nov. 3, 1998, by Prop. 11. Res.Ch. 133, 1998.)

SEC. 30.

Every tax shall be conclusively presumed to have been paid after 30 years from the time it became a lien unless the property subject to the lien has been sold in the manner provided by the Legislature for the payment of the tax.

(Sec. 30 added Nov. 5, 1974, by Prop. 8. Res.Ch. 70. 1974.)

SEC. 31.

The power to tax may not be surrendered or suspended by grant or contract.

(Sec. 31 added Nov. 5, 1974, by Prop. 8. Res.Ch. 70, 1974.)

SEC. 32.

No legal or equitable process shall issue in any proceeding in any court against this State or any officer thereof to prevent or enjoin the collection of any tax. After payment of a tax claimed to be illegal, an action may be maintained

to recover the tax paid, with interest, in such manner as may be provided by the Legislature.
(Sec. 32 added Nov. 5, 1974, by Prop. 8. Res.Ch. 70, 1974.)

SEC. 33.

The Legislature shall pass all laws necessary to carry out the provisions of this article.
(Sec. 33 added Nov. 5, 1974, by Prop. 8. Res.Ch. 70, 1974.)

SEC. 34.

Neither the State of California nor any of its political subdivisions shall levy or collect a sales or use tax on the sale of, or the storage, use or other consumption in this State of food products for human consumption except as provided by statute as of the effective date of this section.
(Sec. 34 added Nov. 3, 1992, by Prop. 163. Initiative measure. Effective Jan. 1, 1993.)

SEC. 35.

(a) The people of the State of California find and declare all of the following:
(1) Public safety services are critically important to the security and well-being of the State's citizens and to the growth and revitalization of the State's economic base.
(2) The protection of the public safety is the first responsibility of local government and local officials have an obligation to give priority to the provision of adequate public safety services.
(3) In order to assist local government in maintaining a sufficient level of public safety services, the proceeds of the tax enacted pursuant to this section shall be designated exclusively for public safety.

(b) In addition to any sales and use taxes imposed by the Legislature, the following sales and use taxes are hereby imposed:

(1) For the privilege of selling tangible personal property at retail, a tax is hereby imposed upon all retailers at the rate of $1/_2$ percent of the gross receipts of any retailer from the sale of all tangible personal property sold at retail in this State on and after January 1, 1994.

(2) An excise tax is hereby imposed on the storage, use, or other consumption in this State of tangible personal property purchased from any retailer on and after January 1, 1994, for storage, use, or other consumption in this State at the rate of $1/_2$ percent of the sales price of the property.

(c) The Sales and Use Tax Law, including any amendments made thereto on or after the effective date of this section, shall be applicable to the taxes imposed by subdivision (b).

(d) (1) All revenues, less refunds, derived from the taxes imposed pursuant to subdivision (b) shall be transferred to the Local Public Safety Fund for allocation by the Legislature, as prescribed by statute, to counties in which either of the following occurs:

(A) The board of supervisors, by a majority vote of its membership, requests an allocation from the Local Public Safety Fund in a manner prescribed by statute.

(B) A majority of the county's voters voting thereon approve the addition of this section.

(2) Moneys in the Local Public Safety Fund shall be allocated for use exclusively for public safety services of local agencies.

(e) Revenues derived from the taxes imposed pursuant to subdivision (b) shall not be considered proceeds of taxes for purposes of Article XIII B or State General Fund proceeds of taxes within the meaning of Article XVI.

(f) Except for the provisions of Section 34, this section shall supersede any other provisions of this Constitution that are in conflict with the provisions of this section, including, but not limited to, Section 9 of Article II.

(Sec. 35 added Nov. 2, 1993, by Prop. 172. Res.Ch. 41, 1993.)

SEC. 36.

(a) For purposes of this section:

(1) "Public Safety Services" includes the following:

(A) Employing and training public safety officials, including law enforcement personnel, attorneys assigned to criminal proceedings, and court security staff.

(B) Managing local jails and providing housing, treatment, and services for, and supervision of, juvenile and adult offenders.

(C) Preventing child abuse, neglect, or exploitation; providing services to children and youth who are abused, neglected, or exploited, or who are at risk of abuse, neglect, or exploitation, and the families of those children; providing adoption services; and providing adult protective services.

(D) Providing mental health services to children and adults to reduce failure in school, harm to self or others, homelessness, and preventable incarceration or institutionalization.

(E) Preventing, treating, and providing recovery services for substance abuse.

(2) "2011 Realignment Legislation" means legislation enacted on or before September 30, 2012, to implement the state budget plan, that is entitled 2011 Realignment and provides for the assignment of Public Safety Services responsibilities to local agencies, including related reporting responsibilities. The legislation shall provide local agencies with maximum flexibility and control over the design, administration, and delivery of Public Safety Services consistent with federal law and funding requirements, as determined by the Legislature. However, 2011 Realignment Legislation shall include no new programs assigned to local agencies after January 1, 2012, except for the early periodic screening, diagnosis, and treatment (EPSDT) program and mental health managed care.

(b) (1) Except as provided in subdivision (d), commencing in the 2011–12 fiscal year and continuing thereafter, the following amounts shall be deposited into the Local

Revenue Fund 2011, as established by Section 30025 of the Government Code, as follows:

(A) All revenues, less refunds, derived from the taxes described in Sections 6051.15 and 6201.15 of the Revenue and Taxation Code, as those sections read on July 1, 2011.

(B) All revenues, less refunds, derived from the vehicle license fees described in Section 11005 of the Revenue and Taxation Code, as that section read on July 1, 2011.

(2) On and after July 1, 2011, the revenues deposited pursuant to paragraph (1) shall not be considered General Fund revenues or proceeds of taxes for purposes of Section 8 of Article XVI of the California Constitution.

(c) (1) Funds deposited in the Local Revenue Fund 2011 are continuously appropriated exclusively to fund the provision of Public Safety Services by local agencies. Pending full implementation of the 2011 Realignment Legislation, funds may also be used to reimburse the State for program costs incurred in providing Public Safety Services on behalf of local agencies. The methodology for allocating funds shall be as specified in the 2011 Realignment Legislation.

(2) The county treasurer, city and county treasurer, or other appropriate official shall create a County Local Revenue Fund 2011 within the treasury of each county or city and county. The money in each County Local Revenue Fund 2011 shall be exclusively used to fund the provision of Public Safety Services by local agencies as specified by the 2011 Realignment Legislation.

(3) Notwithstanding Section 6 of Article XIII B, or any other constitutional provision, a mandate of a new program or higher level of service on a local agency imposed by the 2011 Realignment Legislation, or by any regulation adopted or any executive order or administrative directive issued to implement that legislation, shall not constitute a mandate requiring the State to provide a subvention of funds within the meaning of that section. Any requirement that a local agency comply with Chapter 9 (commencing with Section 54950) of Part 1 of Division 2 of Title 5 of the Government Code, with respect to performing its Public Safety Services responsibilities, or any other matter, shall

not be a reimbursable mandate under Section 6 of Article XIII B.

(4) (A) Legislation enacted after September 30, 2012, that has an overall effect of increasing the costs already borne by a local agency for programs or levels of service mandated by the 2011 Realignment Legislation shall apply to local agencies only to the extent that the State provides annual funding for the cost increase. Local agencies shall not be obligated to provide programs or levels of service required by legislation, described in this subparagraph, above the level for which funding has been provided.

(B) Regulations, executive orders, or administrative directives, implemented after October 9, 2011, that are not necessary to implement the 2011 Realignment Legislation, and that have an overall effect of increasing the costs already borne by a local agency for programs or levels of service mandated by the 2011 Realignment Legislation, shall apply to local agencies only to the extent that the State provides annual funding for the cost increase. Local agencies shall not be obligated to provide programs or levels of service pursuant to new regulations, executive orders, or administrative directives, described in this subparagraph, above the level for which funding has been provided.

(C) Any new program or higher level of service provided by local agencies, as described in subparagraphs (A) and (B), above the level for which funding has been provided, shall not require a subvention of funds by the State nor otherwise be subject to Section 6 of Article XIII B. This paragraph shall not apply to legislation currently exempt from subvention under paragraph (2) of subdivision (a) of Section 6 of Article XIII B as that paragraph read on January 2, 2011.

(D) The State shall not submit to the federal government any plans or waivers, or amendments to those plans or waivers, that have an overall effect of increasing the cost borne by a local agency for programs or levels of service mandated by the 2011 Realignment Legislation, except to the extent that the plans, waivers, or amendments are required by federal law, or the State provides annual funding for the cost increase.

(E) The State shall not be required to provide a subvention of funds pursuant to this paragraph for a mandate that is imposed by the State at the request of a local agency or to comply with federal law. State funds required by this paragraph shall be from a source other than those described in subdivisions (b) and (d), ad valorem property taxes, or the Social Services Subaccount of the Sales Tax Account of the Local Revenue Fund.

(5) (A) For programs described in subparagraphs (C) to (E), inclusive, of paragraph (1) of subdivision (a) and included in the 2011 Realignment Legislation, if there are subsequent changes in federal statutes or regulations that alter the conditions under which federal matching funds as described in the 2011 Realignment Legislation are obtained, and have the overall effect of increasing the costs incurred by a local agency, the State shall annually provide at least 50 percent of the nonfederal share of those costs as determined by the State.

(B) When the State is a party to any complaint brought in a federal judicial or administrative proceeding that involves one or more of the programs described in subparagraphs (C) to (E), inclusive, of paragraph (1) of subdivision (a) and included in the 2011 Realignment Legislation, and there is a settlement or judicial or administrative order that imposes a cost in the form of a monetary penalty or has the overall effect of increasing the costs already borne by a local agency for programs or levels of service mandated by the 2011 Realignment Legislation, the State shall annually provide at least 50 percent of the nonfederal share of those costs as determined by the State. Payment by the State is not required if the State determines that the settlement or order relates to one or more local agencies failing to perform a ministerial duty, failing to perform a legal obligation in good faith, or acting in a negligent or reckless manner.

(C) The state funds provided in this paragraph shall be from funding sources other than those described in subdivisions (b) and (d), ad valorem property taxes, or the Social Services Subaccount of the Sales Tax Account of the Local Revenue Fund.

(6) If the State or a local agency fails to perform a duty or obligation under this section or under the 2011 Realignment Legislation, an appropriate party may seek judicial relief. These proceedings shall have priority over all other civil matters.

(7) The funds deposited into a County Local Revenue Fund 2011 shall be spent in a manner designed to maintain the State's eligibility for federal matching funds, and to ensure compliance by the State with applicable federal standards governing the State's provision of Public Safety Services.

(8) The funds deposited into a County Local Revenue Fund 2011 shall not be used by local agencies to supplant other funding for Public Safety Services.

(d) If the taxes described in subdivision (b) are reduced or cease to be operative, the State shall annually provide moneys to the Local Revenue Fund 2011 in an amount equal to or greater than the aggregate amount that otherwise would have been provided by the taxes described in subdivision (b). The method for determining that amount shall be described in the 2011 Realignment Legislation, and the State shall be obligated to provide that amount for so long as the local agencies are required to perform the Public Safety Services responsibilities assigned by the 2011 Realignment Legislation. If the State fails to annually appropriate that amount, the Controller shall transfer that amount from the General Fund in pro rata monthly shares to the Local Revenue Fund 2011. Thereafter, the Controller shall disburse these amounts to local agencies in the manner directed by the 2011 Realignment Legislation. The state obligations under this subdivision shall have a lower priority claim to General Fund money than the first priority for money to be set apart under Section 8 of Article XVI and the second priority to pay voter-approved debts and liabilities described in Section 1 of Article XVI.

(e) (1) To ensure that public education is not harmed in the process of providing critical protection to local Public Safety Services, the Education Protection Account is hereby created in the General Fund to receive and disburse the revenues derived from the incremental increases in taxes imposed by this section, as specified in subdivision (f).

(2) (A) Before June 30, 2013, and before June 30 of each year from 2014 to 2030, inclusive, the Director of Finance shall estimate the total amount of additional revenues, less refunds, that will be derived from the incremental increases in tax rates made in subdivision (f) that will be available for transfer into the Education Protection Account during the next fiscal year. The Director of Finance shall make the same estimate by January 10, 2013, for additional revenues, less refunds, that will be received by the end of the 2012–13 fiscal year.

(B) During the last 10 days of the quarter of each of the first three quarters of each fiscal year from 2013–14 to 2030–31, inclusive, the Controller shall transfer into the Education Protection Account one-fourth of the total amount estimated pursuant to subparagraph (A) for that fiscal year, except as this amount may be adjusted pursuant to subparagraph (D).

(C) In each of the fiscal years from 2012–13 to 2032–33, inclusive, the Director of Finance shall calculate an adjustment to the Education Protection Account, as specified by subparagraph (D), by adding together the following amounts, as applicable:

(i) In the last quarter of each fiscal year from 2012–13 to 2030–31, inclusive, the Director of Finance shall recalculate the estimate made for the fiscal year pursuant to subparagraph (A), and shall subtract from this updated estimate the amounts previously transferred to the Education Protection Account for that fiscal year.

(ii) In June 2015 and in every June from 2016 to 2033, inclusive, the Director of Finance shall make a final determination of the amount of additional revenues, less refunds, derived from the incremental increases in tax rates made in subdivision (f) for the fiscal year ending two years prior. The amount of the updated estimate calculated in clause (i) for the fiscal year ending two years prior shall be subtracted from the amount of this final determination.

(D) If the sum determined pursuant to subparagraph (C) is positive, the Controller shall transfer an amount equal to that sum into the Education Protection Account within 10 days preceding the end of the fiscal year. If that amount is negative, the Controller shall suspend or reduce subsequent quarterly transfers, if any, to the Education Protection Account until the total reduction equals the negative amount herein described. For purposes of any calculation made pursuant to clause (i) of subparagraph (C), the amount of a quarterly transfer shall not be modified to reflect any suspension or reduction made pursuant to this subparagraph.

(E) Before June 30, 2018, and before June 30 of each year from 2019 to 2030, inclusive, the Director of Finance shall estimate the amount of the additional revenues, less refunds, to be derived in the following fiscal year from the incremental increases in tax rates made in subdivision (f), that, when combined with all other available General Fund revenues, will be required to meet:

(i) The minimum funding guarantee of Section 8 of Article XVI for that following fiscal year; and

(ii) The workload budget for that following fiscal year, excluding any program expenditures already accounted for through clause (i). For purposes of this section, "workload budget" has the meaning set forth in Section 13308.05 of the Government Code, as that section read and was interpreted by the Department of Finance on January 1, 2016, provided, however, that "currently authorized services" shall mean only those services that would have been considered "currently authorized services" under Section 13308.05 of the Government Code as of January 1, 2016.

(F) In order to enhance the ability of all California school children and their families to receive regular, quality health care and thereby minimize school absenteeism due to health-related problems, whenever the Director of Finance estimates that the amount available for transfer into the Education Protection Account during the following fiscal year exceeds the amount of revenues required from that account pursuant to subparagraph (E) for that following fiscal year, the director shall identify the remaining amount. Fifty percent of that remainder, up to a maximum of two billion dollars in any single fiscal year, shall be allocated by the Controller from the Education Protection Account to the California Department of Health Care Services on a quarterly basis to increase funding for the existing health care programs and services described in Chapter 7 (commencing with Section 14000) to Chapter 8.9 (commencing with Section 14700), inclusive, of Part 3 of Division 9 of the Welfare and Institutions Code. The funding shall be used only for critical, emergency, acute, and preventive health care services to children and their families, provided by health care professionals and health facilities that are licensed pursuant to Section 1250 of the Health and Safety Code, and to health plans or others that manage the provision of health care for Medi-Cal beneficiaries that are contracting with the California Department of Health Care Services to provide health benefits pursuant to this section.

(G) The allocation provided for in subparagraph (F) may be suspended by statute during a fiscal year in which a budget emergency has been declared, provided, however, that the allocation shall not be reduced beyond the proportional reduction in overall General Fund expenditures for that year. For purposes of this section, "budget emergency" has the same meaning as in paragraph (2) of subdivision (b) of Section 22 of Article XVI.

(H) The funding provided pursuant to subparagraph (F) shall not be used to supplant existing state General Funds for the nonfederal share of payments for those programs and, consistent with federal law, shall be used to obtain federal matching Medicaid funds.

(3) All moneys in the Education Protection Account are hereby continuously appropriated for the support of school districts, county offices of education, charter schools, and community college districts as set forth in this paragraph, and for health care as set forth in subparagraph (F) of paragraph (2).

(A) Eleven percent of the moneys appropriated for education pursuant to this paragraph shall be allocated quarterly by the Board of Governors of the California Community Colleges to community college districts to provide general purpose funding to community college districts in proportion to the amounts determined pursuant to Section 84750.5 of the Education Code, as that code section read on November 6, 2012. The allocations calculated pursuant to this subparagraph shall be offset by the amounts specified in subdivisions (a), (c), and (d) of Section 84751 of the Education Code, as that section read on November 6, 2012, that are in excess of the amounts calculated pursuant to Section 84750.5 of the Education Code, as that section read on November 6, 2012, provided that no community college district shall receive less than one hundred dollars ($100) per full time equivalent student.

(B) Eighty-nine percent of the moneys appropriated for education pursuant to this paragraph shall be allocated quarterly by the Superintendent of Public Instruction to provide general purpose funding to school districts, county offices of education, and state general-purpose funding to charter schools in proportion to the revenue limits calculated pursuant to Sections 2558 and 42238 of the Education Code and the amounts calculated pursuant to Section 47633 of the Education Code for county offices of education, school districts, and charter schools, respectively, as those sections read on November 6, 2012. The amounts so calculated shall be offset by the amounts specified in subdivision (c) of Section 2558 of, paragraphs (1) through (7) of subdivision (h) of Section 42238 of, and Section 47635 of, the Education Code for county offices of education, school districts, and charter schools, respectively, as those sections read on November 6, 2012, that are in excess of the amounts calculated pursuant to Sections 2558, 42238, and 47633 of the Education Code for county offices of education, school districts, and charter schools, respectively, as those sections read on November 6, 2012, provided that no school district, county office of education, or charter school shall receive less than two hundred dollars ($200) per unit of average daily attendance.

(4) This subdivision is self-executing and requires no legislative action to take effect. Distribution of the moneys in the Education Protection Account by the Board of Governors of the California Community Colleges and Superintendent of Public Instruction shall not be delayed or otherwise affected by failure of the Legislature and Governor to enact an annual budget bill pursuant to Section 12 of Article IV, by invocation of subdivision (h) of

Section 8 of Article XVI, or by any other action or failure to act by the Legislature or Governor.

(5) Notwithstanding any other provision of law, the moneys deposited in the Education Protection Account for education shall not be used to pay any costs incurred by the Legislature, the Governor, or any agency of state government.

(6) A community college district, county office of education, school district, or charter school shall have sole authority to determine how the moneys received from the Education Protection Account are spent in the school or schools within its jurisdiction, provided, however, that the appropriate governing board or body shall make these spending determinations in open session of a public meeting of the governing board or body and shall not use any of the funds from the Education Protection Account for salaries or benefits of administrators or any other administrative costs. Each community college district, county office of education, school district, and charter school shall annually publish on its Internet Web site an accounting of how much money was received from the Education Protection Account and how that money was spent.

(7) The annual independent financial and compliance audit required of community college districts, county offices of education, school districts, and charter schools shall, in addition to all other requirements of law, ascertain and verify whether the funds provided from the Education Protection Account have been properly disbursed and expended as required by this section. Expenses incurred by those entities to comply with the additional audit requirement of this section may be paid with funding from the Education Protection Account and shall not be considered administrative costs for purposes of this section.

(8) Revenues, less refunds, derived pursuant to subdivision (f) for deposit in the Education Protection Account pursuant to this section shall be deemed "General Fund revenues," "General Fund proceeds of taxes," and "moneys to be applied by the State for the support of school districts and

community college districts" for purposes of Section 8 of Article XVI.

(f) (1) (A) In addition to the taxes imposed by Part 1 (commencing with Section 6001) of Division 2 of the Revenue and Taxation Code, for the privilege of selling tangible personal property at retail, a tax is hereby imposed upon all retailers at the rate of 1/4 percent of the gross receipts of any retailer from the sale of all tangible personal property sold at retail in this State on and after January 1, 2013, and before January 1, 2017.

(B) In addition to the taxes imposed by Part 1 (commencing with Section 6001) of Division 2 of the Revenue and Taxation Code, an excise tax is hereby imposed on the storage, use, or other consumption in this State of tangible personal property purchased from any retailer on and after January 1, 2013, and before January 1, 2017, for storage, use, or other consumption in this state at the rate of 1/4 percent of the sales price of the property.

(C) The Sales and Use Tax Law, including any amendments enacted on or after the effective date of this section, shall apply to the taxes imposed pursuant to this paragraph.

(D) This paragraph shall become inoperative on January 1, 2017.

(2) For any taxable year beginning on or after January 1, 2012, and before January 1, 2031, with respect to the tax imposed pursuant to Section 17041 of the Revenue and Taxation Code, the income tax bracket and the rate of 9.3 percent set forth in paragraph (1) of subdivision (a) of Section 17041 of the Revenue and Taxation Code shall be modified by each of the following:

(A) (i) For that portion of taxable income that is over two hundred fifty thousand dollars ($250,000) but not over three hundred thousand dollars ($300,000), the tax rate is 10.3 percent of the excess over two hundred fifty thousand dollars ($250,000).

(ii) For that portion of taxable income that is over three hundred thousand dollars ($300,000) but not over five hundred thousand dollars ($500,000), the tax rate is 11.3 percent of the excess over three hundred thousand dollars ($300,000).

(iii) For that portion of taxable income that is over five hundred thousand dollars ($500,000), the tax rate is 12.3 percent of the excess over five hundred thousand dollars ($500,000).

(B) The income tax brackets specified in clauses (i), (ii), and (iii) of subparagraph (A) shall be recomputed, as otherwise provided in subdivision (h) of Section 17041 of the Revenue and Taxation Code, only for taxable years beginning on and after January 1, 2013.

(C) (i) For purposes of subdivision (g) of Section 19136 of the Revenue and Taxation Code, this paragraph shall be considered to be chaptered on November 6, 2012.

(ii) For purposes of Part 10 (commencing with Section 17001) of, and Part 10.2 (commencing with Section 18401) of, Division 2 of the Revenue and Taxation Code, the modified tax brackets and tax rates established and imposed by this paragraph shall be deemed to be established and imposed under Section 17041 of the Revenue and Taxation Code.

(D) This paragraph shall become inoperative on December 1, 2031.

(3) For any taxable year beginning on or after January 1, 2012, and before January 1, 2031, with respect to the tax imposed pursuant to Section 17041 of the Revenue and Taxation Code, the income tax bracket and the rate of 9.3 percent set forth in paragraph (1) of subdivision (c) of Section 17041 of the Revenue and Taxation Code shall be modified by each of the following:

(A) (i) For that portion of taxable income that is over three hundred forty thousand dollars ($340,000) but not over four hundred eight thousand dollars ($408,000), the tax rate is 10.3 percent of the excess over three hundred forty thousand dollars ($340,000).

(ii) For that portion of taxable income that is over four hundred eight thousand dollars ($408,000) but not over six hundred eighty thousand dollars ($680,000), the tax rate is 11.3 percent of the excess over four hundred eight thousand dollars ($408,000).

(iii) For that portion of taxable income that is over six hundred eighty thousand dollars ($680,000), the tax rate is 12.3 percent of the excess over six hundred eighty thousand dollars ($680,000).

(B) The income tax brackets specified in clauses (i), (ii), and (iii) of subparagraph (A) shall be recomputed, as otherwise provided in subdivision (h) of Section 17041 of the Revenue and Taxation Code, only for taxable years beginning on and after January 1, 2013.

(C) (i) For purposes of subdivision (g) of Section 19136 of the Revenue and Taxation Code, this paragraph shall be considered to be chaptered on November 6, 2012.

(ii) For purposes of Part 10 (commencing with Section 17001) of, and Part 10.2 (commencing with Section 18401) of, Division 2 of the Revenue and Taxation Code, the modified tax brackets and tax rates established and imposed by this paragraph shall be deemed to be established and imposed under Section 17041 of the Revenue and Taxation Code.

(D) This paragraph shall become inoperative on December 1, 2031.

(g) (1) The Controller, pursuant to his or her statutory authority, may perform audits of expenditures from the Local Revenue Fund 2011 and any County Local Revenue Fund 2011, and shall audit the Education Protection Account to ensure that those funds are used and accounted for in a manner consistent with this section.

(2) The Attorney General or local district attorney shall expeditiously investigate, and may seek civil or criminal penalties for, any misuse of moneys from the County Local Revenue Fund 2011 or the Education Protection Account.

(Sec. 36 amended Nov. 8, 2016, by Prop. 55. Initiative measure.)

ARTICLE XIII A [TAX LIMITATION]

[SECTION 1 - SEC. 7]

(Article 13A added June 6, 1978, by Prop. 13. Initiative measure.)

SECTION 1.

(a) The maximum amount of any ad valorem tax on real property shall not exceed One percent (1%) of the full cash value of such property. The one percent (1%) tax to be collected by the counties and apportioned according to law to the districts within the counties.

(b) The limitation provided for in subdivision (a) shall not apply to ad valorem taxes or special assessments to pay the interest and redemption charges on any of the following:

(1) Indebtedness approved by the voters prior to July 1, 1978.

(2) Bonded indebtedness for the acquisition or improvement of real property approved on or after July 1, 1978, by two-thirds of the votes cast by the voters voting on the proposition.

(3) Bonded indebtedness incurred by a school district, community college district, or county office of education for the construction, reconstruction, rehabilitation, or replacement of school facilities, including the furnishing and equipping of school facilities, or the acquisition or lease of real property for school facilities, approved by 55 percent of the voters of the district or county, as appropriate, voting on the proposition on or after the effective date of the measure adding this paragraph. This paragraph shall apply only if the proposition approved by the voters and resulting in the bonded indebtedness includes all of the following accountability requirements:

(A) A requirement that the proceeds from the sale of the bonds be used only for the purposes specified in Article XIII A, Section 1(b)(3), and not for any other purpose, including teacher and administrator salaries and other school operating expenses.

(B) A list of the specific school facilities projects to be funded and certification that the school district board, community college board, or county office of education has evaluated safety, class size reduction, and information technology needs in developing that list.

(C) A requirement that the school district board, community college board, or county office of education conduct an annual, independent performance audit to ensure that the funds have been expended only on the specific projects listed.

(D) A requirement that the school district board, community college board, or county office of education conduct an annual, independent financial audit of the proceeds from the sale of the bonds until all of those proceeds have been expended for the school facilities projects.

(c) Notwithstanding any other provisions of law or of this Constitution, school districts, community college districts, and county offices of education may levy a 55 percent vote ad valorem tax pursuant to subdivision (b).

(Sec. 1 amended Nov. 7, 2000, by Prop. 39. Initiative measure.)

SEC. 2.

(a) The "full cash value" means the county assessor's valuation of real property as shown on the 1975–76 tax bill under "full cash value" or, thereafter, the appraised value of real property when purchased, newly constructed, or a change in ownership has occurred after the 1975 assessment. All real property not already assessed up to the 1975–76 full cash value may be reassessed to reflect that valuation. For purposes of this section, "newly constructed" does not include real property that is reconstructed after a disaster, as declared by the Governor, where the fair market value of the real property, as reconstructed, is comparable to its fair market value prior to the disaster. For purposes of this section, the term "newly constructed" does not include that portion of an existing structure that consists of the construction or reconstruction of seismic retrofitting components, as defined by the Legislature.

However, the Legislature may provide that, under appropriate circumstances and pursuant to definitions and procedures established by the Legislature, any person over the age of 55 years who resides in property that is eligible for the homeowner's exemption under subdivision (k) of Section 3 of Article XIII and any implementing legislation may transfer the base year value of the property entitled to exemption, with the adjustments authorized by subdivision (b), to any replacement dwelling of equal or lesser value located within the same county and purchased or newly constructed by that person as his or her principal residence within two years of the sale of the original property. For purposes of this section, "any person over the age of 55 years" includes a married couple one member of which is over the age of 55 years. For purposes of this section, "replacement dwelling" means a building, structure, or other shelter constituting a place of abode, whether real property or personal property, and any land on which it may be situated. For purposes of this section, a two-dwelling unit shall be considered as two separate single-family dwellings. This paragraph shall apply to any replacement dwelling that was purchased or newly constructed on or after November 5, 1986.

In addition, the Legislature may authorize each county board of supervisors, after consultation with the local affected agencies within the county's boundaries, to adopt an ordinance making the provisions of this subdivision relating to transfer of base year value also applicable to situations in which the replacement dwellings are located in that county and the original properties are located in another county within this State. For purposes of this paragraph, "local affected agency" means any city, special district, school district, or community college district that receives an annual property tax revenue allocation. This paragraph applies to any replacement dwelling that was purchased or newly constructed on or after the date the county adopted the provisions of this subdivision relating to transfer of base year value, but does not apply to any replacement dwelling that was purchased or newly constructed before November 9, 1988.

The Legislature may extend the provisions of this subdivision relating to the transfer of base year values from original properties to replacement dwellings of homeowners over the age of 55 years to severely disabled homeowners, but only with respect to those replacement dwellings purchased or newly constructed on or after the effective date of this paragraph.

(b) The full cash value base may reflect from year to year the inflationary rate not to exceed 2 percent for any given year or reduction as shown in the consumer price index or comparable data for the area under taxing jurisdiction, or may be reduced to reflect substantial damage, destruction, or other factors causing a decline in value.

(c) For purposes of subdivision (a), the Legislature may provide that the term "newly constructed" does not include any of the following:

(1) The construction or addition of any active solar energy system.

(2) The construction or installation of any fire sprinkler system, other fire extinguishing system, fire detection system, or fire-related egress improvement, as defined by the Legislature, that is constructed or installed after the effective date of this paragraph.

(3) The construction, installation, or modification on or after the effective date of this paragraph of any portion or structural component of a single- or multiple-family dwelling that is eligible for the homeowner's exemption if the construction, installation, or modification is for the purpose of making the dwelling more accessible to a severely disabled person.

(4) The construction, installation, removal, or modification on or after the effective date of this paragraph of any portion or structural component of an existing building or structure if the construction, installation, removal, or modification is for the purpose of making the building more accessible to, or more usable by, a disabled person.

(5) The construction or addition, completed on or after January 1, 2019, of a rain water capture system, as defined by the Legislature.

(d) For purposes of this section, the term "change in ownership" does not include the acquisition of real property as a replacement for comparable property if the person acquiring the real property has been displaced from the property replaced by eminent domain proceedings, by acquisition by a public entity, or governmental action that has resulted in a judgment of inverse condemnation. The real property acquired shall be deemed comparable to the property replaced if it is similar in size, utility, and function, or if it conforms to state regulations defined by the Legislature governing the relocation of persons displaced by governmental actions. This subdivision applies to any property acquired after March 1, 1975, but affects only those assessments of that property that occur after the provisions of this subdivision take effect.

(e) (1) Notwithstanding any other provision of this section, the Legislature shall provide that the base year value of property that is substantially damaged or destroyed by a disaster, as declared by the Governor, may be transferred to comparable property within the same county that is acquired or newly constructed as a replacement for the substantially damaged or destroyed property.

(2) Except as provided in paragraph (3), this subdivision applies to any comparable replacement property acquired or newly constructed on or after July 1, 1985, and to the determination of base year values for the 1985–86 fiscal year and fiscal years thereafter.

(3) In addition to the transfer of base year value of property within the same county that is permitted by paragraph (1), the Legislature may authorize each county board of supervisors to adopt, after consultation with affected local agencies within the county, an ordinance allowing the transfer of the base year value of property that is located within another county in the State and is substantially damaged or destroyed by a disaster, as declared by the Governor, to comparable replacement property of equal or lesser value that is located within the adopting county and is acquired or newly constructed

within three years of the substantial damage or destruction of the original property as a replacement for that property. The scope and amount of the benefit provided to a property owner by the transfer of base year value of property pursuant to this paragraph shall not exceed the scope and amount of the benefit provided to a property owner by the transfer of base year value of property pursuant to subdivision (a). For purposes of this paragraph, "affected local agency" means any city, special district, school district, or community college district that receives an annual allocation of ad valorem property tax revenues. This paragraph applies to any comparable replacement property that is acquired or newly constructed as a replacement for property substantially damaged or destroyed by a disaster, as declared by the Governor, occurring on or after October 20, 1991, and to the determination of base year values for the 1991–92 fiscal year and fiscal years thereafter.

(f) For the purposes of subdivision (e):

(1) Property is substantially damaged or destroyed if it sustains physical damage amounting to more than 50 percent of its value immediately before the disaster. Damage includes a diminution in the value of property as a result of restricted access caused by the disaster.

(2) Replacement property is comparable to the property substantially damaged or destroyed if it is similar in size, utility, and function to the property that it replaces, and if the fair market value of the acquired property is comparable to the fair market value of the replaced property prior to the disaster.

(g) For purposes of subdivision (a), the terms "purchased" and "change in ownership" do not include the purchase or transfer of real property between spouses since March 1, 1975, including, but not limited to, all of the following:

(1) Transfers to a trustee for the beneficial use of a spouse, or the surviving spouse of a deceased transferor, or by a trustee of such a trust to the spouse of the trustor.

(2) Transfers to a spouse that take effect upon the death of a spouse.

(3) Transfers to a spouse or former spouse in connection with a property settlement agreement or decree of dissolution of a marriage or legal separation.

(4) The creation, transfer, or termination, solely between spouses, of any coowner's interest.

(5) The distribution of a legal entity's property to a spouse or former spouse in exchange for the interest of the spouse in the legal entity in connection with a property settlement agreement or a decree of dissolution of a marriage or legal separation.

(h) (1) For purposes of subdivision (a), the terms "purchased" and "change in ownership" do not include the purchase or transfer of the principal residence of the transferor in the case of a purchase or transfer between parents and their children, as defined by the Legislature, and the purchase or transfer of the first one million dollars ($1,000,000) of the full cash value of all other real property between parents and their children, as defined by the Legislature. This subdivision applies to both voluntary transfers and transfers resulting from a court order or judicial decree.

(2) (A) Subject to subparagraph (B), commencing with purchases or transfers that occur on or after the date upon which the measure adding this paragraph becomes effective, the exclusion established by paragraph (1) also applies to a purchase or transfer of real property between grandparents and their grandchild or grandchildren, as defined by the Legislature, that otherwise qualifies under paragraph (1), if all of the parents of that grandchild or those grandchildren, who qualify as the children of the grandparents, are deceased as of the date of the purchase or transfer.

(B) A purchase or transfer of a principal residence shall not be excluded pursuant to subparagraph (A) if the transferee grandchild or grandchildren also received a principal residence, or interest therein, through another purchase or transfer that was excludable pursuant to paragraph (1). The full cash value of any real property, other than a principal residence, that was transferred to the grandchild or grandchildren pursuant to a purchase or transfer that was excludable pursuant to paragraph (1), and the full cash value of a principal residence that fails to qualify for exclusion as a result of the preceding sentence, shall be included in applying, for purposes of subparagraph (A), the one-million-dollar ($1,000,000) full cash value limit specified in paragraph (1).

(i) (1) Notwithstanding any other provision of this section, the Legislature shall provide with respect to a qualified contaminated property, as defined in paragraph (2), that either, but not both, of the following apply:

(A) (i) Subject to the limitation of clause (ii), the base year value of the qualified contaminated property, as adjusted as authorized by subdivision (b), may be transferred to a replacement property that is acquired or newly constructed as a replacement for the qualified contaminated property, if the replacement real property has a fair market value that is equal to or less than the fair market value of the qualified contaminated property if that property were not contaminated and, except as otherwise provided by this clause, is located within the same county. The base year value of the qualified contaminated property may be transferred to a replacement real property located within another county if the board of supervisors of that other county has, after consultation with the affected local agencies within that county, adopted a resolution authorizing an intercounty transfer of base year value as so described.

(ii) This subparagraph applies only to replacement property that is acquired or newly constructed within five years after ownership in the qualified contaminated property is sold or otherwise transferred.

(B) In the case in which the remediation of the environmental problems on the qualified contaminated property requires the destruction of, or results in substantial damage to, a structure located on that property, the term "new construction" does not include the repair of a substantially damaged structure, or the construction of a structure replacing a destroyed structure on the qualified contaminated property, performed after the remediation of the environmental problems on that property, provided that the repaired or replacement structure is similar in size, utility, and function to the original structure.

(2) For purposes of this subdivision, "qualified contaminated property" means residential or nonresidential real property that is all of the following:

(A) In the case of residential real property, rendered uninhabitable, and in the case of nonresidential real property, rendered unusable, as the result of either environmental problems, in the nature of and including, but not limited to, the presence of toxic or hazardous materials, or the remediation of those environmental problems, except where the existence of the environmental problems was known to the owner, or to a related individual or entity as described in paragraph (3), at the time the real property was acquired or constructed. For purposes of this subparagraph, residential real property is "uninhabitable" if that property, as a result of health hazards caused by or associated with the environmental problems, is unfit for human habitation, and nonresidential real property is "unusable" if that property, as a result of health hazards caused by or associated with the environmental problems, is unhealthy and unsuitable for occupancy.

(B) Located on a site that has been designated as a toxic or environmental hazard or as an environmental cleanup site by an agency of the State of California or the federal government.

(C) Real property that contains a structure or structures thereon prior to the completion of environmental cleanup activities, and that structure or structures are substantially damaged or destroyed as a result of those environmental cleanup activities.

(D) Stipulated by the lead governmental agency, with respect to the environmental problems or environmental cleanup of the real property, not to have been rendered uninhabitable or unusable, as applicable, as described in subparagraph (A), by any act or omission in which an owner of that real property participated or acquiesced.

(3) It shall be rebuttably presumed that an owner of the real property participated or acquiesced in any act or omission that rendered the real property uninhabitable or

unusable, as applicable, if that owner is related to any individual or entity that committed that act or omission in any of the following ways:

(A) Is a spouse, parent, child, grandparent, grandchild, or sibling of that individual.

(B) Is a corporate parent, subsidiary, or affiliate of that entity.

(C) Is an owner of, or has control of, that entity.

(D) Is owned or controlled by that entity.

If this presumption is not overcome, the owner shall not receive the relief provided for in subparagraph (A) or (B) of paragraph (1). The presumption may be overcome by presentation of satisfactory evidence to the assessor, who shall not be bound by the findings of the lead governmental agency in determining whether the presumption has been overcome.

(4) This subdivision applies only to replacement property that is acquired or constructed on or after January 1, 1995, and to property repairs performed on or after that date.

(j) Unless specifically provided otherwise, amendments to this section adopted prior to November 1, 1988, are effective for changes in ownership that occur, and new construction that is completed, after the effective date of the amendment. Unless specifically provided otherwise, amendments to this section adopted after November 1, 1988, are effective for changes in ownership that occur, and new construction that is completed, on or after the effective date of the amendment.

(Subdivision (c) amended June 5, 2018, by Prop. 72. Res.Ch. 1, 2018. Subd. (h) inoperative February 16, 2021, pursuant to Section 2.1. Other Source: Entire Sec. 2 was last amended June 8, 2010, by Prop. 13; Res.Ch. 115, 2008.)

SEC. 2.1.

(a) Limitation on Property Tax Increases on Primary Residences for Seniors, the Severely Disabled, Wildfire and Natural Disaster Victims, and Families. It is the intent of the Legislature in proposing, and the people in adopting, this section to do both of the following:

(1) Limit property tax increases on primary residences by removing unfair location restrictions on homeowners who are severely disabled, victims of wildfires or other natural disasters, or seniors over 55 years of age that need to move closer to family or medical care, downsize, find a home that better fits their needs, or replace a damaged home and limit damage from wildfires on homes through dedicated funding for fire protection and emergency response.

(2) Limit property tax increases on family homes used as a primary residence by protecting the right of parents and grandparents to pass on their family home to their children and grandchildren for continued use as a primary residence, while eliminating unfair tax loopholes used by East Coast investors, celebrities, wealthy non-California residents, and trust fund heirs to avoid paying a fair share of property taxes on vacation homes, income properties, and beachfront rentals they own in California.

(b) Property Tax Fairness for Seniors, the Severely Disabled, and Victims of Wildfire and Natural Disasters. Notwithstanding any other provision of this Constitution or any other law, beginning on and after April 1, 2021, the following shall apply:

(1) Subject to applicable procedures and definitions as provided by statute, an owner of a primary residence who is over 55 years of age, severely disabled, or a victim of a wildfire or natural disaster may transfer the taxable value of their primary residence to a replacement primary residence located anywhere in this state, regardless of the location or value of the replacement primary residence, that is purchased or newly constructed as that person's principal residence within two years of the sale of the original primary residence.

(2) For purposes of this subdivision:

(A) For any transfer of taxable value to a replacement primary residence of equal or lesser value than the original primary residence, the taxable value of the replacement primary residence shall be deemed to be the taxable value of the original primary residence.

(B) For any transfer of taxable value to a replacement primary residence of greater value than the original primary residence, the taxable value of the replacement primary residence shall be calculated by adding the difference between the full cash value of the original primary residence and the full cash value of the replacement primary residence to the taxable value of the original primary residence.

(3) An owner of a primary residence who is over 55 years of age or severely disabled shall not be allowed to transfer the taxable value of a primary residence more than three times pursuant to this subdivision.

(4) Any person who seeks to transfer the taxable value of their primary residence pursuant to this subdivision shall file an application with the assessor of the county in which the replacement primary residence is located. The application shall, at minimum, include information comparable to that identified in paragraph (1) of subdivision (f) of Section 69.5 of the Revenue and Taxation Code, as that section read on January 1, 2020.

(c) Property Tax Fairness for Family Homes. Notwithstanding any other provision of this Constitution or any other law, beginning on and after February 16, 2021, the following shall apply:

(1) For purposes of subdivision (a) of Section 2, the terms "purchased" and "change in ownership" do not include the purchase or transfer of a family home of the transferor in the case of a transfer between parents and their children, as defined by the Legislature, if the property continues as the family home of the transferee. This subdivision shall apply to both voluntary transfers and transfers resulting from a court order or judicial decree. The new taxable value of the family home of the transferee shall be the sum of both of the following:

(A) The taxable value of the family home, subject to adjustment as authorized by subdivision (b) of Section 2, determined as of the date immediately prior to the date of the purchase by, or transfer to, the transferee.

(B) The applicable of the following amounts:

(i) If the assessed value of the family home upon purchase by, or transfer to, the transferee is less than the sum of the taxable value described in subparagraph (A) plus one million dollars ($1,000,000), then zero dollars ($0).

(ii) If the assessed value of the family home upon purchase by, or transfer to, the transferee is equal to or more than the sum of the taxable value described in subparagraph (A) plus one million dollars ($1,000,000), an amount equal to the assessed value of the family home upon purchase by, or transfer to, the transferee, minus the sum of the taxable value described in subparagraph (A) and one million dollars ($1,000,000).

(2) Paragraph (1) shall also apply to a purchase or transfer of the family home between grandparents and their grandchildren if all of the parents of those grandchildren, who qualify as children of the grandparents, are deceased as of the date of the purchase or transfer.

(3) Paragraphs (1) and (2) shall also apply to the purchase or transfer of a family farm. For purposes of this paragraph, any reference to a "family home" in paragraph (1) or (2) shall be deemed to instead refer to a "family farm."

(4) Beginning on February 16, 2023, and every other February 16 thereafter, the State Board of Equalization shall adjust the one million dollar ($1,000,000) amount described in paragraph (1) for inflation to reflect the percentage change in the House Price Index for California for the prior calendar year, as determined by the Federal Housing Finance Agency. The State Board of Equalization shall calculate and publish the adjustments required by this paragraph.

(5) (A) Subject to subparagraph (B), in order to receive the property tax benefit provided by this section for the purchase or transfer of a family home, the transferee shall claim the homeowner's exemption or disabled veteran's exemption at the time of the purchase or transfer of the family home.

(B) A transferee who fails to claim the homeowner's exemption or disabled veteran's exemption at the time of the purchase or transfer of the family home may receive the property tax benefit provided by this section by claiming the homeowner's exemption or disabled veteran's exemption within one year of the purchase or transfer of the family home and shall be entitled to a refund of taxes previously owed or paid between the date of the transfer and the date the transferee claims the homeowner's exemption or disabled veteran's exemption.

(d) Subdivision (h) of Section 2 shall apply to any purchase or transfer that occurs on or before February 15, 2021, but shall not apply to any purchase or transfer occurring after that date. Subdivision (h) of Section 2 shall be inoperative as of February 16, 2021.

(e) For purposes of this section:

(1) "Disabled veteran's exemption" means the exemption authorized by subdivision (a) of Section 4 of Article XIII.

(2) "Family farm" means any real property which is under cultivation or which is being used for pasture or grazing, or that is used to produce any agricultural commodity, as that term is defined in Section 51201 of the Government Code as that section read on January 1, 2020.

(3) "Family home" has the same meaning as "principal residence," as that term is used in subdivision (k) of Section 3 of Article XIII.

(4) "Full cash value" has the same meaning as defined in subdivision (a) of Section 2.

(5) "Homeowner's exemption" means the exemption provided by subdivision (k) of Section 3 of Article XIII.

(6) "Natural disaster" means the existence, as declared by the Governor, of conditions of disaster or extreme peril to the safety of persons or property within the affected area caused by conditions such as fire, flood, drought, storm, mudslide, earthquake, civil disorder, foreign invasion, or volcanic eruption.

(7) "Primary residence" means a residence eligible for either of the following:

(A) The homeowner's exemption.

(B) The disabled veteran's exemption.

(8) "Principal residence" as used in subdivision (b) has the same meaning as that term is used in subdivision (a) of Section 2.

(9) "Replacement primary residence" has the same meaning as "replacement dwelling," as that term is defined in subdivision (a) of Section 2.

(10) "Taxable value" means the base year value determined in accordance with subdivision (a) of Section 2

plus any adjustment authorized by subdivision (b) of Section 2.

(11) "Victim of a wildfire or natural disaster" means the owner of a primary residence that has been substantially damaged as a result of a wildfire or natural disaster that amounts to more than 50 percent of the improvement value of the primary residence immediately before the wildfire or natural disaster. For purposes of this paragraph, "damage" includes a diminution in the value of the primary residence as a result of restricted access caused by the wildfire or natural disaster.

(12) "Wildfire" has the same meaning as defined in subdivision (j) of Section 51177 of the Government Code, as that section read on January 1, 2020.

(Sec. 2.1 added Nov. 3, 2020, by Prop. 19. Res.Ch. 31, 2020. Effective December 16, 2020.)

SEC. 2.2.

(a) Protection of Fire Services, Emergency Response, and County Services. It is the intent of the Legislature in proposing, and the people in adopting, this section and Section 2.3 to do both of the following:

(1) Dedicate revenue for fire protection and emergency response, address inequities in underfunded fire districts, ensure all communities are protected from wildfires, and safeguard the lives of millions of Californians.

(2) Protect county revenues and other vital local services.

(b) (1) The California Fire Response Fund is hereby created within the State Treasury.

(2) The County Revenue Protection Fund is hereby created within the State Treasury. Moneys in the County Revenue Protection Fund are continuously appropriated, without regard to fiscal year, for the purpose of reimbursing eligible local agencies that incur a negative gain, and paying the administrative costs of the California Department of Tax and Fee Administration, in accordance with Section 2.3. Moneys in the fund shall only be expended as provided in Section 2.3.

(c) For purposes of the calculations required by Section 8 of Article XVI, moneys in the California Fire Response Fund and the County Revenue Protection Fund shall be deemed to be General Fund revenues which may be appropriated pursuant to Article XIII B.

(d) The Director of Finance shall do the following, as applicable:

(1) On or before September 1, 2022, and on or before each subsequent September 1 through September 1, 2027, calculate the additional revenues and savings that accrued to the state from the implementation of Section 2.1, including, but not limited to, any increase in state income tax revenues and net savings to the state arising from any reduction in the state's funding obligation under Section 8 of Article XVI, during the immediately preceding fiscal year ending on June 30. In making the calculation required by this paragraph, the Director of Finance shall use actual data or best available estimates where actual data is not available. The calculation shall be final and shall not be adjusted for any subsequent changes in the underlying data. The Director of Finance shall certify the results of the calculation to the Legislature and the Controller no later than September 1 of each year.

(2) On or before September 1, 2028, and each subsequent September 1 thereafter, calculate the additional revenues and savings that accrued to the state from the implementation of Section 2.1, including, but not limited to, any increase in state income tax revenues and net savings to the state arising from any reduction in the state's funding obligation under Section 8 of Article XVI during the immediately preceding fiscal year ending on June 30 by multiplying the amount from the immediately preceding fiscal year ending on June 30 by the rate of increase in property tax revenues allocated to local agencies in that fiscal year. In making the calculation required by this paragraph, the Director of Finance shall use actual data or best available estimates where actual data is not available. The calculation shall be final and shall not be adjusted for any subsequent changes in the underlying data. The Director of Finance shall certify the

results of the calculation to the Legislature and the Controller no later than September 1 of each fiscal year.

(e) No later than September 15, 2022, and each subsequent September 15 thereafter, the Controller shall do both of the following:

(1) Transfer from the General Fund to the California Fire Response Fund an amount equal to 75 percent of the amount calculated by the Director of Finance pursuant to subdivision (d) for the applicable year.

(2) Transfer from the General Fund to the County Revenue Protection Fund an amount equal to 15 percent of the amount calculated by the Director of Finance pursuant to subdivision (d) for the applicable year. Moneys transferred to the County Revenue Protection Fund pursuant to this paragraph shall be used to reimburse eligible local agencies with a negative gain, as provided in Section 2.3.

(f) Moneys in the California Fire Response Fund shall be appropriated by the Legislature in each fiscal year exclusively for the purposes of this section and, except as otherwise provided in subdivision (g), shall not be appropriated for any other purpose. Moneys in the California Fire Response Fund may be used upon appropriation without regard to fiscal year and shall be used to expand fire suppression staffing, as set forth in paragraphs (1) to (4), inclusive, and not to supplant existing state or local funds utilized for those purposes.

(1) Twenty percent of the moneys in the California Fire Response Fund shall be appropriated to the Department of Forestry and Fire Protection to fund fire suppression staffing.

(2) Eighty percent of the moneys in the California Fire Response Fund shall be deposited in the Special District Fire Response Fund, which is hereby created as a subaccount within the California Fire Response Fund, and appropriated to special districts that provide fire protection services in accordance with the following criteria:

(A) Fifty percent of the amount described in this paragraph shall be used to fund fire suppression staffing in underfunded special districts that provide fire protection services, were formed after July 1, 1978, and employ full-time or full-time-equivalent station-based personnel who are immediately available to comprise at least 50 percent of an initial full alarm assignment.

(B) Twenty-five percent of the amount described in this paragraph shall be used to fund fire suppression staffing in special districts that provide fire protection services, were formed before July 1, 1978, are underfunded due to a disproportionately low share of property tax revenue and an increase in service level demands since July 1, 1978, and employ full-time or full-time-equivalent station-based personnel who are immediately available to comprise at least 50 percent of an initial full alarm assignment.

(C) Twenty-five percent of the amount described in this paragraph shall be used to fund fire suppression staffing in underfunded special districts that provide fire protection services and employ full-time or full-time-equivalent station-based personnel who are immediately available to comprise at least 30 percent but less than 50 percent of an initial full alarm assignment.

(3) In determining whether a special district that provides fire protection services is underfunded for purposes of paragraph (2), the Legislature shall take into account the following factors, in order of priority:

(A) The degree to which the special district's property tax revenue is insufficient to sustain adequate fire suppression, as measured against the population density, size of the service area, and number of taxpayers within the boundaries of the special district.

(B) Whether the special district, upon formation, received a property tax allocation in accordance with Chapter 282 of the Statutes of 1979.

(C) Geographic diversity.

(4) The allocation of moneys to a special district that qualifies pursuant to paragraph (2) shall be in the form of grants, with a term of not less than 10 years, in order to ensure that the special district can engage in responsible budgeting and sustain adequate fire suppression services over the long term.

(g) Notwithstanding subdivision (f), if in any fiscal year after the first fiscal year for which moneys are transferred from the General Fund to the California Fire Response Fund pursuant to this section the amount transferred exceeds the amount transferred in the previous fiscal year by more than 10 percent, the Controller shall not transfer the amount in excess of that 10 percent, which shall be available for appropriation from the General Fund for any purpose.

(Sec. 2.2 added Nov. 3, 2020, by Prop. 19. Res.Ch. 31, 2020. Effective December 16, 2020.)

SEC. 2.3.

(a) Each county shall annually, no later than the date specified by the California Department of Tax and Fee Administration by regulations adopted pursuant to this section, determine the gain for the county and for each local agency in the county resulting from implementation of Section 2.1 by adding the following amounts:

(1) The revenue increase resulting from the sale and reassessment of original primary residences for outbound intercounty transfers pursuant to subdivision (b) of Section 2.1.

(2) The revenue decrease, which shall be expressed as a negative number, resulting from the transfer of taxable values of original primary residences located in other counties to replacement primary residences located within the county for inbound intercounty transfers pursuant to subdivision (b) of Section 2.1.

(3) The revenue increase resulting from subdivision (c) of Section 2.1.

(b) A county or any local agency in the county that has a positive gain determined pursuant to subdivision (a) shall not be eligible to receive reimbursement from the County Revenue Protection Fund. A county or any local agency in the county that has a negative gain determined pursuant to subdivision (a) shall be deemed to be an eligible local agency entitled to a reimbursement from the County Revenue Protection Fund.

(c) The California Department of Tax and Fee Administration shall determine each eligible local agency's aggregate gain every three years, based on the amounts determined pursuant to subdivision (a) for each of those three years, and provide reimbursement to each eligible local agency with a negative gain from the moneys in the County Revenue Protection Fund equal to that amount. If there are insufficient moneys in that fund to cover the total amount of reimbursements under this section, the California Department of Tax and Fee Administration shall allocate a pro rata share of the moneys in the fund to each eligible local agency based on the amount of the eligible local agency's reimbursement relative to the total amount of reimbursements under this section.

(d) At the end of each three-year period described in subdivision (c), after the California Department of Tax and Fee Administration has reimbursed each eligible local agency that has experienced a negative gain during that three-year period, the Controller shall transfer the remaining balance, if any, in the County Revenue Protection Fund to the General Fund, to be available for appropriation for any purpose.

(e) The California Department of Tax and Fee Administration shall promulgate regulations to implement this section pursuant to the rulemaking provisions of the Administrative Procedure Act (Chapter 3.5 (commencing with Section 11340) of Part 1 of Division 3 of Title 2 of the Government Code), as may be amended from time to time by the Legislature, or any successor to those provisions.

(f) For purposes of this section and Section 2.2, an "eligible local agency" is a county, a city, a city and county, a special district, or a school district as determined pursuant to subdivision (o) of Section 42238.02 of the Education Code as it read on January 8, 2020, that has a negative gain as determined pursuant to this section.

(Sec. 2.3 added Nov. 3, 2020, by Prop. 19. Res.Ch. 31, 2020. Effective December 16, 2020.)

SEC. 3.

(a) Any change in state statute which results in any taxpayer paying a higher tax must be imposed by an act passed by not less than two-thirds of all members elected to each of the two houses of the Legislature, except that no new ad valorem taxes on real property, or sales or transaction taxes on the sales of real property may be imposed.

(b) As used in this section, "tax" means any levy, charge, or exaction of any kind imposed by the State, except the following:

(1) A charge imposed for a specific benefit conferred or privilege granted directly to the payor that is not provided to those not charged, and which does not exceed the reasonable costs to the State of conferring the benefit or granting the privilege to the payor.

(2) A charge imposed for a specific government service or product provided directly to the payor that is not provided to those not charged, and which does not exceed the reasonable costs to the State of providing the service or product to the payor.

(3) A charge imposed for the reasonable regulatory costs to the State incident to issuing licenses and permits, performing investigations, inspections, and audits, enforcing agricultural marketing orders, and the administrative enforcement and adjudication thereof.

(4) A charge imposed for entrance to or use of state property, or the purchase, rental, or lease of state property, except charges governed by Section 15 of Article XI.

(5) A fine, penalty, or other monetary charge imposed by the judicial branch of government or the State, as a result of a violation of law.

(c) Any tax adopted after January 1, 2010, but prior to the effective date of this act, that was not adopted in compliance with the requirements of this section is void 12 months after the effective date of this act unless the tax is reenacted by the Legislature and signed into law by the Governor in compliance with the requirements of this section.

(d) The State bears the burden of proving by a preponderance of the evidence that a levy, charge, or other exaction is not a tax, that the amount is no more than necessary to cover the reasonable costs of the

194

governmental activity, and that the manner in which those costs are allocated to a payor bear a fair or reasonable relationship to the payor's burdens on, or benefits received from, the governmental activity.

(Sec. 3 amended Nov. 2, 2010, by Prop. 26. Initiative measure.)

Section 4.

Cities, Counties and special districts, by a two-thirds vote of the qualified electors of such district, may impose special taxes on such district, except ad valorem taxes on real property or a transaction tax or sales tax on the sale of real property within such City, County or special district.

(Sec. 4 added June 6, 1978, by Prop. 13. Initiative measure.)

Section 5.

This article shall take effect for the tax year beginning on July 1 following the passage of this Amendment, except Section 3 which shall become effective upon the passage of this article.

(Sec. 5 added June 6, 1978, by Prop. 13. Initiative measure.)

Section 6.

If any section, part, clause, or phrase hereof is for any reason held to be invalid or unconstitutional, the remaining sections shall not be affected but will remain in full force and effect.

(Sec. 6 added June 6, 1978, by Prop. 13. Initiative measure.)

SEC. 7.

Section 3 of this article does not apply to the California Children and Families First Act of 1998.

(Sec. 7 added Nov. 3, 1998, by Prop. 10. Initiative measure. Effective on date election results were certified.)

ARTICLE XIII B GOVERNMENT SPENDING LIMITATION

[SEC. 1 - SEC. 15]

(Article 13B added Nov. 6, 1979, by Prop. 4. Initiative measure.)

SEC. 1.

The total annual appropriations subject to limitation of the State and of each local government shall not exceed the appropriations limit of the entity of government for the prior year adjusted for the change in the cost of living and the change in population, except as otherwise provided in this article.

(Sec. 1 amended June 5, 1990, by Prop. 111. Res.Ch. 66, 1989. Effective July 1, 1990.)

SEC. 1.5.

The annual calculation of the appropriations limit under this article for each entity of local government shall be reviewed as part of an annual financial audit.

(Sec. 1.5 added June 5, 1990, by Prop. 111. Res.Ch. 66, 1989. Effective July 1, 1990.)

SEC. 2.

(a) (1) Fifty percent of all revenues received by the State in a fiscal year and in the fiscal year immediately following it in excess of the amount which may be appropriated by the State in compliance with this article during that fiscal year and the fiscal year immediately following it shall be transferred and allocated, from a fund established for that purpose, pursuant to Section 8.5 of Article XVI.

(2) Fifty percent of all revenues received by the State in a fiscal year and in the fiscal year immediately following it in excess of the amount which may be appropriated by the State in compliance with this article during that fiscal year and the fiscal year immediately following it shall be returned by a revision of tax rates or fee schedules within the next two subsequent fiscal years.

(b) All revenues received by an entity of government, other than the State, in a fiscal year and in the fiscal year immediately following it in excess of the amount which may be appropriated by the entity in compliance with this article during that fiscal year and the fiscal year immediately following it shall be returned by a revision of tax rates or fee schedules within the next two subsequent fiscal years.

(Sec. 2 amended June 5, 1990, by Prop. 111. Res.Ch. 66, 1989. Effective July 1, 1990.)

SEC. 3.

The appropriations limit for any fiscal year pursuant to Sec. 1 shall be adjusted as follows:

(a) In the event that the financial responsibility of providing services is transferred, in whole or in part, whether by annexation, incorporation or otherwise, from one entity of government to another, then for the year in which such transfer becomes effective the appropriations limit of the transferee entity shall be increased by such reasonable amount as the said entities shall mutually agree and the appropriations limit of the transferor entity shall be decreased by the same amount.

(b) In the event that the financial responsibility of providing services is transferred, in whole or in part, from an entity of government to a private entity, or the financial source for the provision of services is transferred, in whole or in part, from other revenues of an entity of government, to regulatory licenses, user charges or user fees, then for the year of such transfer the appropriations limit of such entity of government shall be decreased accordingly.

(c) (1) In the event an emergency is declared by the legislative body of an entity of government, the appropriations limit of the affected entity of government may be exceeded provided that the appropriations limits in the following three years are reduced accordingly to prevent an aggregate increase in appropriations resulting from the emergency.

(2) In the event an emergency is declared by the Governor, appropriations approved by a two-thirds vote of the legislative body of an affected entity of government to an emergency account for expenditures relating to that emergency shall not constitute appropriations subject to limitation. As used in this paragraph, "emergency" means the existence, as declared by the Governor, of conditions of disaster or of extreme peril to the safety of persons and property within the State, or parts thereof, caused by such conditions as attack or probable or imminent attack by an enemy of the United States, fire, flood, drought, storm, civil disorder, earthquake, or volcanic eruption.

(Subdivision (c) amended June 5, 1990, by Prop. 111. Res.Ch. 66, 1989. Effective July 1, 1990. Other Source: Entire Sec. 3 was added Nov. 6, 1979, by Prop. 4; initiative measure.)

SEC. 4.

The appropriations limit imposed on any new or existing entity of government by this Article may be established or changed by the electors of such entity, subject to and in conformity with constitutional and statutory voting requirements. The duration of any such change shall be as determined by said electors, but shall in no event exceed four years from the most recent vote of said electors creating or continuing such change.

(Sec. 4 added Nov. 6, 1979, by Prop. 4. Initiative measure.)

SEC. 5.

Each entity of government may establish such contingency, emergency, unemployment, reserve, retirement, sinking fund, trust, or similar funds as it shall deem reasonable and proper. Contributions to any such fund, to the extent that such contributions are derived from the proceeds of taxes, shall for purposes of this Article constitute appropriations subject to limitation in the year of contribution. Neither withdrawals from any such fund, nor expenditures of (or authorizations to expend) such withdrawals, nor transfers between or among such funds, shall for purposes of this Article constitute appropriations subject to limitation.

(Sec. 5 added Nov. 6, 1979, by Prop. 4. Initiative measure.)

SECTION 5.5.

Prudent State Reserve. The Legislature shall establish a prudent state reserve fund in such amount as it shall deem reasonable and necessary. Contributions to, and withdrawals from, the fund shall be subject to the provisions of Section 5 of this Article.

(Sec. 5.5 added Nov. 8, 1988, by Prop. 98. Initiative measure.)

SEC. 6.

(a) Whenever the Legislature or any state agency mandates a new program or higher level of service on any local government, the State shall provide a subvention of funds to reimburse that local government for the costs of the program or increased level of service, except that the Legislature may, but need not, provide a subvention of funds for the following mandates:

(1) Legislative mandates requested by the local agency affected.

(2) Legislation defining a new crime or changing an existing definition of a crime.

(3) Legislative mandates enacted prior to January 1, 1975, or executive orders or regulations initially implementing legislation enacted prior to January 1, 1975.

(4) Legislative mandates contained in statutes within the scope of paragraph (7) of subdivision (b) of Section 3 of Article I.

(b) (1) Except as provided in paragraph (2), for the 2005–06 fiscal year and every subsequent fiscal year, for a mandate for which the costs of a local government claimant have been determined in a preceding fiscal year to be payable by the State pursuant to law, the Legislature shall either appropriate, in the annual Budget Act, the full payable amount that has not been previously paid, or suspend the operation of the mandate for the fiscal year for which the annual Budget Act is applicable in a manner prescribed by law.

(2) Payable claims for costs incurred prior to the 2004–05 fiscal year that have not been paid prior to the 2005–06 fiscal year may be paid over a term of years, as prescribed by law.

(3) Ad valorem property tax revenues shall not be used to reimburse a local government for the costs of a new program or higher level of service.

(4) This subdivision applies to a mandate only as it affects a city, county, city and county, or special district.

(5) This subdivision shall not apply to a requirement to provide or recognize any procedural or substantive protection, right, benefit, or employment status of any local government employee or retiree, or of any local government employee organization, that arises from, affects, or directly relates to future, current, or past local government employment and that constitutes a mandate subject to this section.

(c) A mandated new program or higher level of service includes a transfer by the Legislature from the State to cities, counties, cities and counties, or special districts of complete or partial financial responsibility for a required program for which the State previously had complete or partial financial responsibility.

(Sec. 6 amended June 3, 2014, by Prop. 42. Res.Ch. 123, 2013.)

SEC. 7.

Nothing in this Article shall be construed to impair the ability of the State or of any local government to meet its obligations with respect to existing or future bonded indebtedness.
(Sec. 7 added Nov. 6, 1979, by Prop. 4. Initiative measure.)

SEC. 8.

As used in this article and except as otherwise expressly provided herein:

(a) "Appropriations subject to limitation" of the State means any authorization to expend during a fiscal year the proceeds of taxes levied by or for the State, exclusive of state subventions for the use and operation of local government (other than subventions made pursuant to Section 6) and further exclusive of refunds of taxes, benefit payments from retirement, unemployment insurance, and disability insurance funds.

(b) "Appropriations subject to limitation" of an entity of local government means any authorization to expend during a fiscal year the proceeds of taxes levied by or for that entity and the proceeds of state subventions to that entity (other than subventions made pursuant to Section 6) exclusive of refunds of taxes.

(c) "Proceeds of taxes" shall include, but not be restricted to, all tax revenues and the proceeds to an entity of government, from (1) regulatory licenses, user charges, and user fees to the extent that those proceeds exceed the costs reasonably borne by that entity in providing the regulation, product, or service, and (2) the investment of tax revenues. With respect to any local government, "proceeds of taxes" shall include subventions received from the State, other than pursuant to Section 6, and, with respect to the State, proceeds of taxes shall exclude such subventions.

(d) "Local government" means any city, county, city and county, school district, special district, authority, or other political subdivision of or within the State.

(e) (1) "Change in the cost of living" for the State, a school district, or a community college district means the percentage change in California per capita personal income from the preceding year.

(2) "Change in the cost of living" for an entity of local government, other than a school district or a community college district, shall be either (A) the percentage change in California per capita personal income from the preceding year, or (B) the percentage change in the local assessment roll from the preceding year for the jurisdiction due to the addition of local nonresidential new construction. Each entity of local government shall select its change in the cost of living pursuant to this paragraph annually by a recorded vote of the entity's governing body.

(f) "Change in population" of any entity of government, other than the State, a school district, or a community college district, shall be determined by a method prescribed by the Legislature.

"Change in population" of a school district or a community college district shall be the percentage change in the average daily attendance of the school district or community college district from the preceding fiscal year, as determined by a method prescribed by the Legislature.

"Change in population" of the State shall be determined by adding (1) the percentage change in the State's population multiplied by the percentage of the State's budget in the prior fiscal year that is expended for other than educational purposes for kindergarten and grades one to 12, inclusive, and the community colleges, and (2) the percentage change in the total statewide average daily attendance in kindergarten and grades one to 12, inclusive, and the community colleges, multiplied by the percentage of the State's budget in the prior fiscal year that is expended for educational purposes for kindergarten and grades one to 12, inclusive, and the community colleges.

Any determination of population pursuant to this subdivision, other than that measured by average daily attendance, shall be revised, as necessary, to reflect the periodic census conducted by the United States Department of Commerce, or successor department.

(g) "Debt service" means appropriations required to pay the cost of interest and redemption charges, including the funding of any reserve or sinking fund required in connection therewith, on indebtedness existing or legally authorized as of January 1, 1979, or on bonded indebtedness thereafter approved according to law by a vote of the electors of the issuing entity voting in an election for that purpose.

(h) The "appropriations limit" of each entity of government for each fiscal year is that amount which total annual appropriations subject to limitation may not exceed under Sections 1 and 3. However, the "appropriations limit" of each entity of government for fiscal year 1978–79 is the total of the appropriations subject to limitation of the entity for that fiscal year. For fiscal year 1978–79, state subventions to local governments, exclusive of federal grants, are deemed to have been derived from the proceeds of state taxes.

(i) Except as otherwise provided in Section 5, "appropriations subject to limitation" do not include local agency loan funds or indebtedness funds, investment (or authorizations to invest) funds of the State, or of an entity of local government in accounts at banks or savings and loan associations or in liquid securities.

(Sec. 8 amended June 5, 1990, by Prop. 111. Res.Ch. 66, 1989. Effective July 1, 1990.)

SEC. 9.

"Appropriations subject to limitation" for each entity of government do not include:

(a) Appropriations for debt service.

(b) Appropriations required to comply with mandates of the courts or the federal government which, without discretion, require an expenditure for additional services or which unavoidably make the provision of existing services more costly.

(c) Appropriations of any special district which existed on January 1, 1978, and which did not as of the 1977–78 fiscal year levy an ad valorem tax on property in excess of 12½ cents per $100 of assessed value; or the appropriations of any special district then existing or thereafter created by a vote of the people, which is totally funded by other than the proceeds of taxes.

(d) Appropriations for all qualified capital outlay projects, as defined by the Legislature.

(e) Appropriations of revenue which are derived from any of the following:

(1) That portion of the taxes imposed on motor vehicle fuels for use in motor vehicles upon public streets and highways at a rate of more than nine cents ($0.09) per gallon.

(2) Sales and use taxes collected on that increment of the tax specified in paragraph (1).

(3) That portion of the weight fee imposed on commercial vehicles which exceeds the weight fee imposed on those vehicles on January 1, 1990.

(Sec. 9 amended June 5, 1990, by Prop. 111. Res.Ch. 66, 1989. Effective July 1, 1990.)

SEC. 10.

This Article shall be effective commencing with the first day of the fiscal year following its adoption.

(Sec. 10 added Nov. 6, 1979, by Prop. 4. Initiative measure.)

SEC. 10.5.

For fiscal years beginning on or after July 1, 1990, the appropriations limit of each entity of government shall be the appropriations limit for the 1986–87 fiscal year adjusted for the changes made from that fiscal year pursuant to this article, as amended by the measure adding this section, adjusted for the changes required by Section 3.

(Sec. 10.5 added June 5, 1990, by Prop. 111. Res.Ch. 66, 1989. Effective July 1, 1990.)

SEC. 11.

If any appropriation category shall be added to or removed from appropriations subject to limitation, pursuant to final judgment of any court of competent jurisdiction and any appeal therefrom, the appropriations limit shall be adjusted accordingly. If any section, part, clause or phrase in this Article is for any reason held invalid or unconstitutional, the remaining portions of this Article shall not be affected but shall remain in full force and effect.

(Sec. 11 added Nov. 6, 1979, by Prop. 4. Initiative measure.)

SEC. 12.

"Appropriations subject to limitation" of each entity of government shall not include appropriations of revenue from the Cigarette and Tobacco Products Surtax Fund created by the Tobacco Tax and Health Protection Act of 1988. No adjustment in the appropriations limit of any entity of government shall be required pursuant to Section 3 as a result of revenue being deposited in or appropriated from the Cigarette and Tobacco Products Surtax Fund created by the Tobacco Tax and Health Protection Act of 1988.

(Sec. 12 added Nov. 8, 1988, by Prop. 99. Initiative measure.)

SEC. 13.

"Appropriations subject to limitation" of each entity of government shall not include appropriations of revenue from the California Children and Families First Trust Fund created by the California Children and Families First Act of 1998. No adjustment in the appropriations limit of any entity of government shall be required pursuant to Section 3 as a result of revenue being deposited in or appropriated from the California Children and Families First Trust Fund. The surtax created by the California Children and Families First Act of 1998 shall not be considered General Fund revenues for the purposes of Section 8 of Article XVI.

(Sec. 13 added Nov. 3, 1998, by Prop. 10. Initiative measure. Effective on date election results were certified.)

SEC. 14.

"Appropriations subject to limitation" of each entity of government shall not include appropriations of revenue from the California Healthcare, Research and Prevention Tobacco Tax Act of 2016 Fund created by the California Healthcare, Research and Prevention Tobacco Tax Act of 2016. No adjustment in the appropriations limit of any entity of government shall be required pursuant to Section 3 as a result of revenue being deposited in or appropriated from the California Healthcare, Research and Prevention Tobacco Tax Act of 2016 Fund.

(Sec. 14 added Nov. 8, 2016, by Prop. 56. Initiative measure.)

SEC. 15.

"Appropriations subject to limitation" of each entity of government shall not include appropriations of revenues from the Road Maintenance and Rehabilitation Account created by the Road Repair and Accountability Act of 2017, or any other revenues deposited into any other funds pursuant to the act. No adjustment in the appropriations limit of any entity of government shall be required pursuant to Section 3 as a result of revenues being deposited in or appropriated from the Road Maintenance and Rehabilitation Account created by the Road Repair and

Accountability Act of 2017 or any other account pursuant to the act.
(Sec. 15 added June 5, 2018, by Prop. 69. Res.Ch. 30, 2017.)

ARTICLE XIII C VOTER APPROVAL FOR LOCAL TAX LEVIES

[SECTION 1 - SEC. 3]

(Article 13C added Nov. 5, 1996, by Prop. 218. Initiative measure.)

SECTION 1.

Definitions. As used in this article:

(a) "General tax" means any tax imposed for general governmental purposes.

(b) "Local government" means any county, city, city and county, including a charter city or county, any special district, or any other local or regional governmental entity.

(c) "Special district" means an agency of the State, formed pursuant to general law or a special act, for the local performance of governmental or proprietary functions with limited geographic boundaries including, but not limited to, school districts and redevelopment agencies.

(d) "Special tax" means any tax imposed for specific purposes, including a tax imposed for specific purposes, which is placed into a general fund.

(e) As used in this article, "tax" means any levy, charge, or exaction of any kind imposed by a local government, except the following:

(1) A charge imposed for a specific benefit conferred or privilege granted directly to the payor that is not provided to those not charged, and which does not exceed the reasonable costs to the local government of conferring the benefit or granting the privilege.

(2) A charge imposed for a specific government service or product provided directly to the payor that is not provided to those not charged, and which does not exceed the reasonable costs to the local government of providing the service or product.

(3) A charge imposed for the reasonable regulatory costs to a local government for issuing licenses and permits,

performing investigations, inspections, and audits, enforcing agricultural marketing orders, and the administrative enforcement and adjudication thereof.

(4) A charge imposed for entrance to or use of local government property, or the purchase, rental, or lease of local government property.

(5) A fine, penalty, or other monetary charge imposed by the judicial branch of government or a local government, as a result of a violation of law.

(6) A charge imposed as a condition of property development.

(7) Assessments and property-related fees imposed in accordance with the provisions of Article XIII D.

The local government bears the burden of proving by a preponderance of the evidence that a levy, charge, or other exaction is not a tax, that the amount is no more than necessary to cover the reasonable costs of the governmental activity, and that the manner in which those costs are allocated to a payor bear a fair or reasonable relationship to the payor's burdens on, or benefits received from, the governmental activity.

(Sec. 1 amended Nov. 2, 2010, by Prop. 26. Initiative measure.)

SEC. 2.

Local Government Tax Limitation. Notwithstanding any other provision of this Constitution:

(a) All taxes imposed by any local government shall be deemed to be either general taxes or special taxes. Special purpose districts or agencies, including school districts, shall have no power to levy general taxes.

(b) No local government may impose, extend, or increase any general tax unless and until that tax is submitted to the electorate and approved by a majority vote. A general tax shall not be deemed to have been increased if it is imposed at a rate not higher than the maximum rate so approved. The election required by this subdivision shall be consolidated with a regularly scheduled general election for members of the governing body of the local government, except in cases of emergency declared by a unanimous vote of the governing body.

(c) Any general tax imposed, extended, or increased, without voter approval, by any local government on or after January 1, 1995, and prior to the effective date of this article, shall continue to be imposed only if approved by a majority vote of the voters voting in an election on the issue of the imposition, which election shall be held within two years of the effective date of this article and in compliance with subdivision (b).

(d) No local government may impose, extend, or increase any special tax unless and until that tax is submitted to the electorate and approved by a two-thirds vote. A special tax shall not be deemed to have been increased if it is imposed at a rate not higher than the maximum rate so approved.

(Sec. 2 added Nov. 5, 1996, by Prop. 218. Initiative measure.)

SEC. 3.

Initiative Power for Local Taxes, Assessments, Fees and Charges. Notwithstanding any other provision of this Constitution, including, but not limited to, Sections 8 and 9 of Article II, the initiative power shall not be prohibited or otherwise limited in matters of reducing or repealing any local tax, assessment, fee or charge. The power of initiative to affect local taxes, assessments, fees and charges shall be applicable to all local governments and neither the Legislature nor any local government charter shall impose a signature requirement higher than that applicable to statewide statutory initiatives.

(Sec. 3 added Nov. 5, 1996, by Prop. 218. Initiative measure.)

ARTICLE XIII D [ASSESSMENT AND PROPERTY-RELATED FEE REFORM]
[SECTION 1 - SEC. 6]

(Article 13D added Nov. 5, 1996, by Prop. 218. Initiative measure.)

SECTION 1.

Application. Notwithstanding any other provision of law, the provisions of this article shall apply to all assessments, fees and charges, whether imposed pursuant to state statute or local government charter authority. Nothing in this article or Article XIII C shall be construed to:

(a) Provide any new authority to any agency to impose a tax, assessment, fee, or charge.

(b) Affect existing laws relating to the imposition of fees or charges as a condition of property development.

(c) Affect existing laws relating to the imposition of timber yield taxes.

(Sec. 1 added Nov. 5, 1996, by Prop. 218. Initiative measure.)

SEC. 2.

Definitions. As used in this article:

(a) "Agency" means any local government as defined in subdivision (b) of Section 1 of Article XIII C.

(b) "Assessment" means any levy or charge upon real property by an agency for a special benefit conferred upon the real property. "Assessment" includes, but is not limited to, "special assessment," "benefit assessment," "maintenance assessment" and "special assessment tax."

(c) "Capital cost" means the cost of acquisition, installation, construction, reconstruction, or replacement of a permanent public improvement by an agency.

(d) "District" means an area determined by an agency to contain all parcels which will receive a special benefit from a proposed public improvement or property-related service.

(e) "Fee" or "charge" means any levy other than an ad valorem tax, a special tax, or an assessment, imposed by an agency upon a parcel or upon a person as an incident of property ownership, including a user fee or charge for a property related service.

(f) "Maintenance and operation expenses" means the cost of rent, repair, replacement, rehabilitation, fuel, power, electrical current, care, and supervision necessary to properly operate and maintain a permanent public improvement.

(g) "Property ownership" shall be deemed to include tenancies of real property where tenants are directly liable to pay the assessment, fee, or charge in question.

(h) "Property-related service" means a public service having a direct relationship to property ownership.

(i) "Special benefit" means a particular and distinct benefit over and above general benefits conferred on real property located in the district or to the public at large. General enhancement of property value does not constitute "special benefit."

(Sec. 2 added Nov. 5, 1996, by Prop. 218. Initiative measure.)

SEC. 3.

Property Taxes, Assessments, Fees and Charges Limited. (a) No tax, assessment, fee, or charge shall be assessed by any agency upon any parcel of property or upon any person as an incident of property ownership except:

(1) The ad valorem property tax imposed pursuant to Article XIII and Article XIII A.

(2) Any special tax receiving a two-thirds vote pursuant to Section 4 of Article XIII A.

(3) Assessments as provided by this article.

(4) Fees or charges for property related services as provided by this article.

(b) For purposes of this article, fees for the provision of electrical or gas service shall not be deemed charges or fees imposed as an incident of property ownership.
(Sec. 3 added Nov. 5, 1996, by Prop. 218. Initiative measure.)

SEC. 4.

Procedures and Requirements for All Assessments. (a) An agency which proposes to levy an assessment shall identify all parcels which will have a special benefit conferred upon them and upon which an assessment will be imposed. The proportionate special benefit derived by each identified parcel shall be determined in relationship to the entirety of the capital cost of a public improvement, the maintenance and operation expenses of a public improvement, or the cost of the property related service being provided. No assessment shall be imposed on any parcel which exceeds the reasonable cost of the proportional special benefit conferred on that parcel. Only special benefits are assessable, and an agency shall separate the general benefits from the special benefits conferred on a parcel. Parcels within a district that are owned or used by any agency, the State of California or the United States shall not be exempt from assessment unless the agency can demonstrate by clear and convincing evidence that those publicly owned parcels in fact receive no special benefit.
(b) All assessments shall be supported by a detailed engineer's report prepared by a registered professional engineer certified by the State of California.
(c) The amount of the proposed assessment for each identified parcel shall be calculated and the record owner of each parcel shall be given written notice by mail of the proposed assessment, the total amount thereof chargeable to the entire district, the amount chargeable to the owner's particular parcel, the duration of the payments, the reason for the assessment and the basis upon which the amount of the proposed assessment was calculated, together with the date, time, and location of a public hearing on the proposed assessment. Each notice shall also include, in a

conspicuous place thereon, a summary of the procedures applicable to the completion, return, and tabulation of the ballots required pursuant to subdivision (d), including a disclosure statement that the existence of a majority protest, as defined in subdivision (e), will result in the assessment not being imposed.

(d) Each notice mailed to owners of identified parcels within the district pursuant to subdivision (c) shall contain a ballot which includes the agency's address for receipt of the ballot once completed by any owner receiving the notice whereby the owner may indicate his or her name, reasonable identification of the parcel, and his or her support or opposition to the proposed assessment.

(e) The agency shall conduct a public hearing upon the proposed assessment not less than 45 days after mailing the notice of the proposed assessment to record owners of each identified parcel. At the public hearing, the agency shall consider all protests against the proposed assessment and tabulate the ballots. The agency shall not impose an assessment if there is a majority protest. A majority protest exists if, upon the conclusion of the hearing, ballots submitted in opposition to the assessment exceed the ballots submitted in favor of the assessment. In tabulating the ballots, the ballots shall be weighted according to the proportional financial obligation of the affected property.

(f) In any legal action contesting the validity of any assessment, the burden shall be on the agency to demonstrate that the property or properties in question receive a special benefit over and above the benefits conferred on the public at large and that the amount of any contested assessment is proportional to, and no greater than, the benefits conferred on the property or properties in question.

(g) Because only special benefits are assessable, electors residing within the district who do not own property within the district shall not be deemed under this Constitution to have been deprived of the right to vote for any assessment. If a court determines that the Constitution of the United States or other federal law requires otherwise, the assessment shall not be imposed unless approved by a two-thirds vote of the electorate in the district in addition to being approved by the property owners as required by subdivision (e).

(Sec. 4 added Nov. 5, 1996, by Prop. 218. Initiative measure.)

SEC. 5.

Effective Date. Pursuant to subdivision (a) of Section 10 of Article II, the provisions of this article shall become effective the day after the election unless otherwise provided. Beginning July 1, 1997, all existing, new, or increased assessments shall comply with this article. Notwithstanding the foregoing, the following assessments existing on the effective date of this article shall be exempt from the procedures and approval process set forth in Section 4:

(a) Any assessment imposed exclusively to finance the capital costs or maintenance and operation expenses for sidewalks, streets, sewers, water, flood control, drainage systems or vector control. Subsequent increases in such assessments shall be subject to the procedures and approval process set forth in Section 4.

(b) Any assessment imposed pursuant to a petition signed by the persons owning all of the parcels subject to the assessment at the time the assessment is initially imposed. Subsequent increases in such assessments shall be subject to the procedures and approval process set forth in Section 4.

(c) Any assessment the proceeds of which are exclusively used to repay bonded indebtedness of which the failure to pay would violate the Contract Impairment Clause of the Constitution of the United States.

(d) Any assessment which previously received majority voter approval from the voters voting in an election on the issue of the assessment. Subsequent increases in those assessments shall be subject to the procedures and approval process set forth in Section 4.

(Sec. 5 added Nov. 5, 1996, by Prop. 218. Initiative measure.)

SEC. 6.

Property Related Fees and Charges. (a) Procedures for New or Increased Fees and Charges. An agency shall follow the procedures pursuant to this section in imposing or increasing any fee or charge as defined pursuant to this article, including, but not limited to, the following:

(1) The parcels upon which a fee or charge is proposed for imposition shall be identified. The amount of the fee or charge proposed to be imposed upon each parcel shall be calculated. The agency shall provide written notice by mail of the proposed fee or charge to the record owner of each identified parcel upon which the fee or charge is proposed for imposition, the amount of the fee or charge proposed to be imposed upon each, the basis upon which the amount of the proposed fee or charge was calculated, the reason for the fee or charge, together with the date, time, and location of a public hearing on the proposed fee or charge.

(2) The agency shall conduct a public hearing upon the proposed fee or charge not less than 45 days after mailing the notice of the proposed fee or charge to the record owners of each identified parcel upon which the fee or charge is proposed for imposition. At the public hearing, the agency shall consider all protests against the proposed fee or charge. If written protests against the proposed fee or charge are presented by a majority of owners of the identified parcels, the agency shall not impose the fee or charge.

(b) Requirements for Existing, New or Increased Fees and Charges. A fee or charge shall not be extended, imposed, or increased by any agency unless it meets all of the following requirements:

(1) Revenues derived from the fee or charge shall not exceed the funds required to provide the property related service.

(2) Revenues derived from the fee or charge shall not be used for any purpose other than that for which the fee or charge was imposed.

(3) The amount of a fee or charge imposed upon any parcel or person as an incident of property ownership shall

not exceed the proportional cost of the service attributable to the parcel.

(4) No fee or charge may be imposed for a service unless that service is actually used by, or immediately available to, the owner of the property in question. Fees or charges based on potential or future use of a service are not permitted. Standby charges, whether characterized as charges or assessments, shall be classified as assessments and shall not be imposed without compliance with Section 4.

(5) No fee or charge may be imposed for general governmental services including, but not limited to, police, fire, ambulance or library services, where the service is available to the public at large in substantially the same manner as it is to property owners. Reliance by an agency on any parcel map, including, but not limited to, an assessor's parcel map, may be considered a significant factor in determining whether a fee or charge is imposed as an incident of property ownership for purposes of this article. In any legal action contesting the validity of a fee or charge, the burden shall be on the agency to demonstrate compliance with this article.

(c) Voter Approval for New or Increased Fees and Charges. Except for fees or charges for sewer, water, and refuse collection services, no property related fee or charge shall be imposed or increased unless and until that fee or charge is submitted and approved by a majority vote of the property owners of the property subject to the fee or charge or, at the option of the agency, by a two-thirds vote of the electorate residing in the affected area. The election shall be conducted not less than 45 days after the public hearing. An agency may adopt procedures similar to those for increases in assessments in the conduct of elections under this subdivision.

(d) Beginning July 1, 1997, all fees or charges shall comply with this section.

(Sec. 6 added Nov. 5, 1996, by Prop. 218. Initiative measure.)

ARTICLE XIV LABOR RELATIONS

[SECTION 1 - SECTION 5]
(Article 14 added June 8, 1976, by Prop. 14. Res.Ch. 5, 1976.)

SECTION 1.

The Legislature may provide for minimum wages and for the general welfare of employees and for those purposes may confer on a commission legislative, executive, and judicial powers.
(Sec. 1 added June 8, 1976, by Prop. 14. Res.Ch. 5, 1976.)

SEC. 2.

Worktime of mechanics or workers on public works may not exceed eight hours a day except in wartime or extraordinary emergencies that endanger life or property. The Legislature shall provide for enforcement of this section.
(Sec. 2 added June 8, 1976, by Prop. 14. Res.Ch. 5, 1976.)

SEC. 3.

Mechanics, persons furnishing materials, artisans, and laborers of every class, shall have a lien upon the property upon which they have bestowed labor or furnished material for the value of such labor done and material furnished; and the Legislature shall provide, by law, for the speedy and efficient enforcement of such liens.
(Sec. 3 added June 8, 1976, by Prop. 14. Res.Ch. 5, 1976.)

SEC. 4.

The Legislature is hereby expressly vested with plenary power, unlimited by any provision of this Constitution, to create, and enforce a complete system of workers' compensation, by appropriate legislation, and in that behalf to create and enforce a liability on the part of any or all persons to compensate any or all of their workers for injury or disability, and their dependents for death incurred or sustained by the said workers in the course of their employment, irrespective of the fault of any party. A complete system of workers' compensation includes adequate provisions for the comfort, health and safety and general welfare of any and all workers and those dependent upon them for support to the extent of relieving from the consequences of any injury or death incurred or sustained by workers in the course of their employment, irrespective of the fault of any party; also full provision for securing safety in places of employment; full provision for such medical, surgical, hospital and other remedial treatment as is requisite to cure and relieve from the effects of such injury; full provision for adequate insurance coverage against liability to pay or furnish compensation; full provision for regulating such insurance coverage in all its aspects, including the establishment and management of a state compensation insurance fund; full provision for otherwise securing the payment of compensation; and full provision for vesting power, authority and jurisdiction in an administrative body with all the requisite governmental functions to determine any dispute or matter arising under such legislation, to the end that the administration of such legislation shall accomplish substantial justice in all cases expeditiously, inexpensively, and without incumbrance of any character; all of which matters are expressly declared to be the social public policy of this State, binding upon all departments of the state government.
The Legislature is vested with plenary powers, to provide for the settlement of any disputes arising under such legislation by arbitration, or by an industrial accident commission, by the courts, or by either, any, or all of these

agencies, either separately or in combination, and may fix and control the method and manner of trial of any such dispute, the rules of evidence and the manner of review of decisions rendered by the tribunal or tribunals designated by it; provided, that all decisions of any such tribunal shall be subject to review by the appellate courts of this State. The Legislature may combine in one statute all the provisions for a complete system of workers' compensation, as herein defined.

The Legislature shall have power to provide for the payment of an award to the State in the case of the death, arising out of and in the course of the employment, of an employee without dependents, and such awards may be used for the payment of extra compensation for subsequent injuries beyond the liability of a single employer for awards to employees of the employer.

Nothing contained herein shall be taken or construed to impair or render ineffectual in any measure the creation and existence of the industrial accident commission of this State or the state compensation insurance fund, the creation and existence of which, with all the functions vested in them, are hereby ratified and confirmed.

(Sec. 4 added June 8, 1976, by Prop. 14. Res.Ch. 5, 1976.)

SECTION 5.

(a) The Director of Corrections or any county Sheriff or other local government official charged with jail operations, may enter into contracts with public entities, nonprofit or for profit organizations, entities, or businesses for the purpose of conducting programs which use inmate labor. Such programs shall be operated and implemented pursuant to statutes enacted by or in accordance with the provisions of the Prison Inmate Labor Initiative of 1990, and by rules and regulations prescribed by the Director of Corrections and, for county jail programs, by local ordinances.

(b) No contract shall be executed with an employer that will initiate employment by inmates in the same job classification as non-inmate employees of the same employer who are on strike, as defined in Section 1132.6 of the Labor Code, as it reads on January 1, 1990, or who are subject to lockout, as defined in Section 1132.8 of the Labor Code, as it reads on January 1, 1990. Total daily hours worked by inmates employed in the same job classification as non-inmate employees of the same employer who are on strike, as defined in Section 1132.6 of the Labor Code, as it reads on January 1, 1990, or who are subject to lockout, as defined in Section 1132.8 of the Labor Code, as it reads on January 1, 1990, shall not exceed, for the duration of the strike, the average daily hours worked for the preceding six months, or if the program has been in operation for less than six months, the average for the period of operation.

(c) Nothing in this section shall be interpreted as creating a right of inmates to work.

(Sec. 5 repealed and added Nov. 6, 1990, by Prop. 139. Initiative measure.)

ARTICLE XV USURY

[SECTION 1- SECTION 1.]
*(Article 15 added June 8, 1976, by Prop. 14, clause 35. Res.Ch. 5, 1976.
)*

SECTION 1.

The rate of interest upon the loan or forbearance of any money, goods, or things in action, or on accounts after demand, shall be 7 percent per annum but it shall be competent for the parties to any loan or forbearance of any money, goods or things in action to contract in writing for a rate of interest:
(1) For any loan or forbearance of any money, goods, or things in action, if the money, goods, or things in action are for use primarily for personal, family, or household purposes, at a rate not exceeding 10 percent per annum; provided, however, that any loan or forbearance of any money, goods or things in action the proceeds of which are used primarily for the purchase, construction or improvement of real property shall not be deemed to be a use primarily for personal, family or household purposes; or
(2) For any loan or forbearance of any money, goods, or things in action for any use other than specified in paragraph (1), at a rate not exceeding the higher of (a) 10 percent per annum or (b) 5 percent per annum plus the rate prevailing on the 25th day of the month preceding the earlier of (i) the date of execution of the contract to make the loan or forbearance, or (ii) the date of making the loan or forbearance established by the Federal Reserve Bank of San Francisco on advances to member banks under Sections 13 and 13a of the Federal Reserve Act as now in effect or hereafter from time to time amended (or if there is no such single determinable rate of advances, the closest counterpart of such rate as shall be designated by the Superintendent of Banks of the State of California

unless some other person or agency is delegated such authority by the Legislature).

No person, association, copartnership or corporation shall by charging any fee, bonus, commission, discount or other compensation receive from a borrower more than the interest authorized by this section upon any loan or forbearance of any money, goods or things in action.

However, none of the above restrictions shall apply to any obligations of, loans made by, or forbearances of, any building and loan association as defined in and which is operated under that certain act known as the "Building and Loan Association Act," approved May 5, 1931, as amended, or to any corporation incorporated in the manner prescribed in and operating under that certain act entitled "An act defining industrial loan companies, providing for their incorporation, powers and supervision," approved May 18, 1917, as amended, or any corporation incorporated in the manner prescribed in and operating under that certain act entitled "An act defining credit unions, providing for their incorporation, powers, management and supervision," approved March 31, 1927, as amended or any duly licensed pawnbroker or personal property broker, or any loans made or arranged by any person licensed as a real estate broker by the State of California and secured in whole or in part by liens on real property, or any bank as defined in and operating under that certain act known as the "Bank Act," approved March 1, 1909, as amended, or any bank created and operating under and pursuant to any laws of this State or of the United States of America or any nonprofit cooperative association organized under Chapter 1 (commencing with Section 54001) of Division 20 of the Food and Agricultural Code in loaning or advancing money in connection with any activity mentioned in said title or any corporation, association, syndicate, joint stock company, or partnership engaged exclusively in the business of marketing agricultural, horticultural, viticultural, dairy, live stock, poultry and bee products on a cooperative nonprofit basis in loaning or advancing money to the members thereof or in connection with any such business or any corporation securing money or credit from any federal intermediate credit bank, organized and existing pursuant to the provisions of an act of Congress entitled "Agricultural Credits Act of 1923," as amended in loaning or advancing credit so secured, or any other class of persons authorized by statute, or to any successor in interest to any loan or forbearance exempted under this article, nor shall any such charge of any said exempted classes of persons be considered in any action or for any purpose as increasing or affecting or as connected with the rate of interest hereinbefore fixed. The Legislature may from time to time prescribe the maximum rate per annum of, or provide for the supervision, or the filing of a schedule of, or in any manner fix, regulate or limit, the fees, bonuses, commissions, discounts or other compensation which all or any of the said exempted classes of persons may charge or receive from a borrower in connection with any loan or forbearance of any money, goods or things in action.

The rate of interest upon a judgment rendered in any court of this State shall be set by the Legislature at not more than 10 percent per annum. Such rate may be variable and based upon interest rates charged by federal agencies or economic indicators, or both.

In the absence of the setting of such rate by the Legislature, the rate of interest on any judgment rendered in any court of the State shall be 7 percent per annum.

The provisions of this section shall supersede all provisions of this Constitution and laws enacted thereunder in conflict therewith.

(Sec. 1 amended Nov. 6, 1979, by Prop. 2. Res.Ch. 49, 1979.)

ARTICLE XVI PUBLIC FINANCE

[SECTION 1 - SEC. 23]

(Article 16 heading amended Nov. 5, 1974, by Prop. 8. Res.Ch. 70, 1974.)

SECTION 1.

The Legislature shall not, in any manner create any debt or debts, liability or liabilities, which shall, singly or in the aggregate with any previous debts or liabilities, exceed the sum of three hundred thousand dollars ($300,000), except in case of war to repel invasion or suppress insurrection, unless the same shall be authorized by law for some single object or work to be distinctly specified therein which law shall provide ways and means, exclusive of loans, for the payment of the interest of such debt or liability as it falls due, and also to pay and discharge the principal of such debt or liability within 50 years of the time of the contracting thereof, and shall be irrepealable until the principal and interest thereon shall be paid and discharged, and such law may make provision for a sinking fund to pay the principal of such debt or liability to commence at a time after the incurring of such debt or liability of not more than a period of one-fourth of the time of maturity of such debt or liability; but no such law shall take effect unless it has been passed by a two-thirds vote of all the members elected to each house of the Legislature and until, at a general election or at a direct primary, it shall have been submitted to the people and shall have received a majority of all the votes cast for and against it at such election; and all moneys raised by authority of such law shall be applied only to the specific object therein stated or to the payment of the debt thereby created. Full publicity as to matters to be voted upon by the people is afforded by the setting out of the complete text of the proposed laws, together with the arguments for and against them, in the ballot pamphlet mailed to each elector preceding the election at which they are submitted, and the only requirement for publication of such law shall be that it be set out at length in ballot pamphlets which the Secretary of State shall cause to be printed. The Legislature may, at any time after the approval of such law by the people, reduce the amount of the indebtedness authorized by the law to an amount not less than the amount contracted at the time of the reduction, or it may repeal the law if no debt shall have been contracted in pursuance thereof.

Notwithstanding any other provision of this Constitution, Members of the Legislature who are required to meet with the State Allocation Board shall have equal rights and duties with the nonlegislative members to vote and act upon matters pending or coming before such board for the allocation and apportionment of funds to school districts for school construction purposes or purposes related thereto.

Notwithstanding any other provision of this constitution, or of any bond act to the contrary, if any general obligation bonds of the State heretofore or hereafter authorized by vote of the people have been offered for sale and not sold, the Legislature may raise the maximum rate of interest payable on all general obligation bonds authorized but not sold, whether or not such bonds have been offered for sale, by a statute passed by a two-thirds vote of all members elected to each house thereof.

The provisions of Senate Bill No. 763 of the 1969 Regular Session, which authorize an increase of the state general obligation bond maximum interest rate from 5 percent to an amount not in excess of 7 percent and eliminate the maximum rate of interest payable on notes given in anticipation of the sale of such bonds, are hereby ratified.
(Sec. 1 amended June 2, 1970, by Prop. 7. Res.Ch. 299, 1969.)

SEC. 1.3.

(a) For the purposes of Section 1, a "single object or work," for which the Legislature may create a debt or liability in excess of three hundred thousand dollars

($300,000) subject to the requirements set forth in Section 1, includes the funding of an accumulated state budget deficit to the extent, and in the amount, that funding is authorized in a measure submitted to the voters at the March 2, 2004, statewide primary election.

(b) As used in subdivision (a), "accumulated state budget deficit" means the aggregate of both of the following, as certified by the Director of Finance:

(1) The estimated negative balance of the Special Fund for Economic Uncertainties arising on or before June 30, 2004, not including the effect of the estimated amount of net proceeds of any bonds issued or to be issued pursuant to the California Fiscal Recovery Financing Act (Title 17 (commencing with Section 99000) of the Government Code) and any bonds issued or to be issued pursuant to the measure submitted to the voters at the March 2, 2004, statewide primary election as described in subdivision (a).

(2) Other General Fund obligations incurred by the State prior to June 30, 2004, to the extent not included in that negative balance.

(c) Subsequent to the issuance of any state bonds described in subdivision (a), the State may not obtain moneys to fund a year-end state budget deficit, as may be defined by statute, pursuant to any of the following: (1) indebtedness incurred pursuant to Section 1 of this article, (2) a debt obligation under which funds to repay that obligation are derived solely from a designated source of revenue, or (3) a bond or similar instrument for the borrowing of moneys for which there is no legal obligation of repayment. This subdivision does not apply to funding obtained through a short-term obligation incurred in anticipation of the receipt of tax proceeds or other revenues that may be applied to the payment of that obligation, for the purposes and not exceeding the amounts of existing appropriations to which the resulting proceeds are to be applied. For purposes of this subdivision, "year-end state budget deficit" does not include an obligation within the accumulated state budget deficit as defined by subdivision (b).

(Sec. 1.3 added March 2, 2004, by Prop. 58. Res.Ch. 1, 2003-04 5th Ex. Sess.)

SEC. 1.5.

The Legislature may create and establish a "General Obligation Bond Proceeds Fund" in the State Treasury, and may provide for the proceeds of the sale of general obligation bonds of the State heretofore or hereafter issued, including any sums paid as accrued interest thereon, under any or all acts authorizing the issuance of such bonds, to be paid into or transferred to, as the case may be, the "General Obligation Bond Proceeds Fund." Accounts shall be maintained in the "General Obligation Bond Proceeds Fund" of all moneys deposited in the State Treasury to the credit of that fund and the proceeds of each bond issue shall be maintained as a separate and distinct account and shall be paid out only in accordance with the law authorizing the issuance of the particular bonds from which the proceeds were derived. The Legislature may abolish, subject to the conditions of this section, any fund in the State Treasury heretofore or hereafter created by any act for the purpose of having deposited therein the proceeds from the issuance of bonds if such proceeds are transferred to or paid into the "General Obligation Bond Proceeds Fund" pursuant to the authority granted in this section; provided, however, that nothing in this section shall prevent the Legislature from re-establishing any bond proceeds fund so abolished and transferring back to its credit all proceeds in the "General Obligation Bond Proceeds Fund" which constitute the proceeds of the particular bond fund being re-established.
(Sec. 1.5 added Nov. 6, 1962, by Prop. 9. Res.Ch. 223, 1961.)

SEC. 2.

(a) No amendment to this Constitution which provides for the preparation, issuance and sale of bonds of the State of California shall hereafter be submitted to the electors, nor shall any such amendment to the Constitution hereafter submitted to or approved by the electors become effective for any purpose.

Each measure providing for the preparation, issuance and sale of bonds of the State of California shall hereafter be submitted to the electors in the form of a bond act or statute.

(b) The provisions of this Constitution enumerated in subdivision (c) of this section are repealed and such provisions are continued as statutes which have been approved, adopted, legalized, ratified, validated, and made fully and completely effective, by means of the adoption by the electorate of a ratifying constitutional amendment, except that the Legislature, in addition to whatever powers it possessed under such provisions, may amend or repeal such provisions when the bonds issued thereunder have been fully retired and when no rights thereunder will be damaged.

(c) The enumerated provisions of this Constitution are: Article XVI, Sections 2, 3, 4, $4^{1}/_{2}$, 5, 6, 8, $8^{1}/_{2}$, 15, 16, 16.5, 17, 18, 19, 19.5, 20 and 21.

(Sec. 2 added Nov. 6, 1962, by Prop. 6. Res.Ch. 221, 1961.)

SEC. 3.

No money shall ever be appropriated or drawn from the State Treasury for the purpose or benefit of any corporation, association, asylum, hospital, or any other institution not under the exclusive management and control of the State as a state institution, nor shall any grant or donation of property ever be made thereto by the State, except that notwithstanding anything contained in this or any other section of the Constitution:

(1) Whenever federal funds are made available for the construction of hospital facilities by public agencies and nonprofit corporations organized to construct and maintain such facilities, nothing in this Constitution shall prevent the Legislature from making state money available for that purpose, or from authorizing the use of such money for the

construction of hospital facilities by nonprofit corporations organized to construct and maintain such facilities.

(2) The Legislature shall have the power to grant aid to the institutions conducted for the support and maintenance of minor orphans, or half-orphans, or abandoned children, or children of a father who is incapacitated for gainful work by permanent physical disability or is suffering from tuberculosis in such a stage that he cannot pursue a gainful occupation, or aged persons in indigent circumstances—such aid to be granted by a uniform rule, and proportioned to the number of inmates of such respective institutions.

(3) The Legislature shall have the power to grant aid to needy blind persons not inmates of any institution supported in whole or in part by the State or by any of its political subdivisions, and no person concerned with the administration of aid to needy blind persons shall dictate how any applicant or recipient shall expend such aid granted him, and all money paid to a recipient of such aid shall be intended to help him meet his individual needs and is not for the benefit of any other person, and such aid when granted shall not be construed as income to any person other than the blind recipient of such aid, and the State Department of Social Welfare shall take all necessary action to enforce the provisions relating to aid to needy blind persons as heretofore stated.

(4) The Legislature shall have power to grant aid to needy physically handicapped persons not inmates of any institution under the supervision of the Department of Mental Hygiene and supported in whole or in part by the State or by any institution supported in whole or part by any political subdivision of the State.

(5) The State shall have at any time the right to inquire into the management of such institutions.

(6) Whenever any county, or city and county, or city, or town, shall provide for the support of minor orphans, or half-orphans, or abandoned children, or children of a father who is incapacitated for gainful work by permanent physical disability or is suffering from tuberculosis in such a stage that he cannot pursue a gainful occupation, or aged persons in indigent circumstances, or needy blind persons

not inmates of any institution supported in whole or in part by the State or by any of its political subdivisions, or needy physically handicapped persons not inmates of any institution under the supervision of the Department of Mental Hygiene and supported in whole or in part by the State or by any institution supported in whole or part by any political subdivision of the State; such county, city and county, city, or town shall be entitled to receive the same pro rata appropriations as may be granted to such institutions under church, or other control.

An accurate statement of the receipts and expenditures of public moneys shall be attached to and published with the laws at every regular session of the Legislature.

(Sec. 3 added Nov. 5, 1974, by Prop. 8. Res.Ch. 70, 1974.)

SEC. 3.5.

(a) No statute amending or adding to the provisions of the Medi-Cal Hospital Reimbursement Improvement Act of 2013 shall become effective unless approved by the electors in the same manner as statutes amending initiative statutes pursuant to subdivision (c) of Section 10 of Article II, except that the Legislature may, by statute passed in each house by roll call vote entered into the journal, two-thirds of the membership concurring, amend or add provisions that further the purposes of the act.

(b) For purposes of this section:

(1) "Act" means the Medi-Cal Hospital Reimbursement Improvement Act of 2013 (enacted by Senate Bill 239 of the 2013–14 Regular Session of the Legislature, and any nonsubstantive amendments to the act enacted by a later bill in the same session of the Legislature).

(2) "Nonsubstantive amendments" shall only mean minor, technical, grammatical, or clarifying amendments.

(3) "Provisions that further the purposes of the act" shall only mean:

(A) Amendments or additions necessary to obtain or maintain federal approval of the implementation of the act,

232

including the fee imposed and related quality assurance payments to hospitals made pursuant to the act;

(B) Amendments or additions to the methodology used for the development of the fee and quality assurance payments to hospitals made pursuant to the act.

(c) Nothing in this section shall prohibit the Legislature from repealing the act in its entirety by statute passed in each house by roll call vote entered into the journal, two-thirds of the membership concurring, except that the Legislature shall not be permitted to repeal the act and replace it with a similar statute imposing a tax, fee, or assessment unless that similar statute is either:

(1) A provision that furthers the purposes of the act as defined herein;

(2) Is approved by the electors in the same manner as statutes amending initiative statutes pursuant to subdivision (c) of Section 10 of Article II.

(d) The proceeds of the fee imposed by the act and all interest earned on such proceeds shall not be considered revenues, General Fund revenues, General Fund proceeds of taxes, or allocated local proceeds of taxes, for purposes of Sections 8 and 8.5 of this article or for the purposes of Article XIII B. The appropriation of the proceeds in the trust fund referred to in the act for hospital services to Medi-Cal beneficiaries or other beneficiaries in any other similar federal program shall not be subject to the prohibitions or restrictions in Sections 3 or 5 of this article.

(Sec. 3.5 added Nov. 8, 2016, by Prop. 52. Initiative measure.)

SEC. 4.

The Legislature shall have the power to insure or guarantee loans made by private or public lenders to nonprofit corporations and public agencies, the proceeds of which are to be used for the construction, expansion, enlargement, improvement, renovation or repair of any public or nonprofit hospital, hospital facility, or extended care facility, facility for the treatment of mental illness, or all of them, including any outpatient facility and any other facility useful and convenient in the operation of the hospital and any original equipment for any such hospital or facility, or both.

No provision of this Constitution, including but not limited to, Section 1 of Article XVI and Section 14 of Article XI, shall be construed as a limitation upon the authority granted to the Legislature by this section.

(Sec. 4 added Nov. 5, 1974, by Prop. 8. Res.Ch. 70, 1974.)

SEC. 5.

Neither the Legislature, nor any county, city and county, township, school district, or other municipal corporation, shall ever make an appropriation, or pay from any public fund whatever, or grant anything to or in aid of any religious sect, church, creed, or sectarian purpose, or help to support or sustain any school, college, university, hospital, or other institution controlled by any religious creed, church, or sectarian denomination whatever; nor shall any grant or donation of personal property or real estate ever be made by the State, or any city, city and county, town, or other municipal corporation for any religious creed, church, or sectarian purpose whatever; provided, that nothing in this section shall prevent the Legislature granting aid pursuant to Section 3 of Article XVI.

(Sec. 5 added Nov. 5, 1974, by Prop. 8. Res.Ch. 70, 1974.)

SEC. 6.

The Legislature shall have no power to give or to lend, or to authorize the giving or lending, of the credit of the State, or of any county, city and county, city, township or other political corporation or subdivision of the State now existing, or that may be hereafter established, in aid of or to any person, association, or corporation, whether municipal or otherwise, or to pledge the credit thereof, in any manner whatever, for the payment of the liabilities of any individual, association, municipal or other corporation whatever; nor shall it have power to make any gift or authorize the making of any gift, of any public money or thing of value to any individual, municipal or other corporation whatever; provided, that nothing in this section shall prevent the Legislature granting aid pursuant to Section 3 of Article XVI; and it shall not have power to authorize the State, or any political subdivision thereof, to subscribe for stock, or to become a stockholder in any corporation whatever; provided, further, that irrigation districts for the purpose of acquiring the control of any entire international water system necessary for its use and purposes, a part of which is situated in the United States, and a part thereof in a foreign country, may in the manner authorized by law, acquire the stock of any foreign corporation which is the owner of, or which holds the title to the part of such system situated in a foreign country; provided, further, that irrigation districts for the purpose of acquiring water and water rights and other property necessary for their uses and purposes, may acquire and hold the stock of corporations, domestic or foreign, owning waters, water rights, canals, waterworks, franchises or concessions subject to the same obligations and liabilities as are imposed by law upon all other stockholders in such corporation; and

Provided, further, that this section shall not prohibit any county, city and county, city, township, or other political corporation or subdivision of the State from joining with other such agencies in providing for the payment of workers' compensation, unemployment compensation, tort liability, or public liability losses incurred by such agencies, by entry into an insurance pooling arrangement under a joint exercise of powers agreement, or by membership in such publicly-owned nonprofit corporation or other public agency as may be authorized by the Legislature; and

Provided, further, that nothing contained in this Constitution shall prohibit the use of state money or credit, in aiding veterans who served in the military or naval service of the United States during the time of war, in the acquisition of, or payments for, (1) farms or homes, or in projects of land settlement or in the development of such farms or homes or land settlement projects for the benefit of such veterans, or (2) any business, land or any interest therein, buildings, supplies, equipment, machinery, or tools, to be used by the veteran in pursuing a gainful occupation; and

Provided, further, that nothing contained in this Constitution shall prohibit the State, or any county, city and county, city, township, or other political corporation or subdivision of the State from providing aid or assistance to persons, if found to be in the public interest, for the purpose of clearing debris, natural materials, and wreckage from privately owned lands and waters deposited thereon or therein during a period of a major disaster or emergency, in either case declared by the President. In such case, the public entity shall be indemnified by the recipient from the award of any claim against the public entity arising from the rendering of such aid or assistance. Such aid or assistance must be eligible for federal reimbursement for the cost thereof.

And provided, still further, that notwithstanding the restrictions contained in this Constitution, the treasurer of any city, county, or city and county shall have power and the duty to make such temporary transfers from the funds in custody as may be necessary to provide funds for meeting the obligations incurred for maintenance purposes by any city, county, city and county, district, or other political subdivision whose funds are in custody and are paid out solely through the treasurer's office. Such temporary transfer of funds to any political subdivision shall be made only upon resolution adopted by the governing body of the city, county, or city and county directing the treasurer of such city, county, or city and county to make such temporary transfer. Such temporary transfer of funds to any political subdivision shall not exceed 85 percent of the anticipated revenues accruing to such political subdivision, shall not be made prior to the first day of the fiscal year nor after the last Monday in April of the current fiscal year, and shall be replaced from the revenues accruing to such political subdivision before any other obligation of such political subdivision is met from such revenue.

(Sec. 6 amended Nov. 2, 1982, by Prop. 8. Res.Ch. 60, 1982.)

<u>SEC. 7.</u>

Money may be drawn from the Treasury only through an appropriation made by law and upon a Controller's duly drawn warrant.

(Sec. 7 added Nov. 5, 1974, by Prop. 8. Res.Ch. 70, 1974.)

<u>SEC. 8.</u>

(a) From all state revenues there shall first be set apart the moneys to be applied by the State for support of the public school system and public institutions of higher education.

(b) Commencing with the 1990–91 fiscal year, the moneys to be applied by the State for the support of school districts and community college districts shall be not less than the greater of the following amounts:

(1) The amount which, as a percentage of General Fund revenues which may be appropriated pursuant to Article XIII B, equals the percentage of General Fund revenues appropriated for school districts and community college districts, respectively, in fiscal year 1986–87.

(2) The amount required to ensure that the total allocations to school districts and community college districts from General Fund proceeds of taxes appropriated pursuant to Article XIII B and allocated local proceeds of taxes shall not be less than the total amount from these sources in the prior fiscal year, excluding any revenues allocated pursuant to subdivision (a) of Section 8.5, adjusted for changes in enrollment and adjusted for the change in the cost of living pursuant to paragraph (1) of subdivision (e) of Section 8 of Article XIII B. This paragraph shall be operative only in a fiscal year in which the

percentage growth in California per capita personal income is less than or equal to the percentage growth in per capita General Fund revenues plus one half of one percent.

(3) (A) The amount required to ensure that the total allocations to school districts and community college districts from General Fund proceeds of taxes appropriated pursuant to Article XIII B and allocated local proceeds of taxes shall equal the total amount from these sources in the prior fiscal year, excluding any revenues allocated pursuant to subdivision (a) of Section 8.5, adjusted for changes in enrollment and adjusted for the change in per capita General Fund revenues.

(B) In addition, an amount equal to one-half of one percent times the prior year total allocations to school districts and community colleges from General Fund proceeds of taxes appropriated pursuant to Article XIII B and allocated local proceeds of taxes, excluding any revenues allocated pursuant to subdivision (a) of Section 8.5, adjusted for changes in enrollment.

(C) This paragraph (3) shall be operative only in a fiscal year in which the percentage growth in California per capita personal income in a fiscal year is greater than the percentage growth in per capita General Fund revenues plus one half of one percent.

(c) In any fiscal year, if the amount computed pursuant to paragraph (1) of subdivision (b) exceeds the amount computed pursuant to paragraph (2) of subdivision (b) by a difference that exceeds one and one-half percent of General Fund revenues, the amount in excess of one and one-half percent of General Fund revenues shall not be considered allocations to school districts and community colleges for purposes of computing the amount of state aid pursuant to paragraph (2) or 3 of subdivision (b) in the subsequent fiscal year.

(d) In any fiscal year in which school districts and community college districts are allocated funding pursuant to paragraph (3) of subdivision (b) or pursuant to subdivision (h), they shall be entitled to a maintenance factor, equal to the difference between (1) the amount of General Fund moneys which would have been appropriated pursuant to paragraph (2) of subdivision (b) if that paragraph had been operative or the amount of General Fund moneys which would have been appropriated pursuant to subdivision (b) had subdivision (b) not been suspended, and (2) the amount of General Fund moneys actually appropriated to school districts and community college districts in that fiscal year.

(e) The maintenance factor for school districts and community college districts determined pursuant to subdivision (d) shall be adjusted annually for changes in enrollment, and adjusted for the change in the cost of living pursuant to paragraph (1) of subdivision (e) of Section 8 of Article XIII B, until it has been allocated in full. The maintenance factor shall be allocated in a manner determined by the Legislature in each fiscal year in which the percentage growth in per capita General Fund revenues exceeds the percentage growth in California per capita personal income. The maintenance factor shall be reduced each year by the amount allocated by the Legislature in that fiscal year. The minimum maintenance factor amount to be allocated in a fiscal year shall be equal to the product of General Fund revenues from proceeds of taxes and one-half of the difference between the percentage growth in per capita General Fund revenues from proceeds of taxes and in California per capita personal income, not to exceed the total dollar amount of the maintenance factor.

(f) For purposes of this section, "changes in enrollment" shall be measured by the percentage change in average daily attendance. However, in any fiscal year, there shall be no adjustment for decreases in enrollment between the prior fiscal year and the current fiscal year unless there have been decreases in enrollment between the second prior fiscal year and the prior fiscal year and between the third prior fiscal year and the second prior fiscal year.

(h) Subparagraph (B) of paragraph (3) of subdivision (b) may be suspended for one year only when made part of or included within any bill enacted pursuant to Section 12 of Article IV. All other provisions of subdivision (b) may be suspended for one year by the enactment of an urgency statute pursuant to Section 8 of Article IV, provided that the urgency statute may not be made part of or included within any bill enacted pursuant to Section 12 of Article IV.

(Sec. 8 amended June 5, 1990, by Prop. 111. Res.Ch. 66, 1989. Effective July 1, 1990.)

SEC. 8.5.

(a) In addition to the amount required to be applied for the support of school districts and community college districts pursuant to Section 8, the Controller shall during each fiscal year transfer and allocate all revenues available pursuant to paragraph 1 of subdivision (a) of Section 2 of Article XIII B to that portion of the State School Fund restricted for elementary and high school purposes, and to that portion of the State School Fund restricted for community college purposes, respectively, in proportion to the enrollment in school districts and community college districts respectively.

(1) With respect to funds allocated to that portion of the State School Fund restricted for elementary and high school purposes, no transfer or allocation of funds pursuant to this section shall be required at any time that the Director of Finance and the Superintendent of Public Instruction mutually determine that current annual expenditures per student equal or exceed the average annual expenditure per student of the 10 states with the highest annual expenditures per student for elementary and high schools, and that average class size equals or is less than the average class size of the 10 states with the lowest class size for elementary and high schools.

(2) With respect to funds allocated to that portion of the State School Fund restricted for community college purposes, no transfer or allocation of funds pursuant to this section shall be required at any time that the Director of Finance and the Chancellor of the California Community Colleges mutually determine that current annual expenditures per student for community colleges in this State equal or exceed the average annual expenditure per student of the 10 states with the highest annual expenditures per student for community colleges.

(b) Notwithstanding the provisions of Article XIII B, funds allocated pursuant to this section shall not constitute appropriations subject to limitation.

(c) From any funds transferred to the State School Fund pursuant to subdivision (a), the Controller shall each year allocate to each school district and community college district an equal amount per enrollment in school districts from the amount in that portion of the State School Fund restricted for elementary and high school purposes and an equal amount per enrollment in community college districts from that portion of the State School Fund restricted for community college purposes.

(d) All revenues allocated pursuant to subdivision (a) shall be expended solely for the purposes of instructional improvement and accountability as required by law.

(e) Any school district maintaining an elementary or secondary school shall develop and cause to be prepared an annual audit accounting for such funds and shall adopt a School Accountability Report Card for each school.

(Sec. 8.5 amended June 5, 1990, by Prop. 111. Res.Ch. 66, 1989. Effective July 1, 1990.)

SEC. 9.

Money collected under any state law relating to the protection or propagation of fish and game shall be used for activities relating thereto.

(Sec. 9 added Nov. 5, 1974, by Prop. 8. Res.Ch. 70, 1974.)

SEC. 10.

Whenever the United States government or any officer or agency thereof shall provide pensions or other aid for the aged, co-operation by the State therewith and therein is hereby authorized in such manner and to such extent as may be provided by law.

The money expended by any county, city and county, municipality, district or other political subdivision of this State made available under the provisions of this section shall not be considered as a part of the base for determining the maximum expenditure for any given year permissible under Section 20 of Article XI of this Constitution independent of the vote of the electors or authorization by the State Board of Equalization.

(Sec. 10 amended Nov. 6, 1962, by Prop. 16. Res.Ch. 255, 1961.)

SEC. 11.

The Legislature has plenary power to provide for the administration of any constitutional provisions or laws heretofore or hereafter enacted concerning the administration of relief, and to that end may modify, transfer, or enlarge the powers vested in any state agency or officer concerned with the administration of relief or laws appertaining thereto. The Legislature, or the people by initiative, shall have power to amend, alter, or repeal any law relating to the relief of hardship and destitution, whether such hardship and destitution results from unemployment or from other causes, or to provide for the administration of the relief of hardship and destitution, whether resulting from unemployment or from other causes, either directly by the State or through the counties of the State, and to grant such aid to the counties therefor, or make such provision for reimbursement of the counties by the State, as the Legislature deems proper.

(Sec. 11 amended Nov. 6, 1962, by Prop. 16. Res.Ch. 255, 1961.)

SEC. 13.

Notwithstanding any other provision of this Constitution, the Legislature shall have power to release, rescind, cancel, or otherwise nullify in whole or in part any encumbrance on property, personal obligation, or other form of security heretofore or hereafter exacted or imposed by the Legislature to secure the repayment to, or reimbursement of, the State, and the counties or other agencies of the state government, of aid lawfully granted to and received by aged persons.

(Sec. 13 amended Nov. 6, 1962, by Prop. 16. Res.Ch. 255, 1961.)

SEC. 14.

The Legislature may provide for the issuance of revenue bonds to finance the acquisition, construction, and installation of environmental pollution control facilities, including the acquisition of all technological facilities necessary or convenient for pollution control, and for the lease or sale of such facilities to persons, associations, or corporations, other than municipal corporations; provided, that such revenue bonds shall not be secured by the taxing power of the State; and provided, further, that the Legislature may, by resolution adopted by either house, prohibit or limit any proposed issuance of such revenue bonds. No provision of this Constitution, including, but not limited to, Section 25 of Article XIII and Sections 1 and 2 of Article XVI, shall be construed as a limitation upon the authority granted to the Legislature pursuant to this section. Nothing herein contained shall authorize any public agency to operate any industrial or commercial enterprise.

(Sec. 14 added Nov. 7, 1972, by Prop. 3. Res.Ch. 91, 1972.)

SEC. 14.5.

The Legislature may provide for the issuance of revenue bonds to finance the acquisition, construction, and installation of facilities utilizing cogeneration technology, solar power, biomass, or any other alternative source the Legislature may deem appropriate, including the acquisition of all technological facilities necessary or convenient for the use of alternative sources, and for the lease or sale of such facilities to persons, associations, or corporations, other than municipal corporations; provided, that such revenue bonds shall not be secured by the taxing power of the State; and provided, further, that the Legislature may, by resolution adopted by both houses, prohibit or limit any proposed issuance of such revenue bonds. No provision of this Constitution, including, but not limited to, Sections 1, 2, and 6, of this article, shall be construed as a limitation upon the authority granted to the Legislature pursuant to this section. Nothing contained herein shall authorize any public agency to operate any industrial or commercial enterprise.

(Sec. 14.5 added June 3, 1980, by Prop. 8. Res.Ch. 1, 1980.)

SEC. 15.

A public body authorized to issue securities to provide public parking facilities and any other public body whose territorial area includes such facilities are authorized to make revenues from street parking meters available as additional security.

(Sec. 15 added Nov. 5, 1974, by Prop. 8. Res.Ch. 70, 1974.)

SEC. 16.

All property in a redevelopment project established under the Community Redevelopment Law as now existing or hereafter amended, except publicly owned property not subject to taxation by reason of that ownership, shall be taxed in proportion to its value as provided in Section 1 of this article, and those taxes (the word "taxes" as used herein includes, but is not limited to, all levies on an ad valorem basis upon land or real property) shall be levied and collected as other taxes are levied and collected by the respective taxing agencies.

The Legislature may provide that any redevelopment plan may contain a provision that the taxes, if any, so levied upon the taxable property in a redevelopment project each year by or for the benefit of the State of California, any city, county, city and county, district, or other public corporation (hereinafter sometimes called "taxing agencies") after the effective date of the ordinance approving the redevelopment plan, shall be divided as follows:

(a) That portion of the taxes which would be produced by the rate upon which the tax is levied each year by or for each of those taxing agencies upon the total sum of the assessed value of the taxable property in the redevelopment project as shown upon the assessment roll used in connection with the taxation of that property by the taxing agency, last equalized prior to the effective date of the ordinance, shall be allocated to, and when collected shall be paid into, the funds of the respective taxing agencies as taxes by or for those taxing agencies on all other property are paid (for the purpose of allocating taxes levied by or for any taxing agency or agencies which did not include the territory in a redevelopment project on the effective date of the ordinance but to which that territory has been annexed or otherwise included after the ordinance's effective date, the assessment roll of the county last equalized on the effective date of that ordinance shall be used in determining the assessed valuation of the taxable property in the project on that effective date); and

(b) Except as provided in subdivision (c), that portion of the levied taxes each year in excess of that amount shall be allocated to and when collected shall be paid into a special fund of the redevelopment agency to pay the principal of and interest on loans, moneys advanced to, or indebtedness (whether funded, refunded, assumed or otherwise) incurred by the redevelopment agency to finance or refinance, in whole or in part, the redevelopment project. Unless and until the total assessed valuation of the taxable property in a redevelopment project exceeds the total assessed value of the taxable property in the project as shown by the last equalized assessment roll referred to in subdivision (a), all of the taxes levied and collected upon the taxable property in the redevelopment project shall be paid into the funds of the respective taxing agencies. When the loans, advances, and indebtedness, if any, and interest thereon, have been paid, then all moneys thereafter received from taxes upon the taxable property in the redevelopment project shall be paid into the funds of the respective taxing agencies as taxes on all other property are paid.

(c) That portion of the taxes identified in subdivision (b) which are attributable to a tax rate levied by a taxing agency for the purpose of producing revenues in an amount sufficient to make annual repayments of the principal of, and the interest on, any bonded indebtedness for the acquisition or improvement of real property shall be allocated to, and when collected shall be paid into, the fund of that taxing agency. This paragraph shall only apply to taxes levied to repay bonded indebtedness approved by the voters of the taxing agency on or after January 1, 1989.

The Legislature may also provide that in any redevelopment plan or in the proceedings for the advance of moneys, or making of loans, or the incurring of any indebtedness (whether funded, refunded, assumed, or otherwise) by the redevelopment agency to finance or refinance, in whole or in part, the redevelopment project, the portion of taxes identified in subdivision (b), exclusive of that portion identified in subdivision (c), may be irrevocably pledged for the payment of the principal of and interest on those loans, advances, or indebtedness.

It is intended by this section to empower any redevelopment agency, city, county, or city and county under any law authorized by this section to exercise the provisions hereof separately or in combination with powers granted by the same or any other law relative to redevelopment agencies. This section shall not affect any other law or laws relating to the same or a similar subject but is intended to authorize an alternative method of procedure governing the subject to which it refers.

The Legislature shall enact those laws as may be necessary to enforce the provisions of this section.

(Sec. 16 amended Nov. 8, 1988, by Prop. 87. Res.Ch. 54, 1988.)

SEC. 17.

The State shall not in any manner loan its credit, nor shall it subscribe to, or be interested in the stock of any company, association, or corporation, except that the State and each political subdivision, district, municipality, and public agency thereof is hereby authorized to acquire and hold shares of the capital stock of any mutual water company or corporation when the stock is so acquired or held for the purpose of furnishing a supply of water for public, municipal or governmental purposes; and the holding of the stock shall entitle the holder thereof to all of the rights, powers and privileges, and shall subject the holder to the obligations and liabilities conferred or imposed by law upon other holders of stock in the mutual water company or corporation in which the stock is so held.

Notwithstanding any other provisions of law or this Constitution to the contrary, the retirement board of a public pension or retirement system shall have plenary authority and fiduciary responsibility for investment of moneys and administration of the system, subject to all of the following:

(a) The retirement board of a public pension or retirement system shall have the sole and exclusive fiduciary responsibility over the assets of the public pension or retirement system. The retirement board shall also have sole and exclusive responsibility to administer the system in a manner that will assure prompt delivery of benefits and related services to the participants and their beneficiaries. The assets of a public pension or retirement system are trust funds and shall be held for the exclusive purposes of providing benefits to participants in the pension or retirement system and their beneficiaries and defraying reasonable expenses of administering the system.

(b) The members of the retirement board of a public pension or retirement system shall discharge their duties with respect to the system solely in the interest of, and for the exclusive purposes of providing benefits to, participants and their beneficiaries, minimizing employer contributions thereto, and defraying reasonable expenses of administering the system. A retirement board's duty to its participants and their beneficiaries shall take precedence over any other duty.

(c) The members of the retirement board of a public pension or retirement system shall discharge their duties with respect to the system with the care, skill, prudence, and diligence under the circumstances then prevailing that a prudent person acting in a like capacity and familiar with these matters would use in the conduct of an enterprise of a like character and with like aims.

(d) The members of the retirement board of a public pension or retirement system shall diversify the investments of the system so as to minimize the risk of loss and to maximize the rate of return, unless under the circumstances it is clearly not prudent to do so.

(e) The retirement board of a public pension or retirement system, consistent with the exclusive fiduciary responsibilities vested in it, shall have the sole and exclusive power to provide for actuarial services in order to assure the competency of the assets of the public pension or retirement system.

(f) With regard to the retirement board of a public pension or retirement system which includes in its composition elected employee members, the number, terms, and method of selection or removal of members of the retirement board which were required by law or otherwise in effect on July 1, 1991, shall not be changed, amended, or modified by the Legislature unless the change, amendment, or modification enacted by the Legislature is ratified by a majority vote of the electors of the jurisdiction in which the participants of the system are or were, prior to retirement, employed.

(g) The Legislature may by statute continue to prohibit certain investments by a retirement board where it is in the public interest to do so, and provided that the prohibition satisfies the standards of fiduciary care and loyalty required of a retirement board pursuant to this section.

(h) As used in this section, the term "retirement board" shall mean the board of administration, board of trustees, board of directors, or other governing body or board of a public employees' pension or retirement system; provided, however, that the term "retirement board" shall not be interpreted to mean or include a governing body or board created after July 1, 1991 which does not administer pension or retirement benefits, or the elected legislative body of a jurisdiction which employs participants in a public employees' pension or retirement system.

(Sec. 17 amended Nov. 3, 1992, by Prop. 162. Initiative measure.)

SEC. 18.

(a) No county, city, town, township, board of education, or school district, shall incur any indebtedness or liability in any manner or for any purpose exceeding in any year the income and revenue provided for such year, without the assent of two-thirds of the voters of the public entity voting at an election to be held for that purpose, except that with respect to any such public entity which is authorized to incur indebtedness for public school purposes, any proposition for the incurrence of indebtedness in the form of general obligation bonds for the purpose of repairing, reconstructing or replacing public school buildings determined, in the manner prescribed by law, to be structurally unsafe for school use, shall be adopted upon the approval of a majority of the voters of the public entity voting on the proposition at such election; nor unless before or at the time of incurring such indebtedness provision shall be made for the collection of an annual tax sufficient to pay the interest on such indebtedness as it falls due, and to provide for a sinking fund for the payment of the principal thereof, on or before maturity, which shall not exceed forty years from the time of contracting the indebtedness.

(b) Notwithstanding subdivision (a), on or after the effective date of the measure adding this subdivision, in the case of any school district, community college district, or county office of education, any proposition for the incurrence of indebtedness in the form of general obligation bonds for the construction, reconstruction, rehabilitation, or replacement of school facilities, including the furnishing and equipping of school facilities, or the acquisition or lease of real property for school facilities, shall be adopted upon the approval of 55 percent of the voters of the district or county, as appropriate, voting on the proposition at an election. This subdivision shall apply only to a proposition for the incurrence of indebtedness in the form of general obligation bonds for the purposes specified in this subdivision if the proposition meets all of the accountability requirements of paragraph (3) of subdivision (b) of Section 1 of Article XIII A.

(c) When two or more propositions for incurring any indebtedness or liability are submitted at the same election, the votes cast for and against each proposition shall be counted separately, and when two-thirds or a majority or 55 percent of the voters, as the case may be, voting on any one of those propositions, vote in favor thereof, the proposition shall be deemed adopted.

(Sec. 18 amended Nov. 7, 2000, by Prop. 39. Initiative measure.)

SEC. 19.

All proceedings undertaken by any chartered city, or by any chartered county or by any chartered city and county for the construction of any public improvement, or the acquisition of any property for public use, or both, where the cost thereof is to be paid in whole or in part by special assessment or other special assessment taxes upon property, whether the special assessment will be specific or a special assessment tax upon property wholly or partially according to the assessed value of such property, shall be undertaken only in accordance with the provisions of law governing: (a) limitations of costs of such proceedings or assessments for such proceedings, or both, in relation to the value of any property assessed therefor; (b) determination of a basis for the valuation of any such property; (c) payment of the cost in excess of such limitations; (d) avoidance of such limitations; (e) postponement or abandonment, or both, of such proceedings in whole or in part upon majority protest, and particularly in accordance with such provisions as contained in Sections 10, 11 and 13a of the Special Assessment Investigation, Limitation and Majority Protest Act of 1931 or any amendments, codification, reenactment or restatement thereof.

Notwithstanding any provisions for debt limitation or majority protest as in this section provided, if, after the giving of such reasonable notice by publication and posting and the holding of such public hearing as the legislative body of any such chartered county, chartered city or chartered city and county shall have prescribed, such legislative body by no less than a four-fifths vote of all members thereof, finds and determines that the public convenience and necessity require such improvements or acquisitions, such debt limitation and majority protest provisions shall not apply.

Nothing contained in this section shall require the legislative body of any such city, county, or city and county to prepare or to cause to be prepared, hear, notice for hearing or report the hearing of any report as to any such proposed construction or acquisition or both.

(Sec. 19 added Nov. 5, 1974, by Prop. 8. Res.Ch. 70, 1974.)

SEC. 20.

(a) (1) The Budget Stabilization Account is hereby created in the General Fund.

(2) For the 2015–16 fiscal year and each fiscal year thereafter, based on the Budget Act for the fiscal year, the Controller shall transfer from the General Fund to the Budget Stabilization Account, no later than October 1, a sum equal to 1.5 percent of the estimated amount of General Fund revenues for that fiscal year.

(b) (1) For the 2015–16 fiscal year and each fiscal year thereafter, based on the Budget Act for the fiscal year, the

Department of Finance shall provide to the Legislature all of the following information:

(A) An estimate of the amount of General Fund proceeds of taxes that may be appropriated pursuant to Article XIII B for that fiscal year.

(B) (i) An estimate of that portion of the General Fund proceeds of taxes identified in subparagraph (A) that is derived from personal income taxes paid on net capital gains.

(ii) The portion of the estimate in clause (i) that exceeds 8 percent of the estimate made under subparagraph (A).

(C) That portion of the state's funding obligation under Section 8 that results from including the amount calculated under clause (ii) of subparagraph (B), if any, as General Fund proceeds of taxes.

(D) The amount of any appropriations described in clause (ii) of subparagraph (B) of paragraph (1) of, or subparagraph (C) of paragraph (2) of, subdivision (c), that are made from the revenues described in clause (ii) of subparagraph (B) of this paragraph.

(E) The amount resulting from subtracting the combined values calculated under subparagraphs (C) and (D) from the value calculated under clause (ii) of subparagraph (B). If less than zero, the amount shall be considered zero for this purpose.

(F) The lesser of the amount calculated under subparagraph (E) or the amount of transfer resulting in the balance in the Budget Stabilization Account reaching the limit specified in subdivision (e).

(2) In the 2016–17 fiscal year, with respect to the 2015–16 fiscal year only, and in the 2017–18 fiscal year and each fiscal year thereafter, separately with respect to each of the two next preceding fiscal years, the Department of Finance shall calculate all of the following, using the same methodology used for the relevant fiscal year, and provide those calculations to the Legislature:

(A) An updated estimate of the amount of General Fund proceeds of taxes that may be appropriated pursuant to Article XIII B.

(B) (i) An updated estimate of that portion of the General Fund proceeds of taxes identified in subparagraph (A) that is derived from personal income taxes paid on net capital gains.

(ii) That portion of the updated estimate in clause (i) that exceeds 8 percent of the updated estimate made under subparagraph (A).

(C) The updated calculation of that portion of the state's funding obligation under Section 8 that results from including the updated amount calculated under clause (ii) of subparagraph (B), if any, as General Fund proceeds of taxes.

(D) The amount of any appropriations described in clause (ii) of subparagraph (B) of paragraph (1) of, or subparagraph (C) of paragraph (2) of, subdivision (c), that are made from the revenues described in clause (ii) of subparagraph (B) of paragraph (1).

(E) The amount resulting from subtracting the combined values calculated under subparagraphs (C) and (D) from the value calculated under clause (ii) of subparagraph (B). If less than zero, the amount shall be considered zero for this purpose.

(F) The amount previously transferred for the fiscal year by the Controller from the General Fund to the Budget Stabilization Account pursuant to subdivisions (c) and (d).

(G) The lesser of (i) the amount, not less than zero, resulting from subtracting, from the amount calculated under subparagraph (E), the value of any suspension or reduction of transfer pursuant to paragraph (1) of subdivision (a) of Section 22 previously approved by the Legislature for the relevant fiscal year, and the amount previously transferred for that fiscal year by the Controller as described in subparagraph (F), or (ii) the amount of transfer resulting in the balance in the Budget Stabilization Account reaching the limit as specified in subdivision (e).

(c) (1) (A) By October 1 of the 2015–16 fiscal year and each fiscal year thereafter to the 2029–30 fiscal year, inclusive, based on the estimates set forth in the annual Budget Act pursuant to paragraphs (2) and (3) of subdivision (h), and the sum identified in paragraph (2) of subdivision (a), the Controller shall transfer amounts from the General Fund and the Budget Stabilization Account, pursuant to a schedule provided by the Director of Finance, as provided in subparagraph (B).

(B) Notwithstanding any other provision of this section, in the fiscal year to which the Budget Act identified in subparagraph (A) applies:

(i) Fifty percent of both the amount identified in paragraph (2) of subdivision (a), and the amount resulting from subtracting the value calculated under subparagraph (C) of paragraph (1) of subdivision (b) from the value calculated under clause (ii) of subparagraph (B) of paragraph (1) of subdivision (b), shall be transferred from the General Fund to the Budget Stabilization Account.

(ii) The remaining 50 percent shall be appropriated by the Legislature for one or more of the following obligations and purposes:

(I) Unfunded prior fiscal year General Fund obligations pursuant to Section 8 that existed on July 1, 2014.

(II) Budgetary loans to the General Fund, from funds outside the General Fund, that had outstanding balances on January 1, 2014.

(III) Payable claims for mandated costs incurred prior to the 2004–05 fiscal year that have not yet been paid, and that pursuant to paragraph (2) of subdivision (b) of Section 6 of Article XIII B are permitted to be paid over a term of years, as prescribed by law.

(IV) Unfunded liabilities for state-level pension plans and prefunding other postemployment benefits, in excess of current base amounts as established for the fiscal year in which the funds would otherwise be transferred to the Budget Stabilization Account. For the purpose of this subclause, current base amounts are those required to be paid pursuant to law, an approved memorandum of understanding, benefit schedules established by the employer or entity authorized to establish those contributions for employees excluded or exempted from collective bargaining, or any combination of these. To qualify under this subclause, the appropriation shall supplement and not supplant funding that would otherwise be made available to pay for the obligations described in this subclause for the fiscal year or the subsequent fiscal year.

(2) (A) By October 1 of the 2030–31 fiscal year and each fiscal year thereafter, based on the estimates set forth in the annual Budget Act pursuant to paragraphs (2) and (3) of subdivision (h), the Controller shall transfer amounts from the General Fund to the Budget Stabilization Account, pursuant to a schedule provided by the Director of Finance, as provided in subparagraph (B).

(B) In the fiscal year to which the Budget Act identified in subparagraph (A) applies, both the amount identified in paragraph (2) of subdivision (a), and the amount resulting from subtracting the value calculated under subparagraph (C) of paragraph (1) of subdivision (b) from the value calculated under clause (ii) of subparagraph (B) of paragraph (1) of subdivision (b), shall be transferred from the General Fund to the Budget Stabilization Account.

(C) Notwithstanding any other provision of this section, the Legislature may appropriate up to 50 percent of both the amount identified in paragraph (2) of subdivision (a), and of the amount resulting from subtracting the value calculated under subparagraph (C) of paragraph (1) of subdivision (b) from the value calculated under clause (ii) of subparagraph (B) of paragraph (1) of subdivision (b), for one or more of the obligations and purposes described in clause (ii) of subparagraph (B) of paragraph (1).

(3) The transfers described in this subdivision are subject to suspension or reduction pursuant to paragraph (1) of subdivision (a) of Section 22.

(d) By October 1 of the 2016–17 fiscal year and each fiscal year thereafter, based on the estimates set forth in the annual Budget Act pursuant to paragraphs (4) and (5) of subdivision (h), the Controller shall transfer amounts between the General Fund and the Budget Stabilization Account pursuant to a schedule provided by the Director of Finance, as follows:

(1) If the amount in subparagraph (G) of paragraph (2) of subdivision (b) is greater than zero, transfer that amount from the General Fund to the Budget Stabilization Account, subject to any suspension or reduction of this transfer pursuant to paragraph (1) of subdivision (a) of Section 22.

(2) If the amount described in subparagraph (F) of paragraph (2) of subdivision (b) is greater than the

amount calculated under subparagraph (E) of paragraph (2) of subdivision (b), transfer that excess amount from the Budget Stabilization Account back to the General Fund.

(e) Notwithstanding any other provision of this section, the amount of a transfer to the Budget Stabilization Account pursuant to paragraph (2) of subdivision (a) and subdivisions (c) and (d) for any fiscal year shall not exceed an amount that would result in a balance in the account that, when the transfer is made, exceeds 10 percent of the amount of General Fund proceeds of taxes for the fiscal year estimated pursuant to subdivision (b). For any fiscal year, General Fund proceeds of taxes that, but for this paragraph, would have been transferred to the Budget Stabilization Account may be expended only for infrastructure, as defined by Section 13101 of the Government Code, as that section read on January 1, 2014, including deferred maintenance thereon.

(f) The funds described in subdivision (b) as General Fund proceeds of taxes are General Fund proceeds of taxes for purposes of Section 8 for the fiscal year to which those proceeds are attributed, but are not deemed to be additional General Fund proceeds of taxes on the basis that the funds are thereafter transferred from the Budget Stabilization Account to the General Fund.

(g) The Controller may utilize funds in the Budget Stabilization Account, that he or she determines to currently be unnecessary for the purposes of this section, to help manage General Fund daily cashflow needs. Any use pursuant to this subdivision shall not interfere with the purposes of the Budget Stabilization Account.

(h) The annual Budget Act shall include the estimates described in all of the following:

(1) Paragraph (2) of subdivision (a).

(2) Clause (ii) of subparagraph (B) of paragraph (1) of subdivision (b).

(3) Subparagraph (F) of paragraph (1) of subdivision (b).

(4) Clause (ii) of subparagraph (B) of paragraph (2) of subdivision (b).

(5) Subparagraph (G) of paragraph (2) of subdivision (b).

(Sec. 20 repealed and added Nov. 4, 2014, by Prop. 2. Res.Ch. 1, 2013-14 2nd Ex. Sess.)

SEC. 21.

(a) The Public School System Stabilization Account is hereby created in the General Fund.

(b) On or before October 1 of each fiscal year, commencing with the 2015–16 fiscal year, based on the amounts identified in the annual Budget Act pursuant to subdivision (b) of Section 20, the Controller shall transfer, pursuant to a schedule provided by the Director of Finance, amounts from the General Fund to the Public School System Stabilization Account as follows:

(1) (A) For the 2015–16 fiscal year, and for each fiscal year thereafter, any positive amount identified in subparagraph (C) of paragraph (1) of subdivision (b) of Section 20 shall be transferred from the General Fund to the Public School System Stabilization Account in the amount calculated under subparagraph (B), subject to any reduction or suspension of this transfer pursuant to any other provision of this section or paragraph (3) of subdivision (a) of Section 22.

(B) The Director of Finance shall calculate the amount by which the positive amount identified in subparagraph (C) of paragraph (1) of subdivision (b) of Section 20, in combination with all other moneys required to be applied by the State for the support of school districts and community college districts for that fiscal year pursuant to Section 8, exceeds the sum of the total allocations to school districts and community college districts from General Fund proceeds of taxes appropriated pursuant to Article XIII B and allocated local proceeds of taxes in the prior fiscal year, plus any allocations from the Public School System Stabilization Account in the prior fiscal year, less any transfers to the Public School System Stabilization Account pursuant to this section in the prior fiscal year and any revenues allocated pursuant to subdivision (a) of Section 8.5, adjusted for the percentage change in average daily attendance and adjusted for the higher of the change in the cost of living pursuant to paragraph (1) of subdivision (e) of Section 8 of Article XIII B or the cost of living adjustment applied to school district and community college district general purpose apportionments.

(2) (A) Commencing with the 2016–17 fiscal year, and for each fiscal year thereafter, to the extent the amount calculated under this paragraph exceeds the amounts previously transferred by the Controller from the General Fund to the Public School System Stabilization Account for a preceding fiscal year, any positive amount calculated pursuant to subparagraph (C) of paragraph (2) of subdivision (b) of Section 20 for that fiscal year shall be transferred from the General Fund to the Public School System Stabilization Account in the amount calculated under subparagraph (B), subject to any reduction or suspension of this transfer pursuant to any other provision of this section or paragraph (3) of subdivision (a) of Section 22.

(B) The Director of Finance shall calculate the amount by which the positive amount identified in subparagraph (C) of paragraph (2) of subdivision (b) of Section 20, in combination with all other moneys required to be applied by the State for the support of school districts and community college districts for that fiscal year pursuant to Section 8, exceeds the sum of the total allocations to school districts and community college districts from General Fund proceeds of taxes appropriated pursuant to Article XIII B and allocated local proceeds of taxes in the prior fiscal year, plus any allocations from the Public School System Stabilization Account in the prior fiscal year, less any transfers to the Public School System Stabilization Account pursuant to this section in the prior fiscal year and any revenues allocated pursuant to subdivision (a) of Section 8.5, adjusted for the percentage change in average daily attendance and adjusted for the higher of the change in the cost of living pursuant to the paragraph (1) of subdivision (e) of Section 8 of Article XIII B or the cost of living adjustment applied to school district and community college district general purpose apportionments.

(c) Commencing with the 2016–17 fiscal year, and for each fiscal year thereafter, if the amount calculated pursuant to subparagraph (C) of paragraph (2) of subdivision (b) of Section 20 for a fiscal year is less than the amounts previously transferred by the Controller from the General Fund to the Public School System Stabilization Account for that fiscal year, the amount of this difference shall be appropriated and allocated by the State from the Public School System Stabilization Account for the support of school districts and community college districts.

(d) Notwithstanding any other provision of this section, the amount transferred to the Public School System Stabilization Account pursuant to subdivision (b) for a fiscal year shall not exceed the amount by which the amount of state support calculated pursuant to paragraph (1) of subdivision (b) of Section 8 exceeds the amount of state support calculated pursuant to paragraph (2) of subdivision (b) of Section 8 for that fiscal year. If the amount of state support calculated pursuant to paragraph (1) of subdivision (b) of Section 8 does not exceed the amount of state support calculated pursuant to paragraph (2) of subdivision (b) of Section 8 for a fiscal year, no amount shall be transferred to the Public School System Stabilization Account pursuant to subdivision (b) for that fiscal year.

(e) Notwithstanding any other provision of this section, no amount shall be transferred to the Public School System Stabilization Account pursuant to subdivision (b) for a fiscal year for which a maintenance factor is determined pursuant to subdivision (d) of Section 8.

(f) Notwithstanding any other provision of this section, no amount shall be transferred to the Public School System Stabilization Account pursuant to subdivision (b) until the maintenance factor determined pursuant to subdivisions (d) and (e) of Section 8 for fiscal years prior to the 2014–15 fiscal year has been fully allocated. Transfers may be made beginning in the fiscal year following the fiscal year in which it is determined, based on the Budget Act for that fiscal year, that this condition will be met. If a transfer is made for a fiscal year for which it is later determined that this condition has not been met, the amount of the transfer shall be appropriated and allocated from the Public School System Stabilization Account for the support of school districts and community college districts. No transfer shall be made for a year for which it was determined, based on the Budget Act for that fiscal year, that this condition would not be met but was subsequently determined to have been met in that year or a prior fiscal year.

(g) Notwithstanding any other provision of this section, no amount shall be transferred to the Public School System Stabilization Account for any fiscal year for which any of the provisions of subdivision (b) of Section 8 are suspended pursuant to subdivision (h) of Section 8.

(h) Notwithstanding any other provision of this section, for any fiscal year, the amount of a transfer to the Public School System Stabilization Account pursuant to subdivision (b) shall not exceed an amount that would result in a balance in the account that is in excess of 10 percent of the total allocations to school districts and community college districts from General Fund proceeds of taxes appropriated pursuant to Article XIII B and allocated local proceeds of taxes for that fiscal year pursuant to Section 8. For any fiscal year, General Fund proceeds of taxes that, but for this subdivision, would have been transferred to the Public School System Stabilization Account shall be applied by the State for the support of school districts and community colleges.

(i) In any fiscal year in which the amount required to be applied by the State for the support of school districts and community college districts for that fiscal year pursuant to Section 8 is less than the total allocations to school districts and community college districts from General Fund proceeds of taxes appropriated pursuant to Article XIII B and allocated local proceeds of taxes in the prior fiscal year, plus any allocations from the Public School System Stabilization Account in the prior fiscal year, less any transfers to the Public School System Stabilization Account in the prior fiscal year and any revenues allocated pursuant to subdivision (a) of Section 8.5, adjusted for the percentage change in average daily attendance and adjusted for the higher of the change in the cost of living pursuant to paragraph (1) of subdivision (e) of Section 8 of Article XIII B or the cost of living adjustment applied to school district and community college district general purpose apportionments, the amount of the deficiency shall be appropriated and allocated by the State from the Public

School System Stabilization Account for the support of school districts and community college districts.

(j) Funds transferred to the Public School System Stabilization Account shall be deemed, for purposes of Section 8, to be moneys applied by the State for the support of school districts and community college districts in the fiscal year for which the transfer is made, and not in the fiscal year in which moneys are appropriated from the account.

(k) Nothing in this section shall be construed to reduce the amount of the moneys required to be applied by the State for the support of school districts and community college districts pursuant to Sections 8 and 8.5.

(l) The Controller may utilize funds in the Public School System Stabilization Account, that he or she determines to currently be unnecessary for the purposes of this section, to help manage General Fund daily cashflow needs. Any use of funds by the Controller pursuant to this subdivision shall not interfere with the purposes of the Public School System Stabilization Account.

(Sec. 21 added Nov. 4, 2014, by Prop. 2. Res.Ch. 1, 2013-14 2nd Ex. Sess.)

SEC. 22.

(a) Upon the Governor's proclamation declaring a budget emergency and identifying the conditions constituting the emergency, the Legislature may pass a bill that does any of the following:

(1) Suspends or reduces by a specified dollar amount for one fiscal year the transfer of moneys from the General Fund to the Budget Stabilization Account required by Section 20.

(2) (A) Returns funds that have been transferred to the Budget Stabilization Account pursuant to Section 20 to the General Fund for appropriation to address the budget emergency.

(B) Not more than 50 percent of the balance in the Budget Stabilization Account may be returned to the General Fund for appropriation pursuant to subparagraph (A) in any fiscal year, unless funds in the Budget Stabilization Account have been returned to the General Fund for appropriation in the immediately preceding fiscal year.

(3) Suspends or reduces by a specified dollar amount for one fiscal year the transfer of moneys from the General Fund to the Public School System Stabilization Account required by Section 21.

(4) Appropriates funds transferred to the Public School System Stabilization Account pursuant to Section 21 and allocates those funds for the support of school districts and community college districts.

(b) For purposes of this section, "budget emergency" means any of the following:

(1) An emergency declared by the Governor, within the meaning of paragraph (2) of subdivision (c) of Section 3 of Article XIII B.

(2) (A) A determination by the Governor that estimated resources are inadequate to fund General Fund expenditures for the current or ensuing fiscal year, after setting aside funds for the reserve for liquidation of encumbrances, at a level equal to the highest amount of total General Fund expenditures estimated at the time of enactment of any of the three most recent Budget Acts, adjusted for both of the following:

(i) The annual percentage change in the cost of living for the State, as measured by the California Consumer Price Index.

(ii) The annual percentage growth in the civilian population of the State pursuant to subdivision (b) of Section 7901 of the Government Code.

(B) The maximum amount that may be withdrawn for a budget emergency determined under this paragraph shall not exceed either an amount that would result in a total General Fund expenditure level for a fiscal year that is greater than the highest amount of total General Fund expenditures estimated at the time of enactment of any of the three most recent Budget Acts, as calculated pursuant to subparagraph (A), or any limit imposed by subparagraph (B) of paragraph (2) of subdivision (a).

(Sec. 22 added Nov. 4, 2014, by Prop. 2. Res.Ch. 1, 2013-14 2nd Ex. Sess.)

SEC. 23.

The tax imposed by the California Healthcare, Research and Prevention Tobacco Tax Act of 2016 and the revenue derived therefrom, including investment interest, shall not be considered General Fund revenues for purposes of Section 8 and its implementing statutes, and shall not be considered "General Fund revenues," "state revenues," or "General Fund proceeds of taxes" for purposes of subdivisions (a) and (b) of Section 8 and its implementing statutes.

(Sec. 23 added Nov. 8, 2016, by Prop. 56. Initiative measure.)

ARTICLE XVIII AMENDING AND REVISING THE CONSTITUTION

[SEC. 1 - SEC. 4]
 (Article 18 added Nov. 3, 1970, by Prop. 16. Res.Ch. 187, 1970.)

SEC. 1.

The Legislature by rollcall vote entered in the journal, two-thirds of the membership of each house concurring, may propose an amendment or revision of the Constitution and in the same manner may amend or withdraw its proposal. Each amendment shall be so prepared and submitted that it can be voted on separately.
(Sec. 1 added Nov. 3, 1970, by Prop. 16. Res.Ch. 187, 1970.)

SEC. 2.

The Legislature by rollcall vote entered in the journal, two-thirds of the membership of each house concurring, may submit at a general election the question whether to call a convention to revise the Constitution. If the majority vote yes on that question, within 6 months the Legislature shall provide for the convention. Delegates to a constitutional convention shall be voters elected from districts as nearly equal in population as may be practicable.
(Sec. 2 added Nov. 3, 1970, by Prop. 16. Res.Ch. 187, 1970.)

SEC. 3.

The electors may amend the Constitution by initiative.
(Sec. 3 added Nov. 3, 1970, by Prop. 16. Res.Ch. 187, 1970.)

SEC. 4.

A proposed amendment or revision shall be submitted to the electors and, if approved by a majority of votes cast thereon, takes effect on the fifth day after the Secretary of State files the statement of the vote for the election at which the measure is voted on, but the measure may provide that it becomes operative after its effective date. If provisions of two or more measures approved at the same election conflict, the provisions of the measure receiving the highest number of affirmative votes shall prevail.

(Sec. 4 amended June 5, 2018, by Prop. 71. Res.Ch. 190, 2017.)

ARTICLE XIX MOTOR VEHICLE REVENUES

[SECTION 1 - SEC. 10]

(Article 19 heading renumbered from Art. 26 on June 8, 1976, by Prop. 14. Res.Ch. 5, 1976.)

SECTION 1.

The Legislature shall not borrow revenue from the Highway Users Tax Account, or its successor, and shall not use these revenues for purposes, or in ways, other than those specifically permitted by this article.

(Sec. 1 added Nov. 2, 2010, by Prop. 22. Initiative measure.)

SEC. 2.

Revenues from taxes imposed by the State on motor vehicle fuels for use in motor vehicles upon public streets and highways, over and above the costs of collection and any refunds authorized by law, shall be deposited into the Highway Users Tax Account (Section 2100 of the Streets and Highways Code) or its successor, which is hereby declared to be a trust fund, and shall be allocated monthly in accordance with Section 4, and shall be used solely for the following purposes:

(a) The research, planning, construction, improvement, maintenance, and operation of public streets and highways (and their related public facilities for nonmotorized traffic), including the mitigation of their environmental effects, the payment for property taken or damaged for such purposes, and the administrative costs necessarily incurred in the foregoing purposes.

(b) The research, planning, construction, and improvement of exclusive public mass transit guideways (and their related fixed facilities), including the mitigation of their environmental effects, the payment for property taken or damaged for such purposes, the administrative costs necessarily incurred in the foregoing purposes, and the maintenance of the structures and the immediate right-of-way for the public mass transit guideways, but excluding the maintenance and operating costs for mass transit power systems and mass transit passenger facilities, vehicles, equipment, and services.

(Sec. 2 renumbered from Sec. 1 on Nov. 2, 2010, by Prop. 22. Initiative measure.)

SEC. 3.

Revenues from fees and taxes imposed by the State upon vehicles or their use or operation, over and above the costs of collection and any refunds authorized by law, shall be used for the following purposes:

(a) The state administration and enforcement of laws regulating the use, operation, or registration of vehicles used upon the public streets and highways of this State, including the enforcement of traffic and vehicle laws by state agencies and the mitigation of the environmental effects of motor vehicle operation due to air and sound emissions.

(b) The purposes specified in Section 2 of this article.

(Sec. 3 renumbered from Sec. 2 on Nov. 2, 2010, by Prop. 22. Initiative measure.)

SEC. 4.

(a) Except as provided in subdivision (b), the statutory formulas in effect on June 30, 2009, which allocate the revenues described in Section 2 to cities, counties, and areas of the State shall remain in effect.

(b) The Legislature shall not modify the statutory allocations in effect on June 30, 2009, unless and until both of the following have occurred:

(1) The Legislature determines in accordance with this subdivision that another basis for an equitable, geographical, and jurisdictional distribution exists. Any future statutory revisions shall (A) provide for the allocation of these revenues, together with other similar revenues, in a manner which gives equal consideration to the transportation needs of all areas of the State and all segments of the population; and (B) be consistent with the orderly achievement of the adopted local, regional, and statewide goals for ground transportation in local general plans, regional transportation plans, and the California Transportation Plan;

(2) The process described in subdivision (c) has been completed.

(c) The Legislature shall not modify the statutory allocation pursuant to subdivision (b) until all of the following have occurred:

(1) The California Transportation Commission has held no less than four public hearings in different parts of the State to receive public input about the local and regional goals for ground transportation in that part of the State;

(2) The California Transportation Commission has published a report describing the input received at the public hearings and how the modification to the statutory allocation is consistent with the orderly achievement of local, regional, and statewide goals for ground transportation in local general plans, regional transportation plans, and the California Transportation Plan; and

(3) Ninety days have passed since the publication of the report by the California Transportation Commission.

(d) A statute enacted by the Legislature modifying the statutory allocations must be by a bill passed in each house of the Legislature by rollcall vote entered in the journal, two-thirds of the membership concurring, provided that the bill does not contain any other unrelated provision.

(e) The revenues allocated by statute to cities, counties, and areas of the State pursuant to this article may be used solely by the entity to which they are allocated, and solely for the purposes described in Sections 2, 5, or 6 of this article.

(f) The Legislature may not take any action which permanently or temporarily does any of the following: (1) changes the status of the Highway Users Tax Account as a trust fund; (2) borrows, diverts, or appropriates these revenues for purposes other than those described in subdivision (e); or (3) delays, defers, suspends, or otherwise interrupts the payment, allocation, distribution, disbursal, or transfer of revenues from taxes described in Section 2 to cities, counties, and areas of the State pursuant to the procedures in effect on June 30, 2009.

(Sec. 4 renumbered from Sec. 3 on Nov. 2, 2010, by Prop. 22. Initiative measure.)

SEC. 5.

Revenues allocated pursuant to Section 4 may not be expended for the purposes specified in subdivision (b) of Section 2, except for research and planning, until such use is approved by a majority of the votes cast on the proposition authorizing such use of such revenues in an election held throughout the county or counties, or a specified area of a county or counties, within which the revenues are to be expended. The Legislature may authorize the revenues approved for allocation or expenditure under this section to be pledged or used for the payment of principal and interest on voter-approved bonds issued for the purposes specified in subdivision (b) of Section 2.

(Sec. 5 renumbered from Sec. 4 on Nov. 2, 2010, by Prop. 22. Initiative measure.)

SEC. 6.

(a) Up to 25 percent of the revenues allocated to the State pursuant to Section 4 for the purposes specified in subdivision (a) of Section 2 of this article may be pledged or used by the State, upon approval by the voters and appropriation by the Legislature, for the payment of principal and interest on voter-approved bonds for such purposes issued by the State on and after November 2, 2010.

(b) Up to 25 percent of the revenues allocated to any city or county pursuant to Section 4 for the purposes specified in subdivision (a) of Section 2 of this article may be pledged or used only by any city or county for the payment of principal and interest on voter-approved bonds issued by that city or county for such purposes.

(Sec. 6 renumbered from Sec. 5 on Nov. 2, 2010, by Prop. 22. Initiative measure.)

SEC. 7.

If the Legislature reduces or repeals the taxes described in Section 2 and adopts an alternative source of revenue to replace the moneys derived from those taxes, the replacement revenue shall be deposited into the Highway Users Tax Account, dedicated to the purposes listed in Section 2, and allocated to cities, counties, and areas of the State pursuant to Section 4. All other provisions of this article shall apply to any revenues adopted by the Legislature to replace the moneys derived from the taxes described in Section 2.

(Sec. 7 added Nov. 2, 2010, by Prop. 22. Initiative measure.)

SEC. 8.

This article shall not affect or apply to fees or taxes imposed pursuant to the Sales and Use Tax Law or the Vehicle License Fee Law, and all amendments and additions now or hereafter made to such statutes.

(Sec. 8 renumbered from Sec. 7 on Nov. 2, 2010, by Prop. 22. Initiative measure.)

SEC. 9.

Notwithstanding Sections 2 and 3 of this article, any real property acquired by the expenditure of the designated tax revenues by an entity other than the State for the purposes authorized in those sections, but no longer required for such purposes, may be used for local public park and recreational purposes.

(Sec. 9 renumbered from Sec. 8 on Nov. 2, 2010, by Prop. 22. Initiative measure.)

SEC. 10.

Notwithstanding any other provision of this Constitution, the Legislature, by statute, with respect to surplus state property acquired by the expenditure of tax revenues designated in Sections 2 and 3 and located in the coastal zone, may authorize the transfer of such property, for a consideration at least equal to the acquisition cost paid by the State to acquire the property, to the Department of Parks and Recreation for state park purposes, or to the Department of Fish and Game for the protection and preservation of fish and wildlife habitat, or to the Wildlife Conservation Board for purposes of the Wildlife Conservation Law of 1947, or to the State Coastal Conservancy for the preservation of agricultural lands.

As used in this section, "coastal zone" means "coastal zone" as defined by Section 30103 of the Public Resources Code as such zone is described on January 1, 1977.

(Sec. 10 renumbered from Sec. 9 on Nov. 2, 2010, by Prop. 22. Initiative measure.)

ARTICLE XIX A LOANS FROM THE PUBLIC TRANSPORTATION ACCOUNT OR LOCAL TRANSPORTATION FUNDS

[SECTION 1 - SEC. 2]

(Article 19A added Nov. 3, 1998, by Prop. 2. Res.Ch. 77, 1998.)

SECTION 1.

(a) The Legislature shall not borrow revenues from the Public Transportation Account, or any successor account, and shall not use these revenues for purposes, or in ways, other than those specifically permitted by this article.

(b) The Public Transportation Account in the State Transportation Fund, or any successor account, is a trust fund. The Legislature may not change the status of the Public Transportation Account as a trust fund. Funds in the Public Transportation Account may not be loaned or otherwise transferred to the General Fund or any other fund or account in the State Treasury.

(c) All revenues specified in paragraphs (1) through (3), inclusive, of subdivision (a) of Section 7102 of the Revenue and Taxation Code, as that section read on June 1, 2001, shall be deposited no less than quarterly into the Public Transportation Account (Section 99310 of the Public Utilities Code), or its successor. The Legislature may not take any action which temporarily or permanently diverts or appropriates these revenues for purposes other than those described in subdivision (d), or delays, defers, suspends, or otherwise interrupts the quarterly deposit of these funds into the Public Transportation Account.

(d) Funds in the Public Transportation Account may only be used for transportation planning and mass transportation purposes. The revenues described in subdivision (c) are hereby continuously appropriated to the Controller without regard to fiscal years for allocation as follows:

(1) Fifty percent pursuant to subdivisions (a) through (f), inclusive, of Section 99315 of the Public Utilities Code, as that section read on July 30, 2009.

(2) Twenty-five percent pursuant to subdivision (b) of Section 99312 of the Public Utilities Code, as that section read on July 30, 2009.

(3) Twenty-five percent pursuant to subdivision (c) of Section 99312 of the Public Utilities Code, as that section read on July 30, 2009.

(e) For purposes of paragraph (1) of subdivision (d), "transportation planning" means only the purposes described in subdivisions (c) through (f), inclusive, of Section 99315 of the Public Utilities Code, as that section read on July 30, 2009.

(f) For purposes of this article, "mass transportation," "public transit," and "mass transit" have the same meaning as "public transportation." "Public transportation" means:

(1) (A) Surface transportation service provided to the general public, complementary paratransit service provided to persons with disabilities as required by 42 U.S.C. 12143, or similar transportation provided to people with disabilities or the elderly; (B) operated by bus, rail, ferry, or other conveyance on a fixed route, demand response, or otherwise regularly available basis; (C) generally for which a fare is charged; and (D) provided by any transit district, included transit district, municipal operator, included municipal operator, eligible municipal operator, or transit development board, as those terms were defined in Article 1 of Chapter 4 of Part 11 of Division 10 of the Public Utilities Code on January 1, 2009, a joint powers authority formed to provide mass transportation services, an agency described in subdivision (f) of Section 15975 of the Government Code, as that section read on January 1, 2009, any recipient of funds under Sections 99260, 99260.7, 99275, or subdivision (c) of Section 99400 of the Public Utilities Code, as those sections read on January 1, 2009, or a consolidated agency as defined in Section 132353.1 of the Public Utilities Code, as that section read on January 1, 2009.

(2) Surface transportation service provided by the Department of Transportation pursuant to subdivision (a)

of Section 99315 of the Public Utilities Code, as that section read on July 30, 2009.

(3) Public transit capital improvement projects, including those identified in subdivision (b) of Section 99315 of the Public Utilities Code, as that section read on July 30, 2009.

(g) All revenues specified in Sections 6051.8 and 6201.8 of the Revenue and Taxation Code, as those sections read on January 1, 2018, shall be deposited no less than quarterly into the Public Transportation Account, or its successor. Except as provided in Sections 16310 and 16381 of the Government Code, as those sections read on January 1, 2018, the Legislature may not take any action that temporarily or permanently diverts or appropriates these revenues for purposes other than those described in subdivision (d), or delays, defers, suspends, or otherwise interrupts the quarterly deposit of these revenues into the Public Transportation Account.

(Sec. 1 amended June 5, 2018, by Prop. 69. Res.Ch. 30, 2017.)

SEC. 2.

(a) As used in this section, a "local transportation fund" is a fund created under Section 29530 of the Government Code, or any successor to that statute.

(b) All local transportation funds are hereby designated trust funds. The Legislature may not change the status of local transportation funds as trust funds.

(c) A local transportation fund that has been created pursuant to law may not be abolished.

(d) Money in a local transportation fund shall be allocated only by the local government that created the fund, and only for the purposes authorized under Article 11 (commencing with Section 29530) of Chapter 2 of Division 3 of Title 3 of the Government Code and Chapter 4 (commencing with Section 99200) of Part 11 of Division 10 of the Public Utilities Code, as those provisions existed on October 1, 1997. Neither the county nor the Legislature may authorize the expenditure of money in a local transportation fund for purposes other than those specified in this subdivision.

(e) This section constitutes the sole method of allocating, distributing, and using the revenues in a local transportation fund. The purposes described in subdivision (d) are the sole purposes for which the revenues in a local transportation fund may be used. The Legislature may not enact a statute or take any other action which, permanently or temporarily, does any of the following:

(1) Transfers, diverts, or appropriates the revenues in a local transportation fund for any other purpose than those described in subdivision (d);

(2) Authorizes the expenditures of the revenue in a local transportation fund for any other purpose than those described in subdivision (d);

(3) Borrows or loans the revenues in a local transportation fund, regardless of whether these revenues remain in the Retail Sales Tax Fund in the State Treasury or are transferred to another fund or account.

(f) The percentage of the tax imposed pursuant to Section 7202 of the Revenue and Taxation Code allocated to local transportation funds shall not be reduced below the percentage that was transmitted to such funds during the 2008 calendar year. Revenues allocated to local transportation funds shall be transmitted in accordance with Section 7204 of the Revenue and Taxation Code and deposited into local transportation funds in accordance with Section 29530 of the Government Code, as those sections read on June 30, 2009.

(Sec. 2 amended Nov. 2, 2010, by Prop. 22. Initiative measure.)

ARTICLE XIX B MOTOR VEHICLE FUEL SALES TAX REVENUES AND TRANSPORTATION IMPROVEMENT FUNDING

[SECTION 1 - SEC. 2]

(Article 19B added March 5, 2002, by Prop. 42. Res.Ch. 87, 2001.)

SECTION 1.

The Legislature shall not borrow revenues from the Transportation Investment Fund, or its successor, and shall not use these revenues for purposes, or in ways, other than those specifically permitted by this article.

(Sec. 1 added Nov. 2, 2010, by Prop. 22. Initiative measure.)

SEC. 2.

(a) For the 2003–04 fiscal year and each fiscal year thereafter, all revenues that are collected during the fiscal year from taxes under the Sales and Use Tax Law (Part 1 (commencing with Section 6001) of Division 2 of the Revenue and Taxation Code), or any successor to that law, upon the sale, storage, use, or other consumption in this State of motor vehicle fuel, as defined for purposes of the Motor Vehicle Fuel License Tax Law (Part 2 (commencing with Section 7301) of Division 2 of the Revenue and Taxation Code), shall be deposited into the Transportation Investment Fund or its successor, which is hereby created in the State Treasury and which is hereby declared to be a trust fund. The Legislature may not change the status of the Transportation Investment Fund as a trust fund.

(b) (1) For the 2003–04 to 2007–08 fiscal years, inclusive, moneys in the Transportation Investment Fund shall be allocated, upon appropriation by the Legislature, in accordance with Section 7104 of the Revenue and Taxation Code as that section read on March 6, 2002.

(2) For the 2008–09 fiscal year and each fiscal year thereafter, moneys in the Transportation Investment Fund shall be allocated solely for the following purposes:

(A) Public transit and mass transportation. Moneys appropriated for public transit and mass transportation shall be allocated as follows: (i) Twenty-five percent pursuant to subdivision (b) of Section 99312 of the Public Utilities Code, as that section read on July 30, 2009; (ii) Twenty-five percent pursuant to subdivision (c) of Section 99312 of the Public Utilities Code, as that section read on July 30, 2009; and (iii) Fifty percent for the purposes of subdivisions (a) and (b) of Section 99315 of the Public Utilities Code, as that section read on July 30, 2009.

(B) Transportation capital improvement projects, subject to the laws governing the State Transportation Improvement Program, or any successor to that program.

(C) Street and highway maintenance, rehabilitation, reconstruction, or storm damage repair conducted by cities, including a city and county.

(D) Street and highway maintenance, rehabilitation, reconstruction, or storm damage repair conducted by counties, including a city and county.

(c) For the 2008–09 fiscal year and each fiscal year thereafter, moneys in the Transportation Investment Fund are hereby continuously appropriated to the Controller without regard to fiscal years, which shall be allocated as follows:

(A) Twenty percent of the moneys for the purposes set forth in subparagraph (A) of paragraph (2) of subdivision (b).

(B) Forty percent of the moneys for the purposes set forth in subparagraph (B) of paragraph (2) of subdivision (b).

(C) Twenty percent of the moneys for the purposes set forth in subparagraph (C) of paragraph (2) of subdivision (b).

(D) Twenty percent of the moneys for the purposes set forth in subparagraph (D) of paragraph (2) of subdivision (b).

(d) The Legislature may not enact a statute that modifies the percentage shares set forth in subdivision (c) until all of the following have occurred:

(1) The California Transportation Commission has held no less than four public hearings in different parts of the State to receive public input about the need for public transit, mass transportation, transportation capital improvement projects, and street and highway maintenance;

(2) The California Transportation Commission has published a report describing the input received at the public hearings and how the modification to the statutory allocation is consistent with the orderly achievement of local, regional and statewide goals for public transit, mass transportation, transportation capital improvements, and street and highway maintenance in a manner that is consistent with local general plans, regional transportation plans, and the California Transportation Plan;

(3) Ninety days have passed since the publication of the report by the California Transportation Commission.

(4) The statute enacted by the Legislature pursuant to this subdivision must be by a bill passed in each house of the Legislature by rollcall vote entered in the journal, two-thirds of the membership concurring, provided that the bill does not contain any other unrelated provision and that the revenues described in subdivision (a) are expended solely for the purposes set forth in paragraph (2) of subdivision (b).

(e) (1) An amount equivalent to the total amount of revenues that were not transferred from the General Fund of the State to the Transportation Investment Fund, as of July 1, 2007, because of a suspension of transfer of revenues pursuant to this section as it read on January 1, 2006, but excluding the amount to be paid to the Transportation Deferred Investment Fund pursuant to Section 63048.65 of the Government Code, shall be transferred from the General Fund to the Transportation Investment Fund no later than June 30, 2016. Until this total amount has been transferred, the amount of transfer payments to be made in each fiscal year shall not be less than one-tenth of the total amount required to be transferred by June 30, 2016. The transferred revenues shall be allocated solely for the purposes set forth in this section as if they had been received in the absence of a suspension of transfer of revenues.

(2) The Legislature may provide by statute for the issuance of bonds by the state or local agencies, as applicable, that are secured by the minimum transfer payments required by paragraph (1). Proceeds from the sale of those bonds shall be allocated solely for the purposes set forth in this section as if they were revenues subject to allocation pursuant to paragraph (2) of subdivision (b).

(f) This section constitutes the sole method of allocating, distributing, and using the revenues described in subdivision (a). The purposes described in paragraph (2) of subdivision (b) are the sole purposes for which the revenues described in subdivision (a) may be used. The Legislature may not enact a statute or take any other action which, permanently or temporarily, does any of the following:

(1) Transfers, diverts, or appropriates the revenues described in subdivision (a) for any other purposes than those described in paragraph (2) of subdivision (b);

(2) Authorizes the expenditures of the revenues described in subdivision (a) for any other purposes than those described in paragraph (2) of subdivision (b) or;

(3) Borrows or loans the revenues described in subdivision (a), regardless of whether these revenues remain in the Transportation Investment Fund or are transferred to another fund or account such as the Public Transportation Account, a trust fund in the State Transportation Fund.

(g) For purposes of this article, "mass transportation," "public transit" and "mass transit" have the same meanings as "public transportation." "Public transportation" means:

(1) (A) Surface transportation service provided to the general public, complementary paratransit service provided to persons with disabilities as required by 42 U.S.C. 12143, or similar transportation provided to people with disabilities or the elderly; (B) operated by bus, rail, ferry, or other conveyance on a fixed route, demand response, or otherwise regularly available basis; (C) generally for which a fare is charged; and (D) provided by any transit district,

included transit district, municipal operator, included municipal operator, eligible municipal operator, or transit development board, as those terms were defined in Article 1 of Chapter 4 of Part 11 of Division 10 of the Public Utilities Code on January 1, 2009, a joint powers authority formed to provide mass transportation services, an agency described in subdivision (f) of Section 15975 of the Government Code, as that section read on January 1, 2009, any recipient of funds under Sections 99260, 99260.7, 99275, or subdivision (c) of Section 99400 of the Public Utilities Code, as those sections read on January 1, 2009, or a consolidated agency as defined in Section 132353.1 of the Public Utilities Code, as that section read on January 1, 2009.

(2) Surface transportation service provided by the Department of Transportation pursuant to subdivision (a) of Section 99315 of the Public Utilities Code, as that section read on July 30, 2009.

(3) Public transit capital improvement projects, including those identified in subdivision (b) of Section 99315 of the Public Utilities Code, as that section read on July 30, 2009.

(h) If the Legislature reduces or repeals the taxes described in subdivision (a) and adopts an alternative source of revenue to replace the moneys derived from those taxes, the replacement revenue shall be deposited into the Transportation Investment Fund, dedicated to the purposes listed in paragraph (2) of subdivision (b), and allocated pursuant to subdivision (c). All other provisions of this article shall apply to any revenues adopted by the Legislature to replace the moneys derived from the taxes described in subdivision (a).

(Sec. 2 renumbered from Sec. 1 on Nov. 2, 2010, by Prop. 22. Initiative measure.)

ARTICLE XIX C [ENFORCEMENT OF CERTAIN PROVISIONS]

[SECTION 1 - SEC. 4]

(Article 19C added Nov. 2, 2010, by Prop. 22. Initiative measure.)

SECTION 1.

If any challenge to invalidate an action that violates Article XIX, XIX A, or XIX B is successful either by way of a final judgment, settlement, or resolution by administrative or legislative action, there is hereby continuously appropriated from the General Fund to the Controller, without regard to fiscal years, that amount of revenue necessary to restore the fund or account from which the revenues were unlawfully taken or diverted to its financial status had the unlawful action not been taken.

(Sec. 1 added Nov. 2, 2010, by Prop. 22. Initiative measure.)

SEC. 2.

If any challenge to invalidate an action that violates Section 24 or Section 25.5 of Article XIII is successful either by way of a final judgment, settlement, or resolution by administrative or legislative action, there is hereby continuously appropriated from the General Fund to the local government an amount of revenue equal to the amount of revenue unlawfully taken or diverted.

(Sec. 2 added Nov. 2, 2010, by Prop. 22. Initiative measure.)

SEC. 3.

Interest calculated at the Pooled Money Investment Fund rate from the date or dates the revenues were unlawfully taken or diverted shall accrue to the amounts required to be restored pursuant to this section. Within 30 days from the date a challenge is successful, the Controller shall make the transfer required by the continuous appropriation and issue a notice to the parties that the transfer has been completed.

(Sec. 3 added Nov. 2, 2010, by Prop. 22. Initiative measure.)

SEC. 4.

If in any challenge brought pursuant to this section a restraining order or preliminary injunction is issued, the plaintiffs or petitioners shall not be required to post a bond obligating the plaintiffs or petitioners to indemnify the government defendants or the State of California for any damage the restraining order or preliminary injunction may cause.

(Sec. 4 added Nov. 2, 2010, by Prop. 22. Initiative measure.)

ARTICLE XIX D VEHICLE LICENSE FEE REVENUES FOR TRANSPORTATION PURPOSES

[SECTION 1- SECTION 1.]

(Article 19D added June 5, 2018, by Prop. 69. Res.Ch. 30, 2017.)

SECTION 1.

(a) Notwithstanding Section 8 of Article XIX, revenues derived from vehicle fees imposed under the Vehicle License Fee Law pursuant to Chapter 6 (commencing with Section 11050) of Part 5 of Division 2 of the Revenue and Taxation Code, or its successor, over and above the costs of collection and any refunds authorized by law, shall be used solely for transportation purposes, as defined by Section 11050 of the Revenue and Taxation Code, as that section read upon enactment of the Road Repair and Accountability Act of 2017.

(b) The revenues described in subdivision (a) shall not be used for the payment of principal and interest on state transportation general obligation bonds that were authorized by the voters on or before November 8, 2016, nor shall those revenues be used for payment of principal and interest on state transportation general obligation bond acts approved by the voters after that date, unless the bond act expressly authorizes that use.

(c) Except as provided in Sections 16310 and 16381 of the Government Code, as those sections read on January 1, 2018, the Legislature shall not borrow the revenues described in subdivision (a), and shall not use these revenues for purposes, or in ways, other than as authorized in subdivisions (a) or (b).

(Sec. 1 added June 5, 2018, by Prop. 69. Res.Ch. 30, 2017.)

ARTICLE XX MISCELLANEOUS SUBJECTS
[SEC. 1 - SEC. 23]

(Article 20 adopted 1879.)

SEC. 1.

Notwithstanding the provisions of Section 6 of Article XI, the County of Sacramento and all or any of the cities within the County of Sacramento may be consolidated as a charter city and county as provided by statute, with the approval of a majority of the electors of the county voting on the question of such consolidation and upon such other vote as the Legislature may prescribe in such statute. The charter City and County of Sacramento shall be a charter city and a charter county. Its charter city powers supersede conflicting charter county powers.

(Sec. 1 added June 4, 1974, by Prop. 8. Res.Ch. 159, 1973.)

SEC. 1.5.

The Legislature shall protect, by law, from forced sale a certain portion of the homestead and other property of all heads of families.

(Sec. 1.5 added June 8, 1976, by Prop. 14. Res.Ch. 5, 1976, clause 38, as revised by Res.Ch. 24, Amdt. 7.)

SEC. 2.

Except for tax exemptions provided in Article XIII, the rights, powers, privileges, and confirmations conferred by Sections 10 and 15 of Article IX in effect on January 1, 1973, relating to Stanford University and the Huntington Library and Art Gallery, are continued in effect.

(Sec. 2 renumbered from Sec. 6 on June 8, 1976, by Prop. 14. Res.Ch. 5, 1976.)

SEC. 3.

Members of the Legislature, and all public officers and employees, executive, legislative, and judicial, except such inferior officers and employees as may be by law exempted, shall, before they enter upon the duties of their respective offices, take and subscribe the following oath or affirmation:

"I, _____, do solemnly swear (or affirm) that I will support and defend the Constitution of the United States and the Constitution of the State of California against all enemies, foreign and domestic; that I will bear true faith and allegiance to the Constitution of the United States and the Constitution of the State of California; that I take this obligation freely, without any mental reservation or purpose of evasion; and that I will well and faithfully discharge the duties upon which I am about to enter.

"And I do further swear (or affirm) that I do not advocate, nor am I a member of any party or organization, political or otherwise, that now advocates the overthrow of the Government of the United States or of the State of California by force or violence or other unlawful means; that within the five years immediately preceding the taking of this oath (or affirmation) I have not been a member of any party or organization, political or otherwise, that advocated the overthrow of the Government of the United States or of the State of California by force or violence or other unlawful means except as follows:

_____ (If no affiliations, write in the words "No Exceptions")
_____

and that during such time as I hold the office of _____ (name of office) _____

I will not advocate nor become a member of any party or organization, political or otherwise, that advocates the overthrow of the Government of the United States or of the State of California by force or violence or other unlawful means."

And no other oath, declaration, or test, shall be required as a qualification for any public office or employment.

"Public officer and employee" includes every officer and employee of the State, including the University of California, every county, city, city and county, district, and authority, including any department, division, bureau, board, commission, agency, or instrumentality of any of the foregoing.

(Sec. 3 amended Nov. 4, 1952, by Prop. 6. Res.Ch. 69, 1951.)

SEC. 4.

The Legislature shall not pass any laws permitting the leasing or alienation of any franchise, so as to relieve the franchise or property held thereunder from the liabilities of the lessor or grantor, lessee, or grantee, contracted or incurred in the operation, use, or enjoyment of such franchise, or any of its privileges.

(Sec. 4 renumbered from Sec. 7 on June 8, 1976, by Prop. 14. Res.Ch. 5, 1976.)

SEC. 5.

All laws now in force in this State concerning corporations and all laws that may be hereafter passed pursuant to this section may be altered from time to time or repealed.

(Sec. 5 renumbered from Sec. 24 on June 8, 1976, by Prop. 14. Res.Ch. 5, 1976.)

SEC. 6.

Any legislator whose term of office is reduced by operation of the amendment to subdivision (a) of Section 2 of Article IV adopted by the people in 1972 shall, notwithstanding any other provision of this Constitution, be entitled to retirement benefits and compensation as if the term of office had not been so reduced.

(Sec. 6 renumbered from Sec. 25 on June 8, 1976, by Prop. 14. Res.Ch. 5, 1976.)

SEC. 7.

The limitations on the number of terms prescribed by Section 2 of Article IV, Sections 2 and 11 of Article V, Section 2 of Article IX, and Section 17 of Article XIII apply only to terms to which persons are elected or appointed on or after November 6, 1990, except that an incumbent Senator whose office is not on the ballot for the general election on that date may serve only one additional term. Those limitations shall not apply to any unexpired term to which a person is elected or appointed if the remainder of the term is less than half of the full term.

(Sec. 7 added Nov. 6, 1990, by Prop. 140. Initiative measure.)

SEC. 22.

The State of California, subject to the internal revenue laws of the United States, shall have the exclusive right and power to license and regulate the manufacture, sale, purchase, possession and transportation of alcoholic beverages within the State, and subject to the laws of the United States regulating commerce between foreign nations and among the states shall have the exclusive right and power to regulate the importation into and exportation from the State, of alcoholic beverages. In the exercise of these rights and powers, the Legislature shall not constitute the State or any agency thereof a manufacturer or seller of alcoholic beverages.

All alcoholic beverages may be bought, sold, served, consumed and otherwise disposed of in premises which shall be licensed as provided by the Legislature. In providing for the licensing of premises, the Legislature may provide for the issuance of, among other licenses, licenses for the following types of premises where the alcoholic beverages specified in the licenses may be sold and served for consumption upon the premises:

(a) For bona fide public eating places, as defined by the Legislature.

(b) For public premises in which food shall not be sold or served as in a bona fide public eating place, but upon which premises the Legislature may permit the sale or service of food products incidental to the sale and service of alcoholic beverages. No person under the age of 21 years shall be permitted to enter and remain in any such premises without lawful business therein.

(c) For public premises for the sale and service of beers alone.

(d) Under such conditions as the Legislature may impose, for railroad dining or club cars, passenger ships, common carriers by air, and bona fide clubs after such clubs have been lawfully operated for not less than one year.

The sale, furnishing, giving, or causing to be sold, furnished, or giving away of any alcoholic beverage to any person under the age of 21 years is hereby prohibited, and no person shall sell, furnish, give, or cause to be sold, furnished, or given away any alcoholic beverage to any person under the age of 21 years, and no person under the age of 21 years shall purchase any alcoholic beverage.

The Director of Alcoholic Beverage Control shall be the head of the Department of Alcoholic Beverage Control, shall be appointed by the Governor subject to confirmation by a majority vote of all of the members elected to the Senate, and shall serve at the pleasure of the Governor. The director may be removed from office by the Governor, and the Legislature shall have the power, by a majority vote of all members elected to each house, to remove the director from office for dereliction of duty or corruption or incompetency. The director may appoint three persons who shall be exempt from civil service, in addition to the person he is authorized to appoint by Section 4 of Article XXIV.

The Department of Alcoholic Beverage Control shall have the exclusive power, except as herein provided and in accordance with laws enacted by the Legislature, to license the manufacture, importation and sale of alcoholic beverages in this State, and to collect license fees or occupation taxes on account thereof. The department shall have the power, in its discretion, to deny, suspend or revoke any specific alcoholic beverages license if it shall determine for good cause that the granting or continuance of such license would be contrary to public welfare or morals, or that a person seeking or holding a license has violated any law prohibiting conduct involving moral turpitude. It shall be unlawful for any person other than a licensee of said department to manufacture, import or sell alcoholic beverages in this State.

The Alcoholic Beverage Control Appeals Board shall consist of three members appointed by the Governor, subject to confirmation by a majority vote of all of the members elected to the Senate. Each member, at the time of his initial appointment, shall be a resident of a different county from the one in which either of the other members resides. The members of the board may be removed from office by the Governor, and the Legislature shall have the power, by a majority vote of all members elected to each house, to remove any member from office for dereliction of duty or corruption or incompetency.

When any person aggrieved thereby appeals from a decision of the department ordering any penalty assessment, issuing, denying, transferring, suspending or revoking any license for the manufacture, importation, or sale of alcoholic beverages, the board shall review the decision subject to such limitations as may be imposed by the Legislature. In such cases, the board shall not receive evidence in addition to that considered by the department. Review by the board of a decision of the department shall be limited to the questions whether the department has proceeded without or in excess of its jurisdiction, whether the department has proceeded in the manner required by law, whether the decision is supported by the findings, and whether the findings are supported by substantial evidence in the light of the whole record. In appeals where the board finds that there is relevant evidence which, in the exercise of reasonable diligence, could not have been produced or which was improperly excluded at the hearing before the department it may enter an order remanding the matter to the department for reconsideration in the light of such evidence. In all other appeals the board shall enter an order either affirming or reversing the decision of the department. When the order reverses the decision of the department, the board may direct the reconsideration of the matter in the light of its order and may direct the department to take such further action as is specially enjoined upon it by law, but the order shall not limit or control in any way the discretion vested by law in the department. Orders of the board shall be subject to judicial review upon petition of the director or any party aggrieved by such order.

A concurrent resolution for the removal of either the director or any member of the board may be introduced in the Legislature only if five Members of the Senate, or 10 Members of the Assembly, join as authors.

Until the Legislature shall otherwise provide, the privilege of keeping, buying, selling, serving, and otherwise disposing of alcoholic beverages in bona fide hotels, restaurants, cafes, cafeterias, railroad dining or club cars, passenger ships, and other public eating places, and in bona fide clubs after such clubs have been lawfully operated for not less than one year, and the privilege of keeping, buying, selling, serving, and otherwise disposing of beers on any premises open to the general public shall be licensed and regulated under the applicable provisions of the Alcoholic Beverage Control Act, insofar as the same are not inconsistent with the provisions hereof, and excepting that the license fee to be charged bona fide hotels, restaurants, cafes, cafeterias, railroad dining or club cars, passenger ships, and other public eating places, and any bona fide clubs after such clubs have been lawfully operated for not less than one year, for the privilege of keeping, buying, selling, or otherwise disposing of alcoholic beverages, shall be the amounts prescribed as of the operative date hereof, subject to the power of the Legislature to change such fees.

The State Board of Equalization shall assess and collect such excise taxes as are or may be imposed by the Legislature on account of the manufacture, importation and sale of alcoholic beverages in this State.

The Legislature may authorize, subject to reasonable restrictions, the sale in retail stores of alcoholic beverages contained in the original packages, where such alcoholic beverages are not to be consumed on the premises where sold; and may provide for the issuance of all types of licenses necessary to carry on the activities referred to in the first paragraph of this section, including, but not limited to, licenses necessary for the manufacture, production, processing, importation, exportation, transportation, wholesaling, distribution, and sale of any and all kinds of alcoholic beverages.

The Legislature shall provide for apportioning the amounts collected for license fees or occupation taxes under the provisions hereof between the State and the cities, counties and cities and counties of the State, in such manner as the Legislature may deem proper.

All constitutional provisions and laws inconsistent with the provisions hereof are hereby repealed.

The provisions of this section shall be self-executing, but nothing herein shall prohibit the Legislature from enacting laws implementing and not inconsistent with such provisions.

This amendment shall become operative on January 1, 1957.

(Sec. 22 amended Nov. 6, 1956, by Prop. 5. Res.Ch. 252, 1955. Operative Jan. 1, 1957.)

SEC. 23.

Notwithstanding any other provision of this Constitution, the Speaker of the Assembly shall be an ex officio member, having equal rights and duties with the nonlegislative members, of any state agency created by the Legislature in the field of public higher education which is charged with the management, administration, and control of the State College System of California.

(Sec. 23 added Nov. 3, 1970, by Prop. 7. Res.Ch. 169, 1970.)

ARTICLE XXI REDISTRICTING OF SENATE, ASSEMBLY, CONGRESSIONAL AND BOARD OF EQUALIZATION DISTRICTS

[SECTION 1 - SEC. 3]

(Heading of Article 21 amended Nov. 4, 2008, by Prop. 11. Initiative measure.)

SECTION 1.

In the year following the year in which the national census is taken under the direction of Congress at the beginning of each decade, the Citizens Redistricting Commission described in Section 2 shall adjust the boundary lines of the congressional, State Senatorial, Assembly, and Board of Equalization districts (also known as "redistricting") in conformance with the standards and process set forth in Section 2.

(Sec. 1 amended Nov. 2, 2010, by Prop. 20. Initiative measure.)

SEC. 2.

(a) The Citizens Redistricting Commission shall be created no later than December 31 in 2010, and in each year ending in the number zero thereafter.

(b) The commission shall: (1) conduct an open and transparent process enabling full public consideration of and comment on the drawing of district lines; (2) draw district lines according to the redistricting criteria specified in this article; and (3) conduct themselves with integrity and fairness.

(c) (1) The selection process is designed to produce a commission that is independent from legislative influence and reasonably representative of this State's diversity.

(2) The commission shall consist of 14 members, as follows: five who are registered with the largest political party in California based on registration, five who are registered with the second largest political party in California based on registration, and four who are not registered with either of the two largest political parties in California based on registration.

(3) Each commission member shall be a voter who has been continuously registered in California with the same political party or unaffiliated with a political party and who has not changed political party affiliation for five or more years immediately preceding the date of his or her appointment. Each commission member shall have voted in two of the last three statewide general elections immediately preceding his or her application.

(4) The term of office of each member of the commission expires upon the appointment of the first member of the succeeding commission.

(5) Nine members of the commission shall constitute a quorum. Nine or more affirmative votes shall be required for any official action. The four final redistricting maps must be approved by at least nine affirmative votes which must include at least three votes of members registered from each of the two largest political parties in California based on registration and three votes from members who are not registered with either of these two political parties.

(6) Each commission member shall apply this article in a manner that is impartial and that reinforces public confidence in the integrity of the redistricting process. A commission member shall be ineligible for a period of 10 years beginning from the date of appointment to hold elective public office at the federal, state, county, or city level in this State. A member of the commission shall be ineligible for a period of five years beginning from the date of appointment to hold appointive federal, state, or local public office, to serve as paid staff for, or as a paid consultant to, the Board of Equalization, the Congress, the Legislature, or any individual legislator, or to register as a federal, state or local lobbyist in this State.

(d) The commission shall establish single-member districts for the Senate, Assembly, Congress, and State Board of

Equalization pursuant to a mapping process using the following criteria as set forth in the following order of priority:

(1) Districts shall comply with the United States Constitution. Congressional districts shall achieve population equality as nearly as is practicable, and Senatorial, Assembly, and State Board of Equalization districts shall have reasonably equal population with other districts for the same office, except where deviation is required to comply with the federal Voting Rights Act or allowable by law.

(2) Districts shall comply with the federal Voting Rights Act (42 U.S.C. Sec. 1971 and following).

(3) Districts shall be geographically contiguous.

(4) The geographic integrity of any city, county, city and county, local neighborhood, or local community of interest shall be respected in a manner that minimizes their division to the extent possible without violating the requirements of any of the preceding subdivisions. A community of interest is a contiguous population which shares common social and economic interests that should be included within a single district for purposes of its effective and fair representation. Examples of such shared interests are those common to an urban area, a rural area, an industrial area, or an agricultural area, and those common to areas in which the people share similar living standards, use the same transportation facilities, have similar work opportunities, or have access to the same media of communication relevant to the election process. Communities of interest shall not include relationships with political parties, incumbents, or political candidates.

(5) To the extent practicable, and where this does not conflict with the criteria above, districts shall be drawn to encourage geographical compactness such that nearby areas of population are not bypassed for more distant population.

(6) To the extent practicable, and where this does not conflict with the criteria above, each Senate district shall be comprised of two whole, complete, and adjacent Assembly districts, and each Board of Equalization district

shall be comprised of 10 whole, complete, and adjacent Senate districts.

(e) The place of residence of any incumbent or political candidate shall not be considered in the creation of a map. Districts shall not be drawn for the purpose of favoring or discriminating against an incumbent, political candidate, or political party.

(f) Districts for the Congress, Senate, Assembly, and State Board of Equalization shall be numbered consecutively commencing at the northern boundary of the State and ending at the southern boundary.

(g) By August 15 in 2011, and in each year ending in the number one thereafter, the commission shall approve four final maps that separately set forth the district boundary lines for the congressional, Senatorial, Assembly, and State Board of Equalization districts. Upon approval, the commission shall certify the four final maps to the Secretary of State.

(h) The commission shall issue, with each of the four final maps, a report that explains the basis on which the commission made its decisions in achieving compliance with the criteria listed in subdivision (d) and shall include definitions of the terms and standards used in drawing each final map.

(i) Each certified final map shall be subject to referendum in the same manner that a statute is subject to referendum pursuant to Section 9 of Article II. The date of certification of a final map to the Secretary of State shall be deemed the enactment date for purposes of Section 9 of Article II.

(j) If the commission does not approve a final map by at least the requisite votes or if voters disapprove a certified final map in a referendum, the Secretary of State shall immediately petition the California Supreme Court for an order directing the appointment of special masters to adjust the boundary lines of that map in accordance with the redistricting criteria and requirements set forth in subdivisions (d), (e), and (f). Upon its approval of the masters' map, the court shall certify the resulting map to the Secretary of State, which map shall constitute the certified final map for the subject type of district.

(Sec. 2 amended Nov. 2, 2010, by Prop. 20. Initiative measure.)

SEC. 3.

(a) The commission has the sole legal standing to defend any action regarding a certified final map, and shall inform the Legislature if it determines that funds or other resources provided for the operation of the commission are not adequate. The Legislature shall provide adequate funding to defend any action regarding a certified map. The commission has sole authority to determine whether the Attorney General or other legal counsel retained by the commission shall assist in the defense of a certified final map.

(b) (1) The California Supreme Court has original and exclusive jurisdiction in all proceedings in which a certified final map is challenged or is claimed not to have taken timely effect.

(2) Any registered voter in this state may file a petition for a writ of mandate or writ of prohibition, within 45 days after the commission has certified a final map to the Secretary of State, to bar the Secretary of State from implementing the plan on the grounds that the filed plan violates this Constitution, the United States Constitution, or any federal or state statute. Any registered voter in this state may also file a petition for a writ of mandate or writ of prohibition to seek relief where a certified final map is subject to a referendum measure that is likely to qualify and stay the timely implementation of the map.

(3) The California Supreme Court shall give priority to ruling on a petition for a writ of mandate or a writ of prohibition filed pursuant to paragraph (2). If the court determines that a final certified map violates this Constitution, the United States Constitution, or any federal or state statute, the court shall fashion the relief that it deems appropriate, including, but not limited to, the relief set forth in subdivision (j) of Section 2.

(Sec. 3 amended Nov. 2, 2010, by Prop. 20. Initiative measure.)

ARTICLE XXII [ARCHITECTURAL AND ENGINEERING SERVICES]

[SECTION 1 - SEC. 2]

(Article 22 added Nov. 7, 2000, by Prop. 35. Initiative measure.)

SECTION 1.

The State of California and all other governmental entities, including, but not limited to, cities, counties, cities and counties, school districts and other special districts, local and regional agencies and joint power agencies, shall be allowed to contract with qualified private entities for architectural and engineering services for all public works of improvement. The choice and authority to contract shall extend to all phases of project development including permitting and environmental studies, rights-of-way services, design phase services and construction phase services. The choice and authority shall exist without regard to funding sources whether federal, state, regional, local or private, whether or not the project is programmed by a state, regional or local governmental entity, and whether or not the completed project is a part of any state owned or state operated system or facility.

(Sec. 1 added Nov. 7, 2000, by Prop. 35. Initiative measure.)

SEC. 2.

Nothing contained in Article VII of this Constitution shall be construed to limit, restrict or prohibit the State or any other governmental entities, including, but not limited to, cities, counties, cities and counties, school districts and other special districts, local and regional agencies and joint power agencies, from contracting with private entities for the performance of architectural and engineering services.

(Sec. 2 added Nov. 7, 2000, by Prop. 35. Initiative measure.)

ARTICLE XXXIV PUBLIC HOUSING PROJECT LAW

[Section 1 - Section 4]

(Article 34 added Nov. 7, 1950, by Prop. 10. Initiative measure.)

Section 1.

No low rent housing project shall hereafter be developed, constructed, or acquired in any manner by any state public body until, a majority of the qualified electors of the city, town or county, as the case may be, in which it is proposed to develop, construct, or acquire the same, voting upon such issue, approve such project by voting in favor thereof at an election to be held for that purpose, or at any general or special election.

For the purposes of this Article the term "low rent housing project" shall mean any development composed of urban or rural dwellings, apartments or other living accommodations for persons of low income, financed in whole or in part by the Federal Government or a state public body or to which the Federal Government or a state public body extends assistance by supplying all or part of the labor, by guaranteeing the payment of liens, or otherwise. For the purposes of this Article only there shall be excluded from the term "low rent housing project" any such project where there shall be in existence on the effective date hereof, a contract for financial assistance between any state public body and the Federal Government in respect to such project.

For the purposes of this Article only "persons of low income" shall mean persons or families who lack the amount of income which is necessary (as determined by the state public body developing, constructing, or acquiring the housing project) to enable them, without financial assistance, to live in decent, safe and sanitary dwellings, without overcrowding.

For the purposes of this Article the term "state public body" shall mean this State, or any city, city and county, county, district, authority, agency, or any other subdivision or public body of this State.

For the purposes of this Article the term "Federal Government" shall mean the United States of America, or any agency or instrumentality, corporate or otherwise, of the United States of America.

(Sec. 1 added Nov. 7, 1950, by Prop. 10. Initiative measure.)

Section 2.

The provisions of this Article shall be self-executing but legislation not in conflict herewith may be enacted to facilitate its operation.

(Sec. 2 added Nov. 7, 1950, by Prop. 10. Initiative measure.)

Section 3.

If any portion, section or clause of this article, or the application thereof to any person or circumstance, shall for any reason be declared unconstitutional or held invalid, the remainder of this Article, or the application of such portion, section or clause to other persons or circumstances, shall not be affected thereby.

(Sec. 3 added Nov. 7, 1950, by Prop. 10. Initiative measure.)

Section 4.

The provisions of this Article shall supersede all provisions of this Constitution and laws enacted thereunder in conflict therewith.

(Sec. 4 added Nov. 7, 1950, by Prop. 10. Initiative measure.)

ARTICLE XXXV MEDICAL RESEARCH
[SECTION 1 - SEC. 7]

(Article 35 added Nov. 2, 2004, by Prop. 71. Initiative measure.)

SECTION 1.

There is hereby established the California Institute for Regenerative Medicine.

(Sec. 1 added Nov. 2, 2004, by Prop. 71. Initiative measure.)

SEC. 2.

The institute shall have the following purposes:

(a) To make grants and loans for stem cell research, for research facilities, and for other vital research opportunities to realize therapies, protocols, and/or medical procedures that will result in, as speedily as possible, the cure for, and/or substantial mitigation of, major diseases, injuries, and orphan diseases.

(b) To support all stages of the process of developing cures, from laboratory research through successful clinical trials.

(c) To establish the appropriate regulatory standards and oversight bodies for research and facilities development.

(Sec. 2 added Nov. 2, 2004, by Prop. 71. Initiative measure.)

SEC. 3.

No funds authorized for, or made available to, the institute shall be used for research involving human reproductive cloning.

(Sec. 3 added Nov. 2, 2004, by Prop. 71. Initiative measure.)

SEC. 4.

Funds authorized for, or made available to, the institute shall be continuously appropriated without regard to fiscal year, be available and used only for the purposes provided in this article, and shall not be subject to appropriation or transfer by the Legislature or the Governor for any other purpose.

(Sec. 4 added Nov. 2, 2004, by Prop. 71. Initiative measure.)

SEC. 5.

There is hereby established a right to conduct stem cell research which includes research involving adult stem cells, cord blood stem cells, pluripotent stem cells, and/or progenitor cells. Pluripotent stem cells are cells that are capable of self-renewal, and have broad potential to differentiate into multiple adult cell types. Pluripotent stem cells may be derived from somatic cell nuclear transfer or from surplus products of in vitro fertilization treatments when such products are donated under appropriate informed consent procedures. Progenitor cells are multipotent or precursor cells that are partially differentiated, but retain the ability to divide and give rise to differentiated cells.

(Sec. 5 added Nov. 2, 2004, by Prop. 71. Initiative measure.)

SEC. 6.

Notwithstanding any other provision of this Constitution or any law, the institute, which is established in state government, may utilize state issued tax-exempt and taxable bonds to fund its operations, medical and scientific research, including therapy development through clinical trials, and facilities.

(Sec. 6 added Nov. 2, 2004, by Prop. 71. Initiative measure.)

SEC. 7.

Notwithstanding any other provision of this Constitution, including Article VII, or any law, the institute and its employees are exempt from civil service.

(Sec. 7 added Nov. 2, 2004, by Prop. 71. Initiative measure.)